China's Role in a Shared Human Future

中国在人类命运共同体中的角色

Globalization of Chinese Social Sciences book series ④

中国社会科学全球化系列丛书 ④

China's Role in a Shared Human Future

Towards Theory for Global Leadership

中国在人类命运共同体中的角色：
走向全球领导理论

Martin Albrow

Foreword by Anthony Giddens

Globalization of Chinese Social Sciences book series, Vol. 4
Series editor: Xiangqun Chang

China's Role in a Shared Human Future: Towards Theory for Global Leadership
By Martin Albrow

This book first published jointly in 2018 by
Global China Press
4th Floor, Cannongate House, 64 Cannon Street, London EC4N 6AE, UK
and
New World Press
24 Baiwanzhuang Road, Beijing 100037, China

British Library Cataloguing in Publication Data
A catalogue record for this book is available from the British Library

ISBN 978-1-910334-34-8 (paperback, English); DOI https://doi.org/10.24103/GCSS.en.pb.2018
ISBN 978-1-910334-35-5 (hardback, English); DOI https://doi.org/10.24103/GCSS.en.hb.2018
ISBN 978-1-910334-36-2 (paperback, Chinese); DOI https://doi.org/10.24103/GCSS.ch.pb.2018
ISBN 978-1-910334-37-9 (hardback, Chinese); DOI https://doi.org/10.24103/GCSS.ch.hb.2018

中国社会科学全球化系列丛书 第4卷 常向群主编

《中国在人类命运共同体中的角色：走向全球领导理论》
马丁·阿尔布劳 著

此书由以下出版社于2018年合作出版
全球中国出版社
4th Floor, Cannongate House, 64 Cannon St., London EC4N 6AE, UK
新世界出版社
中国北京市西城区百万庄大街24号

该书编入大英图书馆的公开数据中的图书馆编目

ISBN 978-1-910334-34-8 (平装·英文版); DOI https://doi.org/10.24103/GCSS.en.pb.2018
ISBN 978-1-910334-35-5 (精装·英文版); DOI https://doi.org/10.24103/GCSS.en.hb.2018
ISBN 978-1-910334-36-2 (平装·中文版); DOI https://doi.org/10.24103/GCSS.ch.pb.2018
ISBN 978-1-910334-37-9 (精装·中文版); DOI https://doi.org/10.24103/GCSS.ch.hb.2018

Contents

DOI https://doi.org/10.24103/GCSS.en.2018.1

Foreword

Anthony Giddens

Professor Martin Albrow is one of the foremost sociologists in the English-speaking world and one of the greatest experts on globalization, perhaps the most significant driving force of our times. In his pioneering work *The Global Age* (1996), written when the term 'globalization' itself was quite new, he set out the main dimensions of the profound changes that had begun to transform world society. In its most fundamental meaning, 'globalization' refers to the intensifying interdependence of individuals, institutions and states across the globe.

One dimension is economic – the spread of a world marketplace, a massively complex division of labour between and within companies and their workforces, coupled with financial institutions of global scope. However, globalization is also political and cultural. Increasing globalization confers many benefits, at the same time as it opens up new stresses and strains. Think, for example, of the case of China itself which, when the country opened itself out to the wider world some three decades ago, travelled all the way from mass starvation to a level of prosperity that once would have seemed inconceivable. There are still many who live close to the breadline. Yet in China's prospering cities today one of the main health issues is the very opposite: rising levels of obesity, a condition not of scarcity but of abundance.

Many in current times speak of globalization going into reverse. The reverberations of the global economic crisis are still being felt, especially in Western countries. Whole segments of those countries have not shared in the rising levels of abundance experienced by the majority. There are significant cultural divisions too. Cosmopolitan values – a welcoming of cultural diversity, equality between the sexes and a comfort with geographical mobility – have flowered in many larger cities. In other regions, especially those that have not shared in rising prosperity, there has been a marked reaction against these values. Resentment against immigration, hostile or racist attitudes towards 'foreigners', and towards ethnic or cultural minorities, has again become commonplace. These are the attitudes that have helped fuel the rise of populist parties in the West, parties which explicitly set themselves against globalization and wish to return to the more traditional nation-state. The most significant consequence in global terms is the ascent of Donald Trump to power in the United States, a leader who wants to reverse what he sees as America's declining power and who blames globalization for the US's problems rather than seeing it as the source of its relative prosperity.

Make no mistake, however: globalization has not gone into reverse and short of calamity there is no chance of its doing so. Whatever its stresses and strains, the world is more and more interdependent every day. One of the prime reasons is the rise of the digital revolution, which has moved globalization – i.e. interdependence - to a wholly different level. The celebrated Canadian thinker Marshall McLuhan, writing many years ago at the outset of the digital revolution, coined the term 'global village' to describe the trajectory of world society. How right he was, but even he could never have guessed how far that process would develop. Consider on the level of everyday life. Someone takes a plane to London. That trip takes only some ten hours or so, an everyday miracle which depends upon global satellite systems circling high above the earth. On arrival she calls her parents on her smartphone. It is another everyday miracle. She can see them and vice versa; and they can talk almost as if they were in the same room. Moreover, they can do so almost for nothing. And of course political leaders and billions of other ordinary people can do the same thing.

The global village is what I call a 'high opportunity, high risk' world, where we do not know in advance how that balance of opportunity and risk will play out. The opportunities are everywhere, China's rise to world influence, and probably world leadership, being among them. They are of a scale that human beings have not experienced before, as witnessed in myriad scientific and technological advances, moving faster than ever before precisely because of globalization. To take just one example, this could be an era of massive innovation in medicine, because of the capacity of scientists to collaborate across the world and be in instantaneous communication with one another. Yet the risks are also without precedent in previous periods of history, in some large part because they too are globalized – we just do not know at this point whether as a species we can deal with the combined threats of climate change, a world population approaching ten billion, the proliferation of nuclear weapons, mass migration and the potential for global pandemics.

In this book Albrow does a remarkable job of shedding light on these extraordinary changes and on the pivotal role that China is likely to have in shaping their further evolution. As the United States pulls back from its former global role, China not only can, but must, assume a pivotal position in shaping world society for the better. The progress of the 'Belt and Road' initiative will be only one element in determining whether China's new world role will help heal divisions and promote peaceful global cooperation. That initiative has to demonstrate that it is a vehicle for free cooperation, not an imposition of sectional power.

Albrow fruitfully deploys the thinking of Xi Jinping in showing how all this might be achieved, but links that thinking in an impressive way with Western traditions, old and new. Max Weber, who a century ago sought to pinpoint the cultural origins of Western capitalism, at the same time was fascinated with Eastern religion and culture. His writings, the author shows, still provide core ideas for a rethinking of global cooperation today. We should reject the idea that our hypermodern world can be stabilized and pacified only by hypermodern concepts and technologies. Almost the contrary is the case. In rediscovering the deep roots of shared civilizational values, we can shape a global ethics that can be the foundation of a resurgence of global cooperation.

DOI https://doi.org/10.24103/GCSS.en.2018.2

Author's preface

China's rise has astonished the world. Since 1978, plan after plan has been realized. The 13th Five Year Plan extends to 2020. It then achieves a 'moderately prosperous society', fulfilling the goal to mark the centenary of the founding of the Communist Party of China in 1921.

The next great centenary, the founding of the People's Republic of China, comes in 2049. The goal to be achieved by then is a modern socialist country, prosperous, strong, democratic, culturally advanced and harmonious. President Xi Jinping has called this progress the realization of the Chinese Dream of national rejuvenation.

The West looks on with fascination, apprehension and scepticism. It also seeks endlessly to satisfy itself how and why China has fulfilled plan after plan. After all, according to the dominant liberal ideology of the West, it should not work.

So Western explanations for Chinese exceptionalism range over any number of factors: the sheer size of the population and the internal market, rigid authoritarianism, rigorous education, close family ties, importing capitalism, stealing ideas and commercial secrets, the excessive generosity of the West in opening its markets, and so on.

Very rarely mentioned is the quality of Chinese leadership. Even less often cited is that this leadership constantly develops its theory for shaping society and guiding public policy. It includes, but is broader than Marxism, and their phrase 'philosophical social science' captures it better for Western readers.

It is close to what used to be called public philosophy in the West. That has long lost any hold on the direction of public policy in a political climate where opinion is driven by tweets and media headlines. The nearest thing to a coherent set of ideas to guide public policy, Clinton's and Blair's 'Third Way', was eclipsed very soon after by George W. Bush's and Blair's 'War on Terror', and there has been nothing to fill its place.

The passive acceptance of globalization by Western elites has prompted a populist reaction and there is a complete loss of intellectual confidence, or indeed trust in ideas on the part of the political class.

A truly global perspective, on the other hand, actively looks to shape globalization for human purposes and focuses on global issues that threaten the human future. It is neither for nor against globalization, simply wants to make it work for the public good both for countries but also for the world as a whole.

There is so much in China today that leads in that direction. Chinese theory today is work in progress along that road, continually being updated, from Mao Zedong through Deng Xiaoping to Xi Jinping, whose speeches provide the thought leadership that directs China's public policy. In developing policy for engagement in global affairs, it is now moving explicitly towards a 'New Partnership of Mutual Benefit and a Community of Shared Future'.[1]

Leadership for a common human future requires theory that is free from national prejudices and outdated ideologies and can deliver solutions to problems that confront us all. There is an urgent need to explore the theoretical issues that the future world society is bound to face.

The starkness of the contrast between China's activism and Western resignation in the face of globalization was impressed on me when I first read *Xi Jinping: The Governance of China*. It was my privilege to be invited to speak at its launch in London in April 2015.

Then I expressed the hope that 'the ideas behind the governance of China may sometime soon be extended to rethinking the governance of the globe'.[2] Since then I have returned to the theme of China's potential contribution to theory for global governance on several occasions in China and in Europe.

The collection of speeches and journal articles in this book is an outcome and I hope an encouragement to the Chinese leadership and to scholars to have no hesitation in offering their ideas for a new global order.

The reader will find no blueprint for global governance in the following pages. My intention is to point to directions in Chinese thought and policies and in relations with other countries that can lead to benefits for the whole world.

The prompting in this book to Chinese thinkers to continue forward in those directions stems, of course, from my own theoretical standpoint. In brief, this is that I try to write as a citizen of the world, not as a Western academic sympathetic to China, though naturally I am that.

But there is good reason to distance oneself from Western outlooks on China. They have a history. It is not encouraging: from awe and admiration in the eighteenth century; to contempt and exploitation in the nineteenth; to fear and astonishment in the twentieth.

But in common in those reactions has been the conviction that the West has access to universal truths that the rest of the world only needs to learn. I disagree. The world does not need a total universalism. Every culture, each country has its own version.

The results when they clash over universal principles are often devastating. By contrast the future of human society depends on cooperation in tackling global issues that threaten its very existence.

The global outlook invites every culture to contribute to what is necessary to secure a future for human beings on this earth. It involves dialogue between civilizations, across boundaries, and arises from shared perceptions of human need. It

---

[1] Speech to the 70th Session of the General Assembly of the United Nations, 28 September 2015.
[2] The text of the speech is reprinted below as Chapter One.

treats universal principles as yet another factor to be negotiated between cultures. It is a pragmatic universalism for material purposes.

The global outlook is then, at one and the same time, materialist (even Marxist) and idealist, (even religious). China is already well prepared to contribute, since in its own theory it combines Marxism with Confucian and religious ideas and its result is 'socialism with Chinese characteristics'. But it goes still further in calmly assimilating theory and research from Western economic and social sciences too.

This readiness to appreciate and absorb ideas from other cultures and from advancing social sciences is a huge strength in China's development, and I hope the following pages provide helpful illustration. It means too that I hope the idea of transculturality that is advanced in several chapters will gain from serious Chinese examination of its potential contribution to the theory of global governance.

The chapters that follow originally were presented to varied audiences on different occasions. At one extreme, they are fully developed journal papers, at the other, speeches for a wider public. They are arranged in three parts, but the sequence is less important than the reader's interest and the book can be entered at any point.

To aid selective reading, the list of chapters with the details of their original presentation or publication is available at the end of the book, along with abstracts and key terms when they were provided.

President Xi's thought is the starting point for my discussions in Part One, China's Role in the Globalizing World. Part Two, Theory for the Global Social Order, aims to encourage new thinking about global governance, in particular with the ideas of transculturality and pragmatic universalism. Part Three, From Max Weber to Global Sociology, considers the extent and limits of Western understanding of China in the classic account of Max Weber and asks how far his approach can illuminate our world today.

The growing exchanges between Western and Chinese sociology are work in progress, illustrated from the past in my Postscript, developed for the present by Professor Xiangqun Chang who rounds off this volume in an Appendix that shows how the Book Series in which it is included drives the agenda forward.

Just as global leadership requires a standpoint that is valid beyond national boundaries so too theory for the coming age infringes old disciplinary boundaries. The author therefore makes no apology for trespassing into fields beyond his own, only regrets the limitations that an academic specialism imposes on anyone like me who has been privileged enough to enjoy a career serving sociology.

Specialists in history, religion, philosophy, languages, biology, environment, physics, mathematics, economics and the social sciences all must contribute to theory for the new global order. But it will only be validated by the practical efforts of citizens of the world to create a new world social order, and it is to them this book is dedicated.

DOI https://doi.org/10.24103/GCSS.en.2018.3

Acknowledgments

No work on China by a foreign scholar with only a few words of Mandarin would be possible without the generous cooperation, inspiration and advice from Chinese scholars. I am glad to have this chance to record my belated and deep gratitude to those I worked with in the 1980s and 1990s. Dai Kejing and Lu Xueyi, who sadly passed away in 2013, were immensely helpful as the Postscript to this volume details. Li Yong was both my student and indispensable guide for the State Family Planning programme.

In more recent years Sun Youzhong, Li Xuetao, Wang Yuechen, and Jin Wei have all helped me in many different and more ways than they realize, from giving practical advice to sharing philosophical insights. I am grateful to them all.

Officials in the London Embassy of the PRC have taught me that people to people diplomacy is also about making friends. Minister Ma Hui and Minister Counsellor Xiang Xiaowei have been generous both in sharing their knowledge and giving invaluable advice. Second Secretary Ma Lei in the Embassy Cultural Office has been unfailingly helpful, both in London and for my visits to China. In Beijing, Zhu Qi and his staff in the Bureau for External Relations of the Ministry of Culture have been exceptionally hospitable to me and other delegates who had the good fortune to attend the Symposia on China Studies that they organized with the Chinese Academy of Social Sciences.

The Chinese media have taken unusual (to me) interest in my views on China and are courteous in the extreme, to the extent that I feel it is I who learns more from their interviews than they do. I thank Qu Shang (CCTV), Yingqi Li (*People's Daily*), Huang Yong and Zhang Dailei (Xinhua), in particular.

It is to two outstanding Chinese scholars I owe the greatest debt. Over recent years our discussions have led to close collaboration and friendship.

Zhang Xiaoying both heads the School of International Journalism and Communication at the Beijing Foreign Studies University and finds time to join with me in the study of Max Weber, of which our joint authorship of Chapters Twelve and Thirteen is just one of the important results of her work.

Xiangqun Chang has founded the Global China Institute, the *Journal of China in Comparative Perspective*, the Global China Dialogues and the Global China Press. Evidence of my reliance on and participation in these scholarly enterprises will be found in the pages of this book. Without her persistence and commitment to this book it could not have been published.

I want too to express my appreciation not just to the editors but also the staffs of the journals *Max Weber Studies, Journal of China in Comparative Perspective* and *Global Communication*, whose earlier efforts to publish my work in their journals enable the publication of this book now. To Ingrid Cranfield I owe particular thanks for her meticulous copyediting.

All the following friends from academe and from personal life have from time to time been readers of drafts of a text or texts that this volume includes. They have over the years made me sit up and think, removed many defects in my writing, but bear no responsibility for those that remain: Michael Banton, Colin Bradford, Hugh Canham, Olaf Corry, Anthony Giddens, Stephen Kalberg, Graham Leicester, John Nurser, Geoffrey Pleyers, Hakan Seckinelgin, Sam Whimster and Joy Zhang.

Sue Owen has done all these things, and much more besides, in sharing the joys and sorrows of domestic life. To all of them I give my heartfelt thanks and I look forward to many more equally satisfying exchanges in the years to come.

Martin Albrow
London
13 March, 2018

DOI https://doi.org/10.24103/GCSS.en.2018.4

Part One
China's role in the globalizing world

There was a time in mid-twentieth century in the West when the idea of role had a central place in thinking about society. Each country would find a place for the individual to make a contribution to the greater good.

Later the idea of a role became unfashionable. Critics questioned the justice and coherence of social order in a nation-state under capitalist conditions. Roles in such a society were held to constrain rather than enable individual development, and the idea gave way to an emphasis on identity.

But no authority imposes a role in a globalizing world. On the contrary, roles in it are self-imposed sets of obligations to an order that is yet to come, an aspiration, a vision of a future world where its peoples live in peaceful and fulfilling relations with one another.

Many countries, agencies of all kinds, religious, entrepreneurial, charitable, professional and, yes, 'workers of the world', men and women, can shape a role in this future global society. But some will be able to make a more powerful contribution than others. China will be second to none in this respect.

It is then appropriate for an appreciation of the speeches of President Xi Jinping in the collection entitled *Xi Jinping: The Governance of China* to set the tone at the outset. His speeches provide examples of how globalization can be managed for national well-being, illustrate the scope of the ambitions of the Chinese people for themselves but also their potential for shaping the wider world.

This scope and potential are represented in Chapter Two. On the one hand there is the enthusiastic Chinese commitment to theoretical social science, and on the other the huge ambition of the Belt and Road project that extends now to more than 60 countries. In the Chinese vision these are two sides of the same coin, theory and practice, a combination that is vital for global governance.

The pursuit of economic goals in the Belt and Road initiative and the engagement with national cultures it requires are bound to create tensions. Here the abiding concern with harmony in Chinese culture promotes the pragmatic cooperation needed to defuse the potential for conflict arising from differences between values.

At the present time China offers the world qualities that can mobilize other countries to meet global threats. In its domestic achievements in recent years, and building on the heritage of a 5,000-year-old civilization, China has proven qualities for global leadership: effectiveness, efficiency, legitimacy, respect, reciprocity, reverence, transcendence, inventiveness. There is no time to lose in applying these qualities to global issues.

In my view, this is the strongest message that comes through in the *Xi Jinping: The Governance of China,* Volume II. It offers an example of the practice of leadership, based in theory, with a vision for the future.

DOI https://doi.org/10.24103/GCSS.en.2018.5

Chapter One

The architectonic of ideas –
Xi Jinping: The Governance of China

Your Excellency, Ambassador Liu, may I thank you first for allowing me the honour and privilege of speaking at the launch of President Xi Jinping's new book.[1] Not just Western countries should welcome this major initiative to communicate the ideas of China's leadership about the direction of a country that will affect all others over the coming century.

To my lasting regret I have never taken the arduous road that leads to becoming a sinologist. But as a sociologist of global society I wholeheartedly welcome a book that brings China to the rest of the world, and at the same time offers a huge contribution to understanding between nations and towards cooperation in meeting the global challenges of our time.

There is so much to this book that should lead to new thinking in the West in particular, but in the short time available to me I shall draw three lessons from it.

The very title is a triumph. It is a masterstroke to adopt 'governance' as the leading concept. Though it may be very recent compared with the Chinese idea of *li*, it still has a relatively rich history in Western thought.

To take an English example, a manuscript bearing the title *The Governance of England* (Fortescue) dates from the sixteenth century.[2] So the term 'governance' has the merit of predating modern ideological conflicts. Today it enjoys a renewed popularity, I would suggest, because it invites us to examine the relation of government to social order in a spirit free from the preconceptions of the twentieth century.

That is the **first lesson** I draw from this book. It teaches us that to understand the present we have to embrace the past. President Xi evokes China's history and demonstrates how age-old ideas are a motive force in the present, deeply embedded in practices today, even when we don't recognize them.

Western readers may not be surprised by his emphasis on the development of Chinese Marxist ideas, on socialism with Chinese characteristics since Mao Zedong, through Deng Xiaoping, Jiang Zemin, to Hu Jintao. They may, however, open their eyes wider when they read the tribute to Sun Yat-sen, who led the revolution of 1911 and is seen as the forerunner of the Chinese democratic revolution. They may expect quotations from Confucius. But they may be startled by the

---

[1] *Xi Jinping: The Governance of China.* 2014. The launch took place at the Chinese Embassy in London on 15 April 2016.

[2] Fortescue 1885, edited by Charles Plummer, *The Governance of England.*

profound reflections on the theme of harmony from a prime minister living over 2500 years ago.

Ideas live on, and in China they provide both continuity with a prodigiously long and complex history and also the frame for shaping the future. This is the **second lesson** I wish to draw from this book. It demonstrates how much we should value systematic thought in political leadership.

It brings to my mind a word even older than governance, infrequently used today, but exactly appropriate, namely 'architectonic', that is to say, related to building, to making structures, creating an enduring order. The world needs an architectonic of ideas, flexible enough to meet national and global challenges. We have the example here of what President Xi Jinping advocates in his own country and what the world outside in general so grievously lacks.

The West has lost its grip on ideas. They have become a factor of economic production, a key input for the advertising industry, the source of political slogans and the plaything for entertainers. But lost is the belief in a higher ordering of ideas that might provide guidance for our leaders, or in a common frame of concepts for attending to the acute existential problems of the world of today. We have to go back at least a century to Max Weber to find anything meeting this requirement.

Xi Jinping demonstrates that the virtues of Chinese systematic thinking for modern society are not simply a matter of well-chosen quotations from revered sources, though the reader will take pleasure in the colour and imagery they offer. More fundamental is an underlying drive for systematic interconnectedness that characterizes both ancient and modern Chinese thought.

This was recognized in the West as long ago as 1700, when one of its most spectacular minds, Gottfried Wilhelm Leibniz pointed to the ethical superiority of the Chinese, even if the West had recently surpassed them in scientific advances. It should cause us to reflect on our current awareness of the past when a Chinese President feels the need to remind us that Leibniz was an advocate of mutual understanding between peoples.

The overwhelming thrust of this book is to provide the ideas that will mobilize the mass of the Chinese people in a drive towards national rejuvenation, reform and innovation-led growth. With an implicit nod towards the American equivalent, Xi calls it 'the Chinese Dream', but it is a hard-headed, systematic approach to enhancing what he calls national governance capacity, involving the promotion of political stability, economic growth, social harmony and ethnic unity.

The 'Dream' involves principles, goals, values and ideals, all expressed in characteristic Chinese enumerations: the six 'Centring-ons' that give the market a decisive role but endorse political and social structural reform to enhance 'the Party's capacity to govern in a scientific and democratic way in accordance with the law'; the 'three Stricts' for Party members, self-development, limiting the use of power and self-discipline; the 'three Earnests', making plans, opening up new undertakings and upholding personal integrity. They fit with the 'three Furthers' for the country: freeing the mind; releasing and developing productive forces; strengthening the vigour of society.

There will be those in the West who scoff at the implausibility of realizing all these goals and standards. They will miss their point. This is an ordered frame of thought required for guiding action and judging achievement. Its application is in the first instance to China, but implied is a general theory of governance, where government is embedded in a wider system of norms, values and common understandings that create the kind of social order where people can go about their lives with purpose and a sense of security.

This leads to the **third lesson** I draw from Xi's book. The idea of governance prepares us to bring China, the West and the rest of the world together in the idea of global governance. It points to the gross distortion of global affairs when global governance is seen as a matter primarily for the international financial institutions. In the global age the issues that challenge our existence on this planet call for far more than general agreements on trade.

Xi Jinping affirms China's support for the United Nations, for the Eco Forum Global Conference, for the Millennium Development Goals and for the UN Security Council. China, he says, belongs to a world where exchanges and mutual learning make civilizations richer and more colourful. He calls for partnership, cooperation and mutual development with other nations.

This book encourages us to hope that the ideas behind the governance of China may sometime soon be extended to rethinking the governance of the globe. As Mencius said: 'One can never unify the world if the hearts of all the people are not won over.'

DOI https://doi.org/10.24103/GCSS.en.2018.6

Chapter Two

Philosophical social science as a bridge from 'Belt and Road' to global governance

It is only with awe that any individual scholar can respond to an invitation to speak on the theme of Belt and Road in the country of its origin. For what is one voice compared with the initiative launched by the most powerful collective human agency our world has ever seen, namely contemporary China?

Some have debated whether to call China a nation-state or a civilization. I would say it is both, and additionally also a corporate entity. The bonds that hold it and its people together are more intimate than any known to Western states. Its proven capacity to deliver its goals is matched elsewhere in the world only by corporations or military forces and they can draw on a mere fraction of the population that China possesses.

It takes no special insight to recognize China's special role in the world today. Recent events in the West, like the British vote to leave the European Union, the election of Donald Trump to be President of the United States and the widespread advance of nationalist parties in Europe, suggest that Western-inspired globalization is producing a widespread negative reaction within the very countries that have promoted it in the belief that it is in their own interests.

The 'Balkanization' of the West, the fracturing of old relationships between its states, is now an imminent possibility. By contrast China appears as a stable pole of attraction for countries in Asia, Europe and Africa. But we should not be mesmerized by the drama and pace of recent events in the West. Changes that have been long in the making are under way.

Fifty years ago, from the longest comparative and historical perspective, Arnold Toynbee wrote:

> In the twentieth century of the Christian Era, unity and peace were the crying needs of the global world that had been brought into existence by Western technology's feat of 'annihilating distance'. If a 'Middle Empire' was now needed as a nucleus for political unification on a global scale, China was the country that was designated by history for playing this part of world-unifier once again, this time on a literally worldwide stage.[1]

Those prescient remarks deserve close attention. By linking the emergence of a global world with 'annihilating distance', Toynbee was writing of globalization before the invention of the word; in pointing to the political unification that the global world required, he was recognizing that globalization and world unity

---

[1] Toynbee 1966, *Change and Habit: The Challenge of our Time*, p. 158.

were distinct and by no means necessarily supportive of one another. Technology and politics operate from distinct bases in reality and on different principles. Human effort had to bring them together and nothing less than the agency of a great and powerful country could do so. Toynbee was at that time speculating about a possible world state, with a political order underpinned ultimately by the possession of overwhelming force. That did not exclude joint action between states to secure such an order. But the order itself was achieved through the 'cement of a common culture'.[2]

The current configuration of the world's political order has changed in so many ways since Toynbee was writing. The framework of institutions that has developed since his time leads us to speak of global governance rather than a world state. But it is in the spirit of his reflections that I want to point to the distinctive way in which China is now poised to contribute to this order that is called global governance.

Globalization in itself has not produced global governance. Only in Western neo-liberalism have the two sometimes been equated. Rather, global governance has been the product of decades of cooperation between nation-states and other agencies, public and private, ever since the foundation of the United Nations. It consists of institutions and agencies, treaties, laws and practices dealing with a multiplicity of global issues that cross boundaries and exceed the capacities of any single state to address them adequately.

But in the current reaction against globalization in the West, global governance is endangered by the strident calls for the restoration of national sovereignty that drown out the voices calling for international cooperation. In a recent interview with the BBC the French Presidential candidate, Marine Le Pen, said, 'The true division is between patriots and globalists.'[3] In the populist reaction against globalization all things global are regarded as a threat to the nation.

Chinese leadership has advanced the Belt and Road initiative in part as a response to Western globalization, as an alternative way of extending its national influence in world, but also to join with other countries to build a better world. It has a very different character from globalization, which became, as I shall explore in more detail later, more a philosophy of history than a programme of action, one to which states were expected to adapt rather than assume ownership. Belt and Road on the other hand puts China's agency in the forefront, while emphasizing that cooperation with other countries is at the core of the initiative.

That cooperation depends explicitly on recognizing the distinctive histories and cultural identities of other countries. Forging cooperation on the recognition of difference and diversity is itself a prerequisite for global governance, and success with the Belt and Road initiative can therefore be the forerunner of Chinese

---

[2] Ibid. p. 156.
[3] BBC, 'This World: After Brexit – the Battle for Europe'. BBC2 TV broadcast, 9.2.17.

leadership in sustaining global institutions in the face of Western disillusion and disarray.

When he announced the creation of the Maritime Silk Road in Indonesia on 3 October 2013, President Xi spoke of the way the ASEAN countries and China had interacted and built a 'cultural foundation ... to gain from one another's experience'.[4] We should observe that this cultural foundation is a collective project, a pooling of experience, in which something new is created. In the language of recent social science this is a transcultural achievement.

Belt and Road is the most ambitious project yet to link the peaceful development of China with the prosperity and well-being of the world as a whole. Up to now it has been developed primarily as an economic policy. But through it, drawing on its own cultural heritage, China has the potential to make a more far-reaching contribution to global governance.

We recognize this when, in a sign of its newly won self-confidence as a great power, China takes the initiative to invite foreign scholars to contribute to the collective efforts to create a better world. President Xi Jinping said in his speech to the Symposium of Philosophical Social Sciences on 17 May, 2016: 'We should look to foreign countries and explore those key issues that are related to human prospects and destiny.'[5]

That speech set out a wide-ranging agenda not just for established disciplines such as history, economics, politics, sociology and anthropology but also for emerging fields of study and interdisciplinary work. The scope is vast, from military affairs to the oracle bones inscriptions, from Marxism to ecological civilization.

What holds them all together is 'philosophical social science'. Now this is a formula for the unity of the social sciences that in the West in all likelihood will be greeted with little enthusiasm. The Western sceptic will probably mumble something about 'discredited synthetic philosophy' and 'Who now reads Spencer?'[6]

My view is very different. In my understanding the aim of philosophical social science is to engage with the theoretical concepts that underpin research and thereby link it to the ongoing task of building a harmonious society. In the West, Immanuel Kant emphasized the importance of theory for practice in his famous essay 'On the Common Saying: That May Be True in Theory but Not in Practice' (1793).[7] More recently a statement by the social psychologist Kurt Lewin that there's nothing so practical as a good theory has been widely quoted.[8]

---

[4] Xi 2014, op cit., p. 323.

[5] Xi Jinping 2016, 'Speech at the Symposium of Philosophical Social Sciences', 18 May 2016. Xinhua Net. English translation, Appendix of *Fei Xiaotong Studies*, Vol. 2, Globalization of Chinese Social Sciences Book Series. London: Global China Press.

[6] The famous statement referring to Herbert Spencer with which Talcott Parsons opened his seminal study *The Structure of Social Action*, 1937, p. 3.

[7] Immanuel Kant (ed. Ted Humphrey) 1983, *Perpetual Peace and Other Essays*, pp. 61-92.

[8] Kurt Lewin 1951, *Field Theory in Social Science: Selected Theoretical Papers*.

President Xi quotes Engels saying, 'A nation cannot go without theoretical thinking if it wants to be at the peak of science.' He then cites Hu Jintao's emphasis on the need to 'enhance Chinese cultural creativity and national cohesive force, and increase the power of Chinese civilization.'[9] In both cases, Xi links philosophical social science with nation building.

By contrast, public policy and society building in West have been predominantly empirical, pragmatic and detached from any overarching theory, unless one considers the pre-eminence of liberal economics as serving that function. The idea of a coherent public philosophy flourished only for a short time after 1945 and the short-lived celebration of the triumph of social democracy after the collapse of the Soviet Union has long since been overshadowed by the rise of militant Islamic forces, the 2008 financial crash and the subsequent disillusion with globalization.

The combination of philosophical social sciences with Marxism as an open theoretical system and the cultural heritage of Chinese thinkers provides an ongoing unifying discursive frame that has no equivalent in the West. There is no better illustration of this than the collection of addresses and speeches by President Xi that has been published in English as *Xi Jinping: The Governance of China*.

Those speeches aim to inspire the Chinese people towards realizing 'the Chinese Dream', a comprehensive vision of a rejuvenated nation, where 'The CPC is the central force for leading and bringing together people of all ethnic groups in advancing the great cause of building Chinese socialism.'[10] In the same address to the First Session of the 12th National People's Congress, Xi pointed to 'law-based governance', 'community-level self-governance' and 'equal rights to participate in governance', as well as to the need to strengthen the 'Party's art of leadership and governance'.

Xi's vision for the governance of China is entirely in accord with his programme for the philosophical social sciences, and informed in multiple ways by the concepts and problem settings with which those sciences are preoccupied. At the launch of *Xi Jinping: The Governance of China* in the UK, I said it represented 'an architectonic of ideas, flexible enough to meet national and global challenges... what the world outside in general so grievously lacks'.[11]

In its broadest sense, global governance consists of all those processes and institutions that respond to challenges that extend beyond national boundaries and maintain social order on a global scale. When in the West in recent years economic institutions like the IMF, World Bank and WTO have at times been regarded as the institutional core of global governance they have also been seen as enabling and carrying globalization forward.

But globalization and global governance are not the same thing. If today it is common for populist politicians to attack global institutions and globalization

[9] Xi, ibid.

[10] *Xi Jinping: The Governance of China*, 2014. p. 45.

[11] Martin Albrow, 2015 speech, 'The Architectonic of Ideas - *Xi Jinping: The Governance of China'*.

equally as aspects of an all-embracing globalism, it is because both have been wrongly equated with a particular economic doctrine and with the excesses of unrestrained capitalism.

Many, including myself, have criticized the unnecessary limitation of the idea of globalization to economic processes and a fatal restriction of global governance to economic institutions. Neo-liberalism or the Washington Consensus built on long-established theories of free trade to create a comprehensive straitjacket for state management of national economies, for all times and circumstances. The interventions of the international financial institutions were often effectively de-mands on states to conform to their dictates and were seen in that light.

But globalization in itself, whether as the historical direction to world uni-fication or as the process of the local becoming global, is neither confined to the economy, nor, and for my argument more important, is it bound to diminish the roles of the state or dismantle national boundaries. Nation-states can be agents of globalization and, in going global, can strengthen their identities.

At the very least, it is necessary to counterbalance this view with the huge variety of United Nations agencies and interventions in peacekeeping, health, migration and climate change. When the United Nations Security Council acts collectively as it did recently to condemn the new ballistic missile test by North Korea, the participation of both China and Russia in the unanimous resolution was a pure example of global governance to secure the world's political order.

The new Sustainable Development Goals for instance go far beyond eco-nomic considerations. Consider the 17 goals of the 2030 Agenda for Sustainable Development: Goal 3 aims to 'ensure healthy lives; Goal 5 to 'achieve gender equality'; Goal 10 to 'reduce inequality'; Goal 13 to 'combat climate change'. These are aspects of a comprehensive philosophy for human well-being on our planet.

Just as we must clearly distinguish globalization from global governance, so also must we ground global governance in a set of principles, goals, values and ideals that can underpin a global social and political order. For China this means helping to shape an architectonic of ideas appropriate for this order. Anything less would mean Belt and Road being regarded as the Chinese equivalent to American globalization.

Conceived as an answer to globalization, therefore, Belt and Road runs the risk of being regarded as an economic strategy only and, still worse, being regard-ed by the rest of the world as so much of it has viewed globalization, namely as an extension of national hegemony under the pretence of benefiting all nations. For the United States they will read China.

For the long-term success of Belt and Road it is therefore necessary to em-phasize those non-economic features that make it different from globalization and the accompanying contribution China will be making to global governance. It is a part of the larger project of the Chinese Dream, where the cultural strengths of

China and its awareness of the role of philosophical social science can lead to the holistic view of global governance that the world requires today.

Western globalization discourse

The argument that follows will build in the first place on a comparison between globalization and Belt and Road. Vast though that task could be in principle, I will seek to reduce it to broad outlines that highlight the differences.

Globalization has been such a dominant component of Western political discourse for the last thirty years that its scope seems to exclude very little – worldwide communication, consciousness of a common fate, loss of national sovereignty, growing interdependence and, perhaps in recent years predominantly, the expansion and integration of global markets.

All of these have of course been explored in empirical research and the findings continue to mount. But, paralleling all these developments, globalization has also been *discourse*, the stuff of policies, speeches, commentaries and debate. Since Belt and Road is still at a relatively early stage of vision and policy formulation, it is in this respect we can compare it with globalization.

I want to distinguish three versions of the discourse of globalization: as story, as strategy and as ideology. They happen to have developed over more than forty years as successive phases, each assimilating the previous one, without replacing it.

The first version is globalization as *story*. We can trace this back at least to the 1970s, most notably marked by a chapter in George Modelski's textbook on world politics that advocated a transnational view and saw globalization as the culmination of a historic process that had brought the world to be one place.[12] The roots of globalization in this version are lost in time; the present is the culmination of the past.

In sociology, Roland Robertson's early work represented this story of the world becoming singular even as localities became ever more diverse.[13] In 1990, the Madrid World Congress of the International Sociological Association (ISA) gave this view a public endorsement with its chosen conference theme, 'Sociology for One World: Unity and Diversity'.

In its Congress volume, the ISA disseminated the message to 4,000 delegates from that single, diverse world.[14] In this way it was in effect demonstrating that an academic discipline in itself, through its endeavours to find intellectual understanding across cultural boundaries, could contribute to the creation of a particular kind of global society.

The second globalization discourse focuses on *strategy*. Following hot on the heels of the early academic discussion in the 1980s, the idea was leveraged

---

[12] George Modelski 1972, *The Principles of World Politics.*
[13] Roland Robertson 1992, *Globalization: Social Theory and Global Culture.*
[14] Martin Albrow and Elizabeth King (eds.) 1990, *Globalization, Knowledge and Society.*

into the business world, finding it well adapted to be the background narrative for multinational corporations seeking to extend their reach worldwide.

The benchmark text appropriately was published in the *Harvard Business Review* by Theodore Levitt, 'The Globalization of Markets' (1983), where he argued that globalization meant the homogenization of consumer choice providing the basis for firms to develop global strategies. 'Going global' became a standard feature of the corporate plan.

Undoubtedly the experience of business in going global contributed greatly to the reception of global terminology in everyday speech. Robertson noted how the idea of glocalization, adapted from the Japanese business experience of going global, became a buzzword of the 1990s.[15] The requirements for business to find a familiar and predictable milieu anywhere in the world meant going 'glocal'. At the same time localities could themselves promote and differentiate themselves in a global frame.

What is worth emphasizing here is that the idea of globalization is not derived from free market doctrine, rather the reverse. When the OECD Directorate for Science, Technology and Industry published a special issue of its journal in 1993 it defined globalization as the 'widening and deepening of the operations of firms to produce and sell goods and services in more markets'.[16] Of course firms prefer no tariffs, but they jump national boundaries in all kinds of ways, irrespective of customs duties, especially through establishing subsidiaries, franchises and direct investment. Technology, raw materials, production processes, labour supply and consumer preferences are more important for the location of industry and retail outlets than customs barriers.

It was the success of corporations in going global that prepared the way for the third type of globalization discourse, as *ideology*. In the Western democracies the interests of capital will find expression through the discourse of political parties aiming to win the support of the majority of the electorate. Prompted by the neo-liberal triumphalism that followed on from the collapse of the Soviet Union, a series of accounts appeared in the 1990s that predicted the end of the nation-state and the homogenization of national cultures. Kenichi Ohmae was the most emphatic in announcing the borderless world,[17] Francis Fukuyama the most celebrated in declaring the final victory of Western liberal democracy.[18]

For many Americans this new globalization was clearly in their own national interest. The prevailing view was that of Thomas Friedman, whose bestseller *The Lexus and the Olive Tree* (1999) saw globalization as driven by free market capitalism, a system with the United States as 'the sole and dominant superpower',

---

[15] Robertson 1992, op. cit., p. 174.
[16] OECD (Organization for Economic Cooperation and Development) 1993, p. 7.
[17] Kenichi Ohmae 1994, *The End of the Nation-State*.
[18] Francis Fukuyama 1992, *The End of History and the Last Man*.

where 'culturally speaking, globalization is largely, though not entirely, the spread of Americanization'.[19]

The story and the strategy had merged into the American ideology. President Clinton spoke of globalization as the direction of history that could not be turned back ('the forces of history are on our side')[20] and under him American political leadership set about energetically to forge a progressive, social democratic set of policies, generally known as the Third Way.

Clinton and his Vice-President Al Gore adopted globalization as the keyword in a re-orientation of the Democratic Party's electoral programme towards more open markets and reform of public services. The New Democrats in the United States were followed by New Labour in the United Kingdom and for a period in the 1990s into the new millennium there was a loose movement of leftist political leaders in Europe and more widely in the West signed up to the social democratic ideas of the Third Way.[21]

The promotion of globalization as a global policy to benefit all countries was accompanied by a concerted effort to guide international institutions towards global goals of reducing poverty and combatting climate change. The adoption by the United Nations in 2000 of the Millennium Development Goals (MDGs) was in many ways the highpoint of American leadership in world affairs.

Projecting globalization in a way that equated American interests with the global common good was, however, vulnerable both to movements within American democracy and an ideological opposition that crossed boundaries. The rapidly growing international anti-globalization movement culminated in protests that led to the cancellation of the World Trade Organization meeting in Seattle in December 1999 and Clinton remarking that perhaps the demonstrators had a point.

But within the United States there was also a developing feeling that globalization in some ways undermined traditional culture. It was a Hollywood film, *American Beauty*, in the year 2000 that pointed to a sickness in the life of the American community and there was a reaction to it that declared the production of such a film was un-American. The culture industry itself had become a global production process that could reflect back on its country of origin in ways it did not like.[22] Hollywood was now integral to a global culture.

A declining confidence in globalization was reflected in the defeat of the Democratic candidate for the American Presidency, Al Gore, a strong advocate of policies to combat climate change, by George W. Bush. With the destruction of the twin towers of the World Trade Center on the 11 September 2001, globalization

---

[19] Thomas L. Friedman 1999, *The Lexus and the Olive Tree*, pp. 5-11.

[20] Bill Clinton, speech at the University of Nebraska, 8 December 2000.

[21] Anthony Giddens 1998, *The Third Way.*

[22] I drew the implications of this for European culture in a lecture in Helsinki entitled 'Globalization or Americanization: the Fate of European Culture', reprinted in Martin Albrow 2014, *Global Age Essays on Social and Cultural Change.*

discourse ceased to provide the language for American foreign policy and gave way to an older concern to make the world safe for American values.

However, for the rest of the world, China included, globalization to this day is thought of primarily as an American project, underpinned by the international financial institutions, promoting neo-liberal economic policies. In global public opinion its influence persists even as the United States itself has lost faith in the ideology. The election of Donald Trump as the 45th President of the United States after a campaign attacking the globalists inside and outside the country marks the end of American ownership of globalization even as the United States is inextricably bound into the complex processes of the global polity.

Should we then also forget the intellectual ferment of the Third Way years as a matter of mere historical interest? That I think would be a mistake. This was a period of intense theoretical debate that informed both domestic and international public policies. Some of the most prominent Western academics, including Ulrich Beck, Amitai Etzioni, Anthony Giddens and Robert Putnam, contributed to a ferment of ideas about reinventing government, social capital and civil society, with globalization as the underlying driver of change.

The Chinese Belt and Road initiative

What I suggest here is that China needs too to aim for the same kind of intellectual engagement that the West devoted to globalization, but this time to develop a fuller theoretical account of Belt and Road for its potential contribution to the world's social order or, as it is best conceived, to global governance. Belt and Road will require the equivalent intellectual creativity to that which built the response to globalization in the West.

Indeed I hold it would be of immense value to the world if China seeks to fill the theoretical vacuum in the West arising from the loss of faith in globalization. But this time cultural issues, rather than economic ones, should be the centre of attention.

To highlight the differences between Belt and Road and Western economic globalization, I take once more history, strategy and ideology in turn. Plainly, Belt and Road also has a profound anchorage in *history*, specifically in China's explorations and exchanges with the world beyond the Middle Kingdom. President Xi Jinping on 7 September 2013 began his very first speech proposing the Silk Road Economic Belt by recalling two missions more than 2100 years ago made by an envoy of the Han dynasty to Central Asia.[23] When speaking at the 6th China-Arab States cooperation forum on 15 June 2014 he referenced the voyages of Zheng He in the context of the history of exchanges between the two civilizations.[24]

---

[23] Xi, op. cit. p. 315
[24] Xi, op. cit. p. 345.

Compared then with the Western world-historical narrative of globalization, the Chinese Belt and Road initiative depends on a narrative of developing exchanges between countries, cultures and civilizations, not on a story of advancing Western modernity. It therefore escapes the close association between the ideas of progress and the superiority of the West with its resulting imperial expansion and imposition on the rest of the world.

In respect of *strategy,* Belt and Road fits within the Two Centenary Goals of 2021 when the full *xiaokang,* moderately well-off society, will have been achieved, and 2049, by which point China will have become a 'strong, democratic, civilized, harmonious and modern socialist society'. In his speech 'Realize Youthful Dreams', on 4 May 2013, Xi linked those goals to the Chinese Dream of national rejuvenation, a dream for the country and also for 'every ordinary Chinese'.[25]

These goals are of course only the apex of an architecture of goals, targets, plans and timetables, which for Western observers are extraordinary not only in their ambition, detail and comprehensiveness but also in their visibility and public penetration through banners, street signs and the media. Even more impressive is their record of demonstrated success over nearly forty years of the great opening-up policy.

Belt and Road therefore is the extension of a national strategy that can call on the combined resources and energies of the state, businesses and people. For the West, however, always conflicted over the respective powers of the state and business, the direction of globalization as a strategy depended on the business plans of the global corporations, with the international financial institutions serving as enablers rather than goal setters.

Governments then are torn between the demands of business and those of their electorates. This is the intractable dilemma of liberal democracies. But for China there is no question of national strategy being determined by corporate strategies and the partnership it offers to other countries in building Belt and Road offers them great opportunities to develop their own national strategies.

The strategic partnerships with countries such as Pakistan, India, Turkey, Germany, France and the UK provide an incentive for them to strengthen the role of the state in setting national goals. In the UK agreement with China, forging ahead with cooperation on building nuclear power plants goes hand in hand with an explicit commitment to an industrial strategy, something that has been rejected by successive governments ever since Margaret Thatcher was Prime Minister, a rejection that fitted with the move to neo-liberal economics and the ideology of free markets.

Without question, as far as *ideology* is concerned, Belt and Road is grounded in socialism with Chinese characteristics and therein lies a fundamental difference from Western ideas of globalization. Whether as neo-liberalism or in the social

---

[25] Ibid. pp. 53-60.

democratic amendments to its economic doctrines, Western theories neutralized cultural differences and advanced their policies as universally applicable. The so-called Washington Consensus ignored cultural difference and was notoriously inflexible and prescriptive for Russia after the fall of the Soviet Union and in the South East Asian crisis of the 1990s.

The Chinese Belt and Road initiative calls on markets to aid in the achievement of socialism and is confident that socialism can be built in China on the basis of the cultural traditions of Chinese civilization as well as on Marxist principles. But this clearly is a formula that allows for other countries to join Belt and Road on the basis of their own cultural experience and ideological commitments. Chinese socialism is not for export.

All that Belt and Road requires from its partners is that they recognize a mutual interest in investing in infrastructure and connectivity. The most obvious proof that this is beyond ideology must be the commitment of President Trump to a vast infrastructure programme for the United States, basically the same as the defeated Democrats had been offering, though more ambitious.

The contrast then between Western globalization and the Chinese Belt and Road initiative is profound in respect of the different discourses through which they are promoted to the general public. They reach far into the speech writing, policy formulations and daily routines of officials and executives in both West and East. For that reason I call them public philosophies in the sense understood in the West in the 1950s, 'a body of positive principles and precepts which a good citizen cannot deny or ignore'.[26]

In their reception beyond civilizational boundaries they differ too. I hazard the view that Chinese people have a far better understanding of Western globalization than do their counterparts in the West of Belt and Road. Table 1 summarizes my account above and may help each to understand the other better.

	Western globalization	Chinese Belt and Road
Story	The unification of the world	2,000 years of cultural encounters
Strategy	Going global	The Chinese Dream
Ideology	Liberal democracy	Socialism with Chinese characteristics

Table 1 Western and Chinese Public Philosophies

Renewing global governance

Even as China seeks greater understanding and cooperation with the 64 other partner countries, it is inviting them to join together on the basis of their cultural autonomy. The question I ask here is: Can this succeed where Western globalization has largely failed in helping to create a world in which countries can enjoy equal respect and a rightful share in its benefits?

---

[26] Walter Lippmann 1955, *The Public Philosophy*, p. 93.

The complexity of the task ahead is hinted at in a profound yet apparently light-hearted passage in the speech President Xi made to the College of Europe in Bruges in April 2014. In referring to his equal enjoyment of Chinese tea and European beer he contrasted China's belief in 'harmony without uniformity' with the EU's stress on being 'united in diversity'.[27]

He pointed to each as representative of two great civilizations and both as being necessary for a 'common cultural prosperity'. He then appealed, 'Let us work together allowing for all flowers of human civilization to blossom together.' That is a more eloquent way of speaking of global governance and points directly to a basis as vital as understanding between cultures, namely cooperation for common goals.

Understanding and cooperation between people and peoples are the two fundamental axes on which all global governance has to be based. In general there is inadequate recognition that they draw ultimately on different sides both of the human personality and principles of social organization.

Understanding is based in empathy and has its social expression in community. Cooperation is based in cognition and is realized in a wide variety of organizations or associations. It is a contrast that was developed by sociologists at the beginning of the last century as the core distinction to make in classifying types of society.

In practice, both of these aspects of human relations must be realized for any governance to work, within or between countries. Undue emphasis on one at the expense of the other is likely to result in failure. Perfect understanding of the other is ultimately elusive and never guaranteed, while joint projects with common goals are always vulnerable to underlying different interests.

In the last century the most common approach to reconciling both of these aspects of human action in a society that satisfied human needs was to appeal to shared values.[28] These are both intellectually cognizable, open to discussion, as well as evoking emotional engagement. It is a measure of the advance of global society that since 1945 there have been numerous statements of shared values emanating from the international bodies to which both Western and Eastern countries belong.

The result is that it is not far-fetched to speak of the global community, as does the sociologist Amitai Etzioni, where there is both a global normative consensus and legitimate authorities with specified responsibilities and accountability.[29] This is an ongoing, incomplete achievement that owes nothing to the Western ideology of globalization and everything to a shared recognition of threats to human existence on this earth.

---

[27] Xi, op. cit. p. 310.

[28] At a national level the most famous statement of this position was by Talcott Parsons, 1951, *The Social System*.

[29] Amitai Etzioni 2004, *From Empire to Community*.

In this respect there has been in the last twenty years a definite convergence between the Western outlook and Chinese cultural practices in goal setting and pragmatic programmes. The Millennium Development Goals and now the Sustainable Development Goals provide the same basis for cooperation internationally as the five-year plans do in China.

These are markers for our time that highlight the difference between an account that sees the world homogenized by globalization, the age of globalization, and one that sees countries responding variously to common global challenges, the global age. As Ulrich Beck recognized in his *Risk Society* (1986) and I emphasized in my book *The Global Age* (1996), the sense of common threat is the pervasive feature of our time that marks it off from an old modernity.

While sharing this sense of common challenges, we also need to face up to the differences that exist within both the Western and Chinese approaches when it comes to global governance. Building institutional frameworks for large entities, where countries are the constituent parts, that characterizes both Western globalization and the EU, brings with it the risk of overriding and neglecting cultural difference.

I need only mention the recent British vote to leave the European Union to make that point. When Britain joined the developing European institutions, they still formed what was called the European Economic Community. But at the heart of those institutions there has always been the ambition to move towards 'ever closer union' and it has been advocated especially by the unelected officials in the European Commission in Brussels. With the later creation of a European Parliament, the common currency, the Euro, the formation of the European Union and talk of a European army, this dream moved ever closer to what for many in the UK was not a dream but a nightmare, a superstate in which national identity was submerged.

The Chinese approach, however, also brings its own risks, very clearly outlined in the recent account of the Belt and Road initiative by Professor Wang Yiwei.[30] He lists a series of risks, political, security, economic, legal and moral. The construction of community is one strategy for containing them that he highlights and he cites the establishment of the European Economic Community in 1965 as an example at the regional level. As I have just pointed out, that is an exceptionally relevant point in the context of the British exit from the European Union, because a main complaint has been that the Union has departed from the original spirit of a community.

Recognizing the power of the idea of community, the 18th CPC National Congress advanced the concept of a 'community of common destiny' as a formula for global integration. This certainly evokes both the common understanding that characterizes community and the sense of purpose and direction conveyed by the

---

[30] Wang Yiwei 2016, *The Belt and Road Initiative. What Will China Offer the World in its Rise.*

idea of destiny. Finding a formula that resonates effectively across all cultures is of course the translation challenge that exceeds all translation challenges, but this does takes us forward, at least in the English language and I assume in Chinese too.

Eastern and Western, Chinese and European approaches to global govern-ance have to engage with one another. Finding a common language is as important as sharing a common task. 'Community of common destiny' may well succeed in becoming a key concept in a cultural heritage that belongs to all humankind. But let us note how it arises. It does so in the context of dialogues with ASEAN, Africa, Latin America and Caribbean countries, as well as out of the experience of Europe.

It is then a *transcultural* concept, belonging to no national culture in particu-lar, but crossing many and shared by all. It is therefore particularly appropriate that transculturality as a concept was probably born in a colonial culture that had experienced centuries of immigration and cultural encounters, hybridization and fusion. The Cuban social scientist, anthropologist Fernando Ortiz, first employed the idea of transculturalism when exploring the emergence of a new and distinc-tive musical culture arising out of native, African and Spanish roots in Cuba.[31]

Transculturality is a generative process that arises out of the encounter be-tween cultures and results in the creation of new culture, an outcome that can be transformative for the original cultures. For a recent example we can read the account of European and Chinese seventeenth and eighteenth century encounters by the Chinese social anthropologist Shou Yu, who also looks forward to the tran-sition for the Chinese Dream to a world symbiotic dream.[32]

Those early modern encounters had long-term consequences for both West and East. For the West they prompted deep consideration of religion and a rec-ognition of religious experience as profound as, but different from Christianity. For China they served to emphasize that science had applications across cultural boundaries.

From the example of the Jesuits at the court of the Emperor Kangxi and their conversations with Gottfried Leibniz, it is easy to move to the recognition that the world religions, Buddhism, Christianity, Islam, are each transcultural products, independent of any culture, transformed by all, and for that very reason are de-scribed as world religions.

In the modern world, in the secular reaction against religion, Marxism from its beginning and in its development to this day assumed a transcultural character. Marx and Engels, German Jews living in Britain, inspired the International Work-ing Men's Movement, assuming a distinct character wherever it took root, open

---

[31] Ortiz 1951, *Los Bailes y el Teatro de los Negros en el Folklore de Cuba*.

[32] Yu 2015, 'Universal Dream, National Dreams and Symbiotic Dream: Reflections on Transcultural Generativity in China-Europe Encounters', *Journal of China in Comparative Perspective*, Vol. 1, No. 1, pp. 44-81, 201-227.

to every culture, belonging to none in particular. It has achieved its most notable success in China, the most striking recent example of how West and East can discover a common resource arising out of their encounters.

In the global frame it is the recognition of this generative process that led the United Nations to promote its Dialogue of Civilizations and for dialogue to become a guiding principle for relations between nation-states with very different cultural heritage. The results are ongoing, perhaps the most striking being the almost unanimous acceptance of the idea of sustainability in guiding human concern for the preservation of the natural environment on which its future depends.

China has particular strengths that make it an ideal source for contributions to new transcultural concepts for global governance. In a paper in the new journal *Global Communication* I highlighted eight qualities in China's cultural heritage that represent a uniquely appropriate set for a leadership role in our fragmenting world: effectiveness, efficiency, legitimacy, respect, reciprocity, reverence, transcendence and inventiveness.[33] Of these I would single out respect, reciprocity and inventiveness as obvious potential contributions to a recasting of global governance.

Empirical research and philosophical analysis of global interactions between cultures are essential accompaniments of a programme as far-reaching as Belt and Road. The language that is necessary to promote global governance has to develop beyond that which was the medium for understanding in an older modern period of competition between nation-states. The development of concepts for our new age is a necessary professional concern for social scientists and they can all contribute to what we may properly call philosophical social science.

Given the corporate structure of Chinese state and society, the speeches of President Xi are the most authoritative statement of its basic principles, policies and future direction. In two recent speeches on successive days at the World Economic Forum meeting in Davos and at the Geneva Office of the United Nations he provided both an update on the Belt and Road initiative and a statement for a world audience of the policies that will interest it.[34]

On Belt and Road he was able to report that, after three years, over 100 countries and international organizations had given support, and more than 40 had signed cooperation agreements. His answer to the question of Chinese policies towards the rest of the world was very direct. It had four elements:

---

[33] Albrow 2016 (in Chinese), 'Bridging the Divides – China's Role in a Fragmenting World', 《弥合分歧——中国在分化世界中的角色》, *Global Communication*.

[34] Xi 2017, 'Jointly Shoulder Responsibility of Our Times, Promote Global Growth', Davos, 17 January; 'Work Together to Build a Community of Shared Future for Mankind', Geneva, 18 January.

1. Peace ('part of our DNA') and stability 'the only way to development and prosperity';
2. Commitment to common development, 'when you drink water you should remember its source';
3. Partnerships on the basis of the *Five Principles of Peaceful Co-existence*;
4. Multilateralism, upholding an international system with the United Nations as its core.

At different points in those speeches Xi introduced key concepts for any developing system of global governance, including inclusive globalization, a community of shared future, interconnection and interdependence, democracy in international relations, the diversity of civilizations and shared governance. He also cited the recent meeting of the G20 in Hangzhou for having for the first time put development within a macro-policy framework.

All these are concepts at the highest level of generality, each of which at the same time provides an overarching agenda for empirical research and philosophical analysis that is the proper concern of the philosophical social sciences. *Xi Jinping: The Governance of China* provides numerous examples of the way these in turn inform public policy in China as well as in foreign relations.

The full effect of Belt and Road will be felt when it has become the springboard for the extension of this conception of philosophical social science to global governance as a whole, not as a set of prescriptions for others to follow, but as a shared enterprise, prompted by partnerships, that develops new transcultural concepts. The community of common destiny already has a claim to be such a concept at the highest of generality for global governance. Many more will be needed in these turbulent times.

The cultural autonomy of nations will be as jealously guarded in the future as it has been in the past, and there can be no restriction on their right to profess values for themselves and to commend them to all human beings. Yet in a community of common destiny they will only find security for themselves and respect from others when they find a common basis for working together successfully, in the practice of a pragmatic universalism that denies dogmatism and is open to correction through experience and debate.

DOI https://doi.org/10.24103/GCSS.en.2018.7

Chapter Three

Harmonizing goals and values: the challenge for Belt and Road[1]

As one of the organizing committee of this, the 4th Global China Dialogue, may I extend the warmest welcome to our distinguished visitors from the rest of the world and, in particular, from the People's Republic of China.

You have joined us at the midpoint of our series of seven Dialogues. Some of you have already taken part in our debates and demonstrated that your country is a key contributor to the developing awareness of the need for a new global order.

You will notice from our programme that the Dialogues began with China considered in a comparative perspective. They will conclude in three years' time with the reform of global governance.

These are the departure and destination points in our journey over seven years and I would argue that, so far, we have kept pace, if somewhat breathlessly, with the hectic rate of changes in the world around us. We hope we make our own small contribution to ensuring that those changes can be positive.

In 2014 we were reflecting the Western recognition that China's opening-up policy signalled a distinctive and innovative approach to development. Last year we focused on one of the major demands for cooperation across boundaries, namely combating climate change. This year we generalize our concerns to all goals.

We engage in our dialogue at a time when there is a reassertion of nation-state sovereignty within the global order. Some detect in that a dismantling of the multilateral systems that have been built so laboriously over the decades since 1945. It is irresponsible to dismiss those fears as groundless.

Yet, by contrast, this very event here in London is built on something other than national sovereignty. We share a belief in the constructive potential of dialogue, we are concerned to contribute to a global order that extends to all humankind. We recognize dangers that confront us all.

These common understandings exist, even though we may be citizens of countries with leaders who proclaim their own country comes first. What we enjoy here, therefore, is what we have emphasized in our previous dialogues, and will do so again in this one, a *transcultural* experience. With our feet on our countries' earth we lift our eyes to a heaven we all hope to share.

We are then half way on a journey that takes us towards a reshaped global order, with a developing understanding that sovereign countries will each be able

---

[1] Keynote speech at the opening of the 4th Global China Dialogue, at the British Academy in London, 1 December 2017.

to make their distinctive contribution to it. In the case of China it has become such a powerful agency it can exercise a decisive influence on the emerging shape of that order.

'Belt and Road', announced by President Xi Jinping only four years ago, is already a unique contribution, referencing in its name the historic ties between China, East and West, avoiding in that way the summary, soulless anagrams that dominate the language of global governance.

This is not to say China is not also an experienced participant user of the multilateral governance alphabet, in APEC, ASEAN, BRICS, G20, IAEA, IMF, UN and UNESCO and so on. But none of these can offer the poetic resonance and cross-cultural backstory of Belt and Road. This evokes a family history, the family of nations.

Of course China also takes initiatives that extend the multilateral model, for instance by founding the Asian Infrastructure Investment Bank. The financial backing of the AIIB provides a vital function for Belt and Road projects.

But those projects are much more than the financial guarantees that support them. They have an engagement in the culture of the partner countries that no amount of financial leveraging can match.

When China agrees with Kazakhstan to begin the Bright Road Initiative, or with Vietnam on the One Economic Circle, or with the UK to support the Northern Powerhouse, technology and infrastructure are core components. But in each case the demand for these initiatives arises also out of the felt needs of the people in their local environments with their distinct cultural heritages.

Sea trade between France and China began in 1698 with the sailing of the ship *Amphitrite* from La Rochelle to Canton. This September, the Committee for Sailing in La Rochelle joined with the International Yacht Club in Dalian to establish there a French-style school of sailing. Connections made through trade and the opportunities for contact it brings link similar lifestyles from cultures far distant from one another in a mutual understanding of what they each value.

President Xi opened the Belt and Road Forum for International Cooperation in Beijing on 14 May with a keynote speech that included five principles that should steer the Belt and Road Initiative to greater success. They asked for cooperation along five roads: to peace; to prosperity; to opening up; of innovation; connecting different civilizations.

He elaborated the fifth of these, connecting different civilizations, in the following way: 'exchange will replace estrangement, mutual learning will replace clashes, and co-existence will replace a sense of superiority. This will boost mutual understanding, mutual respect and trust among different countries.'

Let us consider the very basic grounding of these connections. In the beginning there is a shared project to build a road, or a railway, or a port. There is clear goal with a specific understood benefit. Our understanding of why others build roads is as intuitive and immediate as our understanding of why birds build nests. Infrastructure is only the forbidding term we use for something as basic as providing the conditions for safeguarding the long-term necessities of social life.

Thus, it is not just for economic reasons that the response of all major economies in recent years since the financial crisis of 2008 has been to invest in infrastructure. Within a country it is possible to achieve political consensus around the renewal of basic requirements for transport and travel. It is a public good delivering benefits to all social classes, even if under capitalism they are distributed as profit for some and wages for others.

But the President of the People's Republic of China is challenging us to see Belt and Road not just as a sharing of technologies for common goals but as a journey towards greater understanding between cultures. Infrastructure across boundaries, crossing seas, linking far distant lands has the potential to create that wider sense of community of a shared future that he has often held up to us as the direction in which we must all travel.

I have little doubt that it is by taking steps along this road that people can begin to tackle the problems that are genuinely global in their reach. The experience of shared technology for common goals is a good preparation for cooperating in sustainable development. We can hope too that it may aid in the spread of nuclear technologies for peaceful use.

This is what President Xi calls 'policy connectivity'. We can add that it is genuinely public policy for the Global Age quite distinct from what is so often regarded as its hallmark, namely globalization.

For me it is quite significant that he confines the use of that term to 'economic globalization', by which we can refer to all those processes that create a single market and promote the worldwide spread of production methods and consumption of goods.

Belt and Road is something else. It is the extension of connectivity that encourages the local culture to find its common features with others and to contribute its distinctive qualities to shaping common ventures. This is what he calls 'people to people connectivity'.

Of course, the advocacy of Belt and Road is also the outstanding example of China 'going global'. Moreover the scope and ambition of the ideas that underpin it make it the most comprehensive initiative for shaping the future global order since the international agreement on the Sustainable Development Goals.

What distinguishes Belt and Road from the SDGs is that it emphasizes processes rather than targets, learning rather than repetition, and innovation rather than standardization. Every country can contribute its own way of going global once it opens up as China has done. The SDGs are still an essential feature of the multilateral system, but Belt and Road is their counterpart contribution to the global order of the family of nations.

This is why I am not as dispirited as so many are by the current worldwide 'my country first' movement. It can also lead to more intensive engagement with global issues, even, at its most paradoxical, to competitive striving to contribute most to their solution. It does not deny cooperation (the 'art of the deal'!) or friendship with other countries.

But the most powerful feature of Belt and Road compared with current contributions to shaping the world order is its consistent determination to bring relevant theoretical ideas into close alignment with the practical problems facing humankind.

It pins the abstract vocabulary of culture, exchange, cooperation, connectivity, co-existence and interdependence to the map of our world today or, as Xi describes it, 'in this increasingly multipolar, economically globalized, digitized and culturally diversified world'.

I can think of no better way to describe the current state of the world with no more than seven descriptors! (Perhaps that could spark a competition for this Dialogue: 'Find seven words to describe our human condition at this time.')

At the same time let us not underestimate the challenge that Belt and Road is taking up. Even as it applauds cultural diversity and aims to find common cause in joint projects, it is facing values that many see as imperilled and announce they will defend 'to the death'.

One only has to think of one of the most contested areas in development policies, population planning. India and China have long looked over one another's shoulders at their respective efforts. China's one-child family policy began in 1979 and was largely effective until it was recently replaced with a two-child policy.

By contrast, India has struggled since the 1950s with a variety of policies in different states, with very different reactions, even trying compulsory sterilization in the mid-1970s, contributing to a national emergency and the attempted assassination of Sanjay Gandhi, the Prime Minister's son who was held largely responsible for the population policies of the time.

These are not insurmountable problems. I recall touring Bangladesh's population programme in the 1980s and finding close cooperation between religious Imams, the state and women's cooperatives. I cherish still my photograph of a Centre for Conjugal Beatitude where family planning knowledge was available to local men and women.

Values are rooted in the historic experience of peoples, shape their identity, daily lives and plans. They differ from the mundane, short-lived practicality of goals. Even when there are common values between nations they can be divisive. Sovereignty is the most obvious example.

For these reasons, in the coming Global Dialogues we will be addressing the issues that arise when shared values result in conflict, how we can transcend competing ideas of justice, overcome the inequalities that endanger peace and reform the current system of global governance.

With these objectives in mind, I believe that One Belt One Road is showing the world a pre-eminently practical way forward with the greatest chance of significant progress in achieving them at the present time. Let us therefore enjoy this day as one where we share in its hopeful endeavour.

DOI https://doi.org/10.24103/GCSS.en.2018.8

Chapter Four
Bridging the divides – China's role in a fragmenting world

Today the world cries out for global leadership. Revolutions in the technology of communication, the growth of social media, the polarization of rich and poor, the globalization of terror and the relentless pressure of global warming all contribute to a sense of a world beyond human control. Impending fragmentation threatens Europe, and the United States suffers grievously from the realization that it no longer dominates the world order which it did most to establish after the Second World War.

A completely new geopolitical situation requires new forms of leadership. Western powers are in disarray and the world needs to look for inspiration from a continuous civilization with roots going back 5,000 years. In the twentieth century China has demonstrated both the capacity to adapt its ancient culture to the processes of modernization and also the resilience needed to withstand the ensuing shocks. No other power possesses a similar range of qualities that make it fit for assuming a global leadership role.

The current need for global leadership

What I am going to argue here is that the current world situation requires a country to assume a role for the world as a whole, to provide leadership dedicated to the development of global public policy to complement the military role of the United States. Together they can lead in partnership with other nations to provide governance of the globe for the benefit of the whole of humankind.

Let me make one thing amply clear at this point. I am not talking of China becoming the sole hegemon. The title of Martin Jacques's well-known book *When China Rules the World* was of course deliberately provocative. Its premise, that it is possible for some agency or other to rule the world, is the weak point in an otherwise outstanding account of contemporary China.[1] For the interconnected, digital world that has arisen over the last generation cannot be ruled as countries were in the past.

Not since the 1930s has the world experienced such a time of division and uncertainty. In those years revolution and war were destroying ordinary life for millions of people in the Soviet Union and China. The new world power, the United States, was immersed in its domestic problems, absenting itself from the extremist aftermath of the First World War that was shaping Europe.

---

[1] Jacques 2009.

Yet in those years of turmoil the United States was also building a new national purpose, the New Deal that underpinned the collective endeavour that the coming Second World War was going to require. It is an irony of history that this collectivism enabled the champion of Western individualism to join with the deeply opposed power ideologically, the Soviet Union, to defeat European Fascism. It also empowered it for the leadership needed to create the new world order after 1945.

Today militant Islam's aspiration for the Caliphate has assumed the form of the self-proclaimed Islamic state, spreading destruction both as a strategy and on principle, taking advantage from divisions between the powers whose commitment to that seventy-year-old settlement has steadily diminished. But whatever divides world powers today, the lesson of the 1930s is that they have an overriding common interest in defeating a movement that rules through fear and celebrates death and destruction.

The paradox of the present time is that an unprecedented recognition of our common human condition, a global consciousness of a shared fate, competes with an ideology of destructiveness that, armed with nuclear or biological weapons, could inflict damage on the world as catastrophic as, and certainly more immediate than even global warming.

The sense of a shared human fate was what I with others sought to characterize as the Global Age, a transformation led by worldwide concern for issues such as climate change and nuclear proliferation that threaten human existence on this planet.[2] This was literally years away from the belief in progress that was central to the optimism of the Modern Age at the outset of the twentieth century.

Now, even as global issues are as pressing as ever, the communications revolution has projected the Digital Age into the headlines, and its accompanying network society signals an interconnectedness that unites people worldwide, not just in beliefs but in everyday social relations.

Yet, in contradictory fashion, however closely networks bond distant parts together, they appear to do nothing to reduce gross inequalities and injustices that globalization has served to intensify. Injustice and inequality are spread across countries in cultural divisions, by generation, gender and occupation, even as the older ones persist, of language, religion and ethnicity

These waves of historical change, the Modern, the Global, the Digital, each successive one overlaying the other, arrive on a rising tide of population growth and environmental degradation that promote massive migratory shifts, putting pressure on national governments and increasing international tension. The new communications hugely increase the integration of the global economy and mean nowhere is safe from the impact of the business cycle that, like the tides, continues to elude human control.

---

[2] Albrow 1996, *The Global Age: State and Society beyond Modernity* (Chinese edition, 2004).

It is a time of fragmentation. Gone are the bipolar world of the Cold War, the three worlds of world development, even the multipolar world. Those past worlds were grounded in hegemonic military power, where nation-states had effective control of the means of destruction and the states with the most powerful military capability secured the geopolitical order.

World leadership to address multiple global challenges is no longer a simple function of military strength. Soft power, the extension of national influence through culture, is frequently seen as a kind of equivalent means in an information age to exercise control over others. China is no exception in promoting its culture in this way worldwide.[3]

But in a fragmented networked world local threats carry destruction far beyond national control. Common challenges require collective cooperation. The reduction of carbon emissions, ending human trafficking, creating communication security, managing space exploration and dealing with non-state violence and criminality across borders fuel the demand for global governance in our Digital Age. Here what the world needs is not the power of the few over the many but the capacity to bring people together in the common cause. It can happen, and does even in our divided world today.

The Paris Agreements to combat climate change of December 2015 were the most dramatic and far-reaching since 1945 in the number of countries (194) involved and the momentous nature of the challenge that they resolved to tackle. They mark the highest point yet in a collective global public policy and China and the United States were the most prominent signatories. Leadership was shared and the power that matters in this case is the capacity to deliver common objectives.

The leadership that led to the founding of the United Nations, the agreement to the Universal Declaration of Human Rights, the new international financial institutions and the transformation of Europe through the Marshall Plan belonged primarily to a country, the United States, that was manifestly ('manifest destiny' has a hallowed place in American public discourse) in charge of its own affairs and capable of framing projects for the declared benefit of the wider world.

At this moment of time, March 2016, the world appears to revisit the twentieth century's pre-world war periods rather than the time of the new world order after 1945. The subsequent tensions of the Cold War have never been entirely dissipated as the continued rivalry of the United States and Russia shows, and the Western powers have allowed their dependence on Middle East oil supplies to inflame centuries-old divisions in Islam.

None of the parties involved in the Middle East conflicts is able to impose its will or to provide a vision of an eventual settlement. A comparison of the inability of the United States to shape the future now compared with its capacity in 1945 is

---

[3] Barr 2011, *Who's Afraid of China? The Challenge of China's Soft Power.*

the starkest reminder of the relative weakness of even the strongest military power to deliver peace.

Moreover, the relative power of any country to shape even its own fate, let alone that of others, is now very much less in this globalizing world. Although nation-states remain as the most powerful human agencies, leadership among them will involve accepting that power is polycentric, belonging both to national and non-national actors, across social and economic sectors that span country boundaries.

A country stepping into a leadership role will work through shared institutions, inspiring others rather than dogmatizing, guiding rather than commanding. The world needs leadership of and for diversity in order to meet the global challenges that threaten us all.

China's leadership profile

The profile of leadership qualities that China offers for a globalized world is complex and unique. Any attempt to summarize it is bound to be both too simple and controversial. I make no apology for that, because its purpose is to focus attention and to promote more developed thought and debate.

Let me then follow the ages-old Chinese tradition of enumerating key principles and propose eight Chinese global leadership qualities. The enumerating tradition may be ancient and hallowed, the actualization of these particular principles, on the other hand, has been frequently interrupted and never equally observed at any one time in China's past.

These qualities are, however, all components of China's cultural heritage. Together they constitute a comprehensive and distinctive profile for leadership in our time of troubles. Some of them will have their counterparts in the West and in other cultures. But it is the **set taken as a whole** that makes what the business community calls its unique selling point.

1. *Effectiveness.* Every year that has passed since 1979 has demonstrated the capacity of Chinese government to achieve its goals, its successive five year plans to industrialize, urbanize and raise the standard of living of its population. There is no equal case in history of such a rapid transformation of the lives of such a huge population.
2. *Efficiency.* The economic successes of the last decades have depended on bridging the divides between socialism and capitalism, creating policies combining regulation and marketization, eliciting individual motivation and providing both for profit taking and investment.
3. *Legitimacy.* The Communist Party supervises the constitutional framework and basic values of the Chinese state within which individual freedom of expression is allowed, a position described as consultative democracy. There is no significant opposition to a constitutional arrange-

ment that has acquired the aura of success that now escapes so many Western democracies.[4]

4. *Respect.* Traditionally respect underpinned authority and inequality. Since 1949 women and minority peoples have been able to invoke equal rights under Chinese law and are finding support for their extension into controversial areas such as reproduction rights and gender bias in the workplace.

5. *Reciprocity.* The ideas of mutual obligation, repaying favours and the necessity of maintaining social relationships in the family and the community have been integral to a Chinese way of life, over millennia, across generations, over distance to persons in their absence.[5]

6. *Reverence.* The sense of connectedness with others includes the dead and those yet to be born, and memory is embodied in the practices of ancestor commemoration and traditional ceremonies and festivals as well as in the study of ancient classics and the preservation of cultural heritage. Since the destruction of the Cultural Revolution, there is a renewed and vigorous drive to connect to China's past.

7. *Transcendence.* This concept been the focus of debate in the West ever since Leibniz discerned a universal basis of natural religion in Chinese philosophy (*tian* and *dao*). It provides for a reconnection with a pre-modern ethos, with non-dogmatic Confucian and Taoist thought, and promotes open-ended debate about the meaning of human existence.

8. *Inventiveness.* The four great inventions, papermaking, gunpowder, printing and the compass, have had worldwide consequences for civilization. Less applauded, though just as important, has been the centuries-old Chinese invention of bureaucracy and formal examinations.

It would be vain to pretend that these qualities have all been represented in their purity over the last decades, let alone since 1949. In most cases, it is easy to think of gross deviations from their requirements. The Great Leap Forward was a case of 'irrational instrumentality',[6] the Cultural Revolution was a grotesque contradiction, the One-Child Policy was contrary to principles of respect and reciprocity, while current policies of westward resettlement appear to prioritize effectiveness over legitimacy.

Indeed, we must not imagine that any one of these qualities can be promoted above and to the exclusion of the others. Harmony between them is the overriding principle. For this very reason, that these qualities are not mutually exclusive and

---

[4] Fang Ning 2014, *China's Democracy Path.*

[5] Chang 2010, *Guanxi or Li Shang Wanglai? Reciprocity, Social Support Networks, & Social Creativity in a Chinese Village.*

[6] Joy Y. Zhang and Michael Barr 2013, *Green Politics in China.*

contain potential contradictions, I have not included harmony on equal terms with them. It is not equal, it occupies **an even higher position**.

The pursuit of harmony involves precisely the recognition that the diversity of human attributes and goals, the precarious relationship between human needs and the natural world, makes conflicts and environmental crises ever present dangers. Harmony is a prerequisite for order and its pursuit is integral to governance, local, national or global.

For that reason, harmony has long been viewed as the overriding concern in thousands of years of Chinese thought and public policy. The durability of the commitment of the Chinese people over the centuries to harmony as the supreme principle, its repeated renewal even after periods of chaos, brings them at this moment of time to be the uniquely qualified candidate for the role of global leadership.

But there is another requirement for leadership without which principles are idle fantasies, and that is power.

Power and the leadership role in a global society

The transition from an old modern age to a new global age was accompanied by a shift in the terms of geopolitical relations between the great powers. From military confrontation the emphasis shifted to economic and cultural competition. One popular way of expressing this change has been with Joseph Nye's concept of soft power, a way to achieve ends by non-military means despite resistance, through cultural influence, media penetration and persuasive ideas.[7]

Soft power is a concept well adapted to the American world-view after the fall of the Soviet Union where the use of military force has been increasingly inadequate as a means to bring other countries under control, and ideas such as globalization have been promoted to secure compliance with an American world order.

The problem with the idea of soft power is that power over others is still the main focus of interest, an extension of a realist view of international relations where nation-states vie for supremacy in a zero-sum game. As such, it expresses a deep current in Western intellectual thought, power over others being the shared concern both of supporters of the established political order and of its radical critics, even dominating thinking about interpersonal relations as much as international relations.

That kind of power, however, is not what is most needed in the world today. There is another kind, the power to achieve goals that extend far beyond the capacities of individuals. We find it in a profound account of power in human society, that of Bertrand Russell. For him, 'Power is the production of intended

---

[7] Nye 2005, *Soft Power: The Means to Success in World Politics.*

effects.'[8] Even though he directed his attention to power over human beings, he explicitly emphasized power over matter or non-human life, and argued that ultimately rule depended on the wisdom of those 'who appeal to the common desires of mankind'.[9]

He would have been entirely unsurprised by the unique power position China occupies today. References to China where he had lived and lectured in 1920 are plentiful. In his words: 'China has always been an exception to all rules.'[10] That China succeeds with a one-party political regime fits the exceptionalist status Russell accorded it. It has what he described as the 'democratic ethic' that was essential to any centrally organized state if it was to avoid the despotism he observed in Soviet Russia and Hitler's Germany.

What organization for a collective goal can achieve in China's case is well represented by the Three Gorges Dam on the Yangtze River. The equivalent in the United States was the Hoover Dam on the Colorado River completed in 1932. It foreshadowed later world leadership but no country deeply divided in itself is capable of assuming global leadership and that rules out the West today, the United States and the countries of Europe, divided within and between themselves.

The story of how the United States lost its confidence in global leadership in recent years is in part one of self-deception, of believing that it provided past leadership through military power when in fact it depended on its collective capacity to get things done on behalf of the world. That decline of belief in the collectivity and its agency, a turning in on itself and intensifying divisiveness have been crucial factors in failing to fulfil the global leadership role.

America still occupies the dominant position in military strength, but the limits on what it can achieve in securing order in the Digital Age are increasingly obvious. The challenges that confront global society as a whole require the kind of leadership that the United States provided after the Second World War. Manifestly, the scope of those demands and the interdependence of countries mean that leadership of that kind must be distributed and shared.

The Sustainable Development Goals need to be the current equivalent for the globe that the Marshall Plan was for Europe in 1947. China, with its unique set of qualities and its newly won strength economically, is currently the only country able to take the lead in partnership with others in ensuring that those goals are delivered. It is the moment for the Middle Kingdom to occupy the global centre stage.

Let me add one more comment on the role before turning to China's potential in it. The concept of role was once central to Western sociology, especially in mid-twentieth century United States. It fell out of favour in large part because it was criticized as a projection of American power while concealing its real nature.

---

[8] Bertrand Russell 1938, *Power: A New Social Analysis*, p.85.
[9] Ibid. p. 284.
[10] Ibid. p. 188.

But as a concept its valuable feature is that it emphasizes that a role is not created by the agent who occupies it, even if it allows for creative activity in its exercise. A role is created by the others: it is their expectations which define its scope and responsibilities. That is as true of a leadership role as of any other. In the case of global leadership, world society expects the occupant of the role to lead on the common tasks that confront them all.

Agency and responsibility of a nation-state

What does it mean for a country to have the global leadership role? At its simplest, it means striving to take the world forward to achieve certain goals and being held responsible for the result of those efforts. Or, put another way, the country has agency, the will and capacity to make a difference. It is regarded by others as responsible for its actions. Those notions reflect both public discourse and common-sense; they are the basis of citizenship and civic rights and hold their validity in international law.

Mention of law, however, brings into focus a range of issues that have a direct bearing on power and leadership for global society. For in international law it is the state rather than the country that has responsibility, and states have very varying degrees of unity, of relationships with their citizens and of citizen identification with their country. State and country are not the same thing and neither is the same as a nation, though the modern term 'nation-state' has become standard usage in order to elide and conceal these differences. Governments everywhere find it convenient to think in nation-state terms.

The state is the cutting edge of a country, the public legal entity recognized by others, controlling an army, imposing taxes. But it is not the same as its people. A country contains self-motivated individuals engaged in private activities sharing in a culture and affirming a collective identity that sometimes is even opposed to the state. We need think only of the way American citizens so often harbour suspicion of central government and at the same time affirm a fervid patriotism. And for others in the rest of the world what is American is much more Hollywood and Wall Street than it is Capitol Hill.

The country is more than the state, the nation, culture or even society. In some sense it contains them all, but as a construct of everyday discourse it is a collective entity, existing in and through its people, a historical actor the subject of grand narratives. Political scientist Benedict Anderson described it as the 'imagined community'.[11] The great historian Arnold Toynbee sought to grasp these features of a country by calling them mythological, represented by figures like Marianne in France or John Bull in the United Kingdom.[12] But then the myth is real – in its effects at least.

---

[11] Benedict Anderson 1983, *Imagined Communities: Reflections on the Origins and Spread of Nationalism.*

[12] Arnold Toynbee 1935, *A Study of History*, Vol. 1, p. 443.

The capacity for collective agency is what all national leaders seek to enhance and use, indeed cannot avoid using to secure their own position, to advance the causes they support and to maintain their state's security in international relations. The power of the state is at their disposal but they will employ all the political arts to mobilize support through public opinion, the media, entertainment and sport, business links, patronage and connections with elites. Leadership to be successful has to add its own qualities to these resources to achieve goals that can command general assent.

President Xi Jinping in his acceptance speech to the session of the National People's Congress that elected him to be President of the People's Republic of China advocated a Chinese Dream, a rejuvenation of the nation based on socialism with Chinese characteristics, relying on the people to achieve modernization and 'moderate prosperity'. The implicit global leadership aspiration in echoing the American Dream is obvious, to be made explicit in the final sentence of his speech invoking 'accelerating socialist modernization, and thus make new and bigger contribution to mankind'.[13]

The place of the Dream in Xi's narrative is clearly modelled on its American equivalent. In the middle of the American century, the dominant sociological theory saw the country as a society integrated around common values, the American Dream, at its core providing a purpose, which, projected into international affairs, was expressed as modernization. The theory reflected the country and its times, preparing for a period of global leadership.

The 'dream' was a fantasy of perfect unity. Academic critiques of that theory of social integration throughout the 1960s and 1970s focused on its failure to render an adequate account of power, social conflict, divisions of class, gender and ethnicity, and market failure. The modernization aspiration projected on to the rest of the world the features that the United States believed held for its own society. The development it offered was an American road to the future led by the dollar, representative democracy and the global corporation. Globalization was the apotheosis of the American Dream.

The 'dream', the theory of integration around common values, modernization and globalization, were all part of American soft power. They served that purpose effectively up to the point where the divisive and polarizing effects of combining individualism with corporate capitalism became apparent. Since then, the American Dream has lost its persuasive appeal, even for the American public.

Different times require different measures. For a country to have the collective capacity to lead the world, it has to have a unity of its parts and its people while inspiring others to follow its example. In China's case, socialist modernization is the substitute for individual aspiration. In the fragmenting world of our time the cooperation and shared mission that this implies may well be the appro-

---

[13] Xi Jinping 2014, p. 46.

priate basis for partnership with other nations, demonstrating capacity in achieving common goals. Leadership by example and through cooperation on common tasks rather than through soft power should underpin China's global leadership, while the Eight Leadership Qualities China possesses are well adapted to address the problems of today without seeking to replicate the American twentieth-century example.

China's role in global leadership

The US achieved its global leadership after the decline of the British Empire, indeed worked hard to displace their old colonial masters. But American twentieth-century hegemony has not been colonial in the old way, even if many have likened it to empire. Military alliances such as NATO, a dominant position in the global economy through the international financial institutions, the dollar as the world reserve currency, American-owned global corporations, client states particularly in Latin America and the Middle East, all have contributed to a singular global pre-eminence, reaching its culminating point in the 1990s.

By then the US had succeeded too in removing its one rival for global leadership, the Soviet Union, confirming in its own eyes the American political system as the gold standard for democracy and individual freedom. It outstripped all others in scientific research and consolidated the global reach of English-speaking culture. Through the mass media, especially the cinema and popular music, the West and American soft power came to be almost synonymous.

In effect, however, as I have argued elsewhere, the cosmopolitanism of the American achievement, epitomized by Hollywood, actually floated off into a transcultural space detached from grassroots American feeling.[14] The very globalization of American culture has left the homeland with a sense of loss of control over what it has created. The global leadership position appears under threat from its own success and the resulting unease has been redirected towards the most successful of the nations that opted into an American-led modernization, namely China.

At an unconscious level, given its historical relations with Britain, the US in its collective psyche may now fear that China seeks to depose it from world leadership in much the same way as once it relegated Britain to a junior role. That is understandable in a psychological sense. However, the new relationship of China and the US bears little similarity to that earlier relationship, which has often been likened to that of ancient Rome and Greece.

The US and China have arrived at superpower status in quite different ways. China's development has not followed in the wake of military success, and the cessation of armed conflict in the Korean peninsula was based in mutual recognition that a victory would come at unacceptable cost for both sides. Their subse-

---

[14] Albrow 2014b, 'Globalization or Americanization: The Fate of European Culture'.

quent rapprochement eventually developed out of shared interest, hostility to the Soviet Union and the benefits for each of investment and the economic development of a vast market.

China's rise is the result of an extraordinary successful mobilization of the whole population for modernization through a combination of skilful political leadership and economic incentives. It has not been the result of humbling defeated foes or a bid for empire in any sense. Certainly it has been motivated in part by the desire to put the 'century of humiliation' behind it, but any British visitor can report being the beneficiary of a remarkable generosity of spirit in 'letting bygones be bygones'. It could not have happened either without a peaceful trading relationship with the United States.

If China's rise is unique, so also is the current world situation in which it has risen. The Digital Age exhibits an unprecedented degree of interconnectedness, through telecommunication, mass media, transport, trade and shared technologies, capped off with the extraordinary way computing and the internet are revolutionizing interpersonal as well as international relations.

The acceleration of this overall process can only be grasped if we think of signal geo-political events such as the fall of the Soviet Union that happened only recently, in 1989, yet effectively before the internet existed, and the destruction of the World Trade Towers, 9/11 in 2001, before Facebook and Baidu.

Vastly enhanced communication technology itself assists migration. Thus, the interconnectedness of the world is paradoxically associated with the dispersion and fragmentation of local community. The contradiction that arises, between individuals seeking to maintain personal privacy and ties across borders and the demands on states to maintain national security, is only one of the many dilemmas that face governments everywhere.

In this globalizing and localizing, individualizing and networking, interconnected and fragmented world, China brings to its superpower position its distinctive set of Eight Global Leadership Qualities that have huge potential for contributing positively to the human future. Returning to them it is straightforward to illustrate how they are already engaged in that task:

- *Effectiveness*, demonstrated in multiple projects, both public as with the Solar City at Dezhou and private as with the largest renewable energy corporation in the world, the Yingli Green Energy Company.
- *Efficiency* in targeted investment was the aim of China's government in bringing 57 countries together to form the Asia Infrastructure Investment Bank which held its inaugural meeting in January 2016.
- *Legitimacy* for international agreements is promoted by Chinese active engagement in United Nations processes, as in policing piracy in the Indian Ocean or sending peacekeepers to Southern Sudan and mediating in the Middle East conflicts.

- *Respect* is demonstrated in recognizing rights of minorities and women. These extend to autonomous regions and special status for ethnic minorities. Women now have achieved 23.4% of representation in the National People's Congress.
- *Reciprocity* as *guanxi* has been praised in the West as the basis of building both trust and corporate strength, and because the social ethic it inspires remains robust into the Digital Age. It also sustains relations with other countries as in the China–Africa Summit of December 2015.
- *Reverence* in the shape of Chinese festivals brings worldwide media coverage. But the Chinese architectural heritage movement is integral to international efforts to safeguard world heritage to the point where in 2011 it is in receipt of the third largest number of World Heritage awards from UNESCO.
- *Transcendence* emphasizes human symbiosis with nature and the universe. It is receptive to religious ideas and practices from outside China, Buddhism and Christianity in particular, but can also embrace religious differences of all kinds. It promotes ideas of harmony and symbiosis that may repair the ravages of modernity and offer hope for the survival of our species on this earth.
- *Inventiveness* characterizes the drive for continuing reform within Chinese institutions and in the development of consultative democracy. It should also extend to the reform of the institutions for global governance, such as the leaders' meetings of the G20 which is to be hosted in China in September 2016.

China is now, on many measures, the best placed state to assume a global leadership role, equal to the United States, making its impact not through military power but by demonstrating solid achievements in global public policy. It can happen through cooperation with multiple partners, countries, corporations and civil society. Recently, the world has had easy access to the principled approach to governance contained in the publication of *Xi Jinping: The Governance of China*. It is clearly based in principles that call for and depend on citizen commitment. Just such an approach extended to global citizens is required to take global public policy forward.

As the single most powerful integrated agency in the contemporary world, the Chinese state has enormous potential for safeguarding the human future. At the same time, a country is much more than its state. Its unique culture lives in every individual Chinese person, and in the expansion of ties and travel abroad each can carry the promise of a better future for the rest of the world. Agency in our time is conveyed as much by the individual citizen as in state projects, and the identity of every country, however small, now has a global presence beyond its own borders. China, on the other hand, is vast and the time has come for its presence to be a global asset of equivalent immensity.

Theoretical postscript: cultural relativism and pragmatic universalism

The reader today, imbued with the spirit of cultural relativism, may well ask how a British author can begin to imagine a role for China in world affairs, let alone as a Western person be objective about the United States.

One ready answer, of course, is that he is an outsider to both countries and lays claim to the status of 'the impartial and well-informed spectator' made so famous by Adam Smith.[15] But that was supported by Smith's belief that the 'higher tribunal' of conscience, based very much in religious faith, could deliver objectivity. This was a classic expression of Western universalism and can no longer carry conviction.

Yet the pervasive relativism of today is not an answer to the conundrum of finding common purpose among nations. 'Live and let live' is not enough to secure cooperation. What we can do is bring our own convictions and understandings of the truth, our own universalisms to engage with one another to find sufficient agreement for the task in hand. That we may call pragmatic universalism, limited to time, place and task.

In global affairs, a pragmatic universalist outlook generates a transcultural space, which some would describe as global culture. In that space, cultures in dialogue can and often do arrive at common understandings to secure the human future, a global universalism. It does not for that reason invalidate personal or national convictions born of personal experience and cultural identity. Like any universalism, the universalism of global affairs is limited, promoted by and debated among countries and global citizens alike, focused on current challenges to human well-being.

---

[15] Adam Smith 1790, *The Theory of Moral Sentiments.*

DOI https://doi.org/10.24103/GCSS.en.2018.9

Chapter Five
Leadership for a people's democracy[1]

The multi-language publication on April 11th of *Xi Jinping: The Governance of China* volume II is an event of global significance. He speaks not only to the Chinese people, but to all who wish to understand how China is contributing to shape a new world order.

In an appreciation of the first volume three years ago I drew three lessons from it. These were:

First, it teaches us that, to understand the present, we have to embrace the past.

Second, it demonstrates how much we should value systematic thought in political leadership.

Third, the idea of governance prepares us to bring China, the West and the Rest of the World together in the idea of global governance.

They are all amply illustrated in this second volume. It expands on and develops all of them. We find old friends in familiar places as the thoughts of Confucius and Aristotle, Leibniz and Locke, Mencius, Marx and Mao flow like tributaries into the great stream of socialism with Chinese characteristics.

They inform what I called the architectonic of the Chinese political system, erected on interconnected concepts of community level self-governance, consultative democracy, the people's political participation, ethnic autonomy, all developed in practice through the continuing cooperation of people, party and government.

As China goes out into the world we find here the further development of ideas behind the Belt and Road initiative and the corresponding high-level global governance concept that Xi proposes, 'Towards a Community of Shared Future for Mankind'. This was the title of the speech he gave at the United Nations Office in Geneva in January 2017, which is a fitting conclusion to the volume.

The recent development of Xi's thought is reflected in big new sections in the second volume, on party discipline, cultural confidence, the people's well-being, and beautiful China. They reflect continuing reform, a still more confident going-out to match the opening-up.

These new sections are coupled with a greater emphasis throughout on the role of the Party in providing direction and motivation for the country as a whole.

---

[1] *Xi Jinping: The Governance of China*, Foreign Languages Press Co. Ltd, Beijing, China, 2017. An abbreviated version of this review was delivered as a speech at the Global Launch of *Xi Jinping: The Governance of China, Volume II*, in London on April 11th, 2018.

This fits well with the observation that, unlike the American Dream of personal success, the Chinese Dream is one of national rejuvenation.

This overall development of ideas since the first volume leads me to propose that there is a further lesson for the West that we can draw from Xi's thought, namely:

> **Fourth**, China's democracy path is the on-going demonstration of how leadership of the people is achieved through the Communist Party.

An on-going process of democratic leadership provides a continual, specifically Chinese reconciliation of socialist principles with those of a market economy. It is no accident then that the introduction to this volume consists of extracts from a tribute by Xi to Deng Xiaoping.

This was a man whose political career was, as Xi declares, 'an inexhaustible source of integrity for all Chinese Communists'. Deng's leadership confronted the party and people with 'truth from facts' and began the reform and opening-up on which the ever-growing prosperity of China is founded.

Such leadership is not the imposition of one person rule. It is an inspirational force that incites emulation. It explores and draws on the potential in people, it encourages them to recognize their own capacities, to work for their own welfare and to become responsible agents in the interests of the wider society.

This is leadership as it can be understood anywhere in the world. In China it is provided by the Communist Party. This is why Xi's second volume offers an even bolder and more challenging vision to the West than the first.

Let me emphasize here that the three lessons I drew from the first volume were for the benefit of Western readers. This fourth lesson is also for them. But it also confronts them with a more emphatic challenge than any of the others. It touches on deeply embedded prejudices about China, socialism and communist parties.

The West still cannot rid itself of preconceptions about communism that stem from the Cold War era, from the fate of the Soviet Union and the Eastern bloc. But Chinese communism is a unique and indigenous product, shaped through struggle in a tumultuous century of Chinese history.

The democratic revolution and end of imperial rule in 1911, the founding of the party in 1921, the Long March, the Japanese occupation, Civil War, the founding of the People's Republic in 1949, the ten years of Cultural Revolution all illustrate how facts on the ground so often dictate ideas.

But the last forty years in China since 1978 demonstrates that ideas, in this case the interplay of Marxism with both Chinese and Western intellectual traditions, can adapt to changing contemporary conditions, lead to a more sophisticated understanding of them, and most importantly can take charge of events.

China today is a showcase for the on-going dialectic of material advance and the advocacy of values. Allow me a personal impression of how this works.

It was my privilege to attend the 2016 Symposium on China Studies hosted by the Chinese Ministry of Culture and the Academy of Social Sciences. It included an observational tour of Qinghai Province. Official visits included the Kumbum Tibetan Buddhist monastery, the Jizie Grand Mosque of the Salar people and the former residence of the 10th Panchen Lama, each an example of Chinese respect for diversity in religion and ethnic culture.

But on such occasions it is not necessarily the organized visit that impresses most. Every traveller entering the provincial capital of Xinin from the county of Xunhua sees array after array of residential tower blocs that house a large proportion of the two million population of the city.

Viewed from afar this economic vitality would seem to be signalled by a gigantic illuminated display towering over the highway. The materialism of the West leads one to expect an advertisement for fast food, or at least the latest high tech device.

Closer proximity reveals that it displays the 12 core socialist values: 'prosperity, democracy, civility, harmony, freedom, equality, justice, the rule of law, patriotism, dedication, integrity and friendship'.

Not just Xinin advertises these. Every committee of the local community party, every branch of the party in an enterprise, private or public, up to the Central Committee and down to and including every party member will have studied and discussed these.

Party members take these values into their daily work, making them real to non-members, who in turn become the agents of national rejuvenation. They respond to the Party, drawing on their practical experience. This is the process known as ideological work, following the 'mass line', 'from the people to the people', resulting in self-examination by officials, 'pooling the wisdom and strength of the whole of society' (pp. 322-323).

This is 'The Broad, Multilevel, and Institutionalized Consultative Democracy' as described by Xi in a speech on the 65th anniversary of its founding to the Central Committee of the Communist Party in September 2014.

In the familiar terms of organizational sociology, this is collective decision making with distributed agency, the whole society gaining a sense of purpose in a way that in the West is associated only with corporate entities at a sub-national level. Thus develops a specifically Chinese concept of democracy quite as powerful intellectually and in practice as any developed in the West.

This book is a record of work in progress, of the direction of and aspirations for the Chinese Dream as spoken by its top leader. But it is not a book just for the Chinese public. It should be read by everyone concerned for the global future of our species.

And, for all those Western people who view China's rise with suspicion and alarm, I say, 'Fear not, for you have nothing to lose but the chains of your own prejudices.'

DOI https://doi.org/10.24103/GCSS.en.2018.10

Part Two
Theory for the global social order

The second part of this volume reflects my confidence that China's respect for theory will compensate for the decline of public philosophy in the West and fill the resulting gap in a rational approach to the world's problems. The world needs Chinese ideas as much as China has adopted ideas from the world.

It begins therefore with a fine example in the study by Xiaoying Qi of Chinese theoretical contributions in social science, where she makes a powerful case for 'paradoxical integration', *xiangfan xianghe* and *xiangfan yiti,* to be recognized as illuminating globalization processes.

Theory is work in progress, never complete, and the chapters that follow offer no blueprints, rather aim to remove obstacles to seeing further ahead. Theory carries forward a global public philosophy by challenging old assumptions, such as the view that there can be no compromise on principles.

The need for paradoxical integration is plain if we consider the different world-views of the two superpowers, the United States and China. However, if we simply linger in the past we may consider their radically different historical experiences create an unbridgeable gulf between the two cultures. The stories of their own identity formation underpin quite different approaches to global governance. But working for global goals they can create a transculture of cooperation.

Chapters Eight to Ten explore the consequences for theory of transcultural engagement, strategies for resolving value conflicts, and the need to accept the co-existence of alternative universalisms in pragmatic accommodation, an attitude of pragmatic universalism.

Chapter Eleven finds the promise for this attitude in President Xi's formula for global governance, *mingyun gongtongti*, a community of common destiny. This long-established Chinese vision can extend to the world as a whole but will depend on exchange and cooperation between nations. We can find support for this direction of thought in a classical line of German reflection on understanding represented by Wilhelm Dilthey. It is the final paradox, an idealist argument that sees peace and well-being dependent on material factors, shared technologies and joint projects.

DOI https://doi.org/10.24103/GCSS.en.2018.11

Chapter Six
Chinese social theory in global social science

In a globalizing world, the aim of social science has to be the increase of mutual understanding between peoples and cultures that are thrown together, whether they want it or not, to overcome conflict and to enhance the possibilities of cooperative responses to the global challenges that confront them all. It is the urgency of the need to co-operate under current conditions that makes intensive examination of the impediments to it so important. Ethnocentrism, the inability to view another culture except through the lens of one's own, is the major impediment that comparative studies seek to remove.

A particular aim is to correct the widely acknowledged limitations of dominant social science concepts embedded in the historical experience of the West. Xiaoying Qi provides us with an exemplary study of the way the wealth of Chinese intellectual traditions can be brought into critical engagement with Western paradigms to develop common conceptual resources that will be to the benefit of all peoples.[1]

A great virtue of this book lies in demonstrating the worth of a multiplicity of methods for disentangling the transcultural potential of concepts from their cultural roots. The author brings an impressively equipped toolbox to her chosen task, to show how 'Western or metropolitan social theory might be reconstituted through the incorporation of particular relevant Chinese concepts'.[2] The first half of the book is devoted to exploring and documenting transcultural flows.

In the first chapter we read an account of the institutional and linguistic hegemony of Western theories and concepts: the second is a case study of the treatment of *guanxi* in 214 Western management journal articles. There follows an account of the reception and use of Western concepts by Chinese intellectual entrepreneurs between 1842 and 1949; and then the fourth chapter depicts the historical interplay of continuity and transformation, from the reception of Buddhism onwards, that makes up the intellectual heritage that is called Chinese today.

The second half of the book offers three examples for the incorporation of Chinese concepts into mainstream social theory. The first is one that has already been received in the West extensively, namely face (*lian* and *mianzi*). The second explains how *xin* (heart/mind) transcends the Western dichotomy of reason and emotion. The third develops a concept of 'paradoxical integration' (*xiangfan xianghe* or *xiangfan yiti*) derived from the classic Daoist text *Daodejing*. The very different ways in which each of these concepts resonates with cognate ideas in

---

[1] Qi 2014, *Globalized Knowledge Flows and Chinese Social Theory*

[2] .Ibid. p. 7.

Western thought stand out in Dr Qi's account and it is one of its great merits that she does not attempt to suggest that there is any simple rule of thumb by which Chinese ideas can be assimilated in the West. Each case involves a unique cultural encounter.

But there are lessons to be drawn for the general tasks of comparative social science in this study of the actual and possible contributions of Chinese concepts to a universally accessible and applicable repertoire. We can identify elementary analytical components for any cultural frame of thought: them and us, living and dead, connected and disconnected, cause and effect, the same and different, new and old, and so on. These are the common features of the human condition so emphatically stressed by Lévi-Strauss in declaring the savage mind operates by the same logic as ours does today.[3]

Yet there are endless variations in the configuration of such basic elements of culture and this is true for social relations too. The result is different prominence being accorded to a particular configuration of elements according to the culture in which it is situated. The vendetta in southern Italian culture as an organizing principle of clan relations has near equivalents in other societies although it may not have acquired in them the recognition as a distinct phenomenon that is accorded a name.

Similarly *guanxi*, when defined (that is dissected into elements) by Qi, as 'carefully constructed and maintained relations between persons that carry mutual obligations and benefits', may render very effectively relations in Western societies that are only alluded to in terms of 'influence', 'patronage', 'old-boy network' or corruption. None of these terms is adequate to describe, for instance, what the British magazine *Private Eye* specializes in revealing, favours given and returned that are outside any formal relations. *Guanxi* is closer to the target of its satire than any other single concept and discloses the ambiguities in public morality lying below the surface of British culture.

The example of 'face', popularized in his account of 'Chinese characteristics' by the American missionary Arthur H. Smith, illustrates a quite different kind of cross-cultural flow.[4] His book went through fifteen editions and was an important source for Max Weber's (1951) study of Chinese religion.[5] It led to the Oxford English Dictionary including 'to lose face' in its Supplement with the note '[tr. Chinese *tiu lien*]'.

Yet, while Smith saw 'face' as the key to Chinese character, Qi shows that it was he who first attracted the attention of Chinese scholars to it and there is now an extensive social scientific discussion of face in Chinese. Qi points here to the intellectual entrepreneurship required to effect this kind of exchange of concepts between cultures and rightly assigns her own work to it.

---

[3] Lévi-Strauss 1966, *The Savage Mind.*
[4] Smith 1894, *Chinese Characteristics.*
[5] Weber 1951, *The Religion of China: Confucianism and Taoism.*

In the chapter on reason and emotion Qi bravely tackles a strategic distinction in Western thought. She makes the case for their effective integration in the Chinese concept of *xin*, documenting its shared recognition in the long series of major thinkers from Guanzi (683-642 BCE) through Laozi, Confucius, Mencius up to Dai Zhen (1723-1777). Serving for the Western comparison, Max Weber is singled out as a prime representative of the view that emotions are irrational.

The contrast between West and East is strongly drawn and richly informative on *xin*. There are, however, two qualifications that should be entered. While the author is explicit about the pitfalls of postulating an undifferentiated West or East, in this chapter there is a marked asymmetry between the treatment of them, one that is not infrequent in West/East comparisons. Namely, classic Chinese thought is contrasted with modern Western thought and the rich diversity of classic and European thought up to the eighteenth century is neglected. The legacy of Aristotle extends beyond logic into ethics and his concepts of virtue and the mean combine reason and emotion, just as does the Christian idea of the soul. Here it would help if Qi made more extensive use of Alasdair MacIntyre's work than she does.[6]

The other qualification relates to the treatment of Max Weber as a proxy for Western thought as a whole. It is true that he opposes rational action to emotion, but this is an analytical distinction within an account that is concerned to identify the features of Western modernity. The main focus of his work is the explanation of formal institutionalized rationalities in the state, economy, science and religion, and to account for the revolutionary impact of modern capitalism. He is above all the theorist of modernity, and for him the traditional societies of West and East equally displayed their own kinds of rationalism. Once modern capitalism had gained its momentum in the West, he had no doubt that the East would be able to adopt its main features – as indeed it has.

If we are going to assimilate the Eastern classics to enrich a shared world culture we need to draw on pre-modern Western ideas also and in this respect set limits on modernity, both before and after the dominance it achieved in the nineteenth and early twentieth centuries, a viewpoint I advance with the concept of the Global Age.[7]

This is a position that requires the advance of new concepts for a new age and, under conditions of globalization, despite the hegemony in science of the English language, it is certain that insights based on the vast intellectual heritage of China and its unique historical development will increasingly enrich a store of concepts belonging to the world community of social scientists.

It is a process that will include the revision of old concepts as well as the invention of new ones. Qi's last chapter illustrates this very effectively. It advances the idea of paradoxical integration (*xiangfan xianghe* and *xiangfan yiti*), drawing

---

[6] MacIntyre 1967, *A Short History of Ethics*, p. 64.
[7] Albrow 1996, *The Global Age* and 2014, *Global Age Essays on Social and Cultural Change*.

on the Daoist tradition, 'the non-contradictory or non-destructive correspondence of opposites in a single thing or event at a given moment of time'.[8]

She suggests that it is particularly helpful methodologically for identifying some of the paradoxes of globalization, as with Roland Robertson's 'glocalization'[9] and Bryan Turner's 'enclave society'.[10] A similar critical approach to older concepts has allowed Xiangqun Chang (2010) to advance the concept of *lishang-wanglai* for a more precise analytical approach to reciprocal social relationships in *guanxi*.[11] The overriding point is that Chinese social theory will not stay in the past but change with the changing times. This indeed is the conclusion Qi reaches: 'transformations in Chinese culture paradoxically draw upon enduring properties of a Chinese intellectual heritage that provides the means through which such change is achieved.'[12]

In a short review, one can only begin to suggest the depth of scholarship and richness of argument and insight that this book contains. It not only provides an extensive exploration of sources for Chinese social theory but also exemplifies the way in which a truly global social science can continue to develop through comparative studies of concept formation. There is more than ample proof here that the author will be in the forefront of those who take this programme forward.

This book should be on the reading lists for all courses in comparative sociology or anthropology, and is essential for courses in social theory or philosophy of social science where there is a main concern (as there should be!) to combat Western ethnocentrism. To this end I would urge the publishers, if they have not already done so, to prepare for paperback publication at a price students can afford.

---

[8] Qi, p. 210.
[9] Robertson 1992, *Globalization.*
[10] Turner 2007, 'The Enclave Society: Towards a Sociology of Immobility'.
[11] Chang 2010, *Guanxi or li shang wanglai?*
[12] Qi, p. 227.

DOI https://doi.org/10.24103/GCSS.en.2018.12

Chapter Seven
The challenge of transculturality
for the USA and China

Sociologists only rarely explore the field of international relations. Raymond Aron was notable exception, as is Amitai Etzioni. That feature of our discipline that Ulrich Beck criticized, methodological nationalism, has channelled our attention to social relations within nation-states. But, just like individuals and communities, nation-states are social entities, and they have relations with one another, and so there is no reason why sociologists should not apply their concepts and methods to international relations too.

> The USA and China have world-views that extend far
> beyond their relations with one another.

As a sociologist I propose to consider the relations of the USA and China in a global context. Since they are currently the two most important agencies for determining the collective fate of humankind, the rest of the world has an interest in seeing them in a global frame. As superpowers they too look to the globe, as well as to the sum of their relations with other countries, before they look to one another.

So I want to consider how the USA and China look outward to the rest of the world before going on to comment on their relations with one another. In any social relationship, we bring our past experience and outlook to it, and they, to varying degrees, will have a big influence on its future course.

Please note, I am not examining prejudices and stereotypes that Americans and Chinese might have about one another. They exist, of course, and may contribute negatively to the possibilities of cooperation for shared goals, even where there is impressive agreement as between Presidents Obama and Xi Jinping on the Paris Agreement to combat global warming.

My concern today is with the ways in which the United States and China view the world or, if one likes, what used to be called their 'world-views', what German scholars at the beginning of the twentieth century called the *Weltanschauung* or, for Max Weber, the *Weltbild*, the 'world picture', which they saw as a vital component in understanding relations between cultures or civilizations.

Such a concept draws us back to the formative period of our academic discipline, to the debates about concepts of society, culture and social relations that were so fierce in Europe and the USA at the time of Ferdinand Tönnies, Max Weber, Emile Durkheim and William Sumner. These were conducted at a time of fervent nationalism that did a lot to shape the methodological nationalism of later thought and research.

Sociologists struggled then, as we do still, to reconcile their commitment to universalistic ideals of science and human values with patriotism and loyalty to the local community. Durkheim's solution was to propose that the nation had a duty promote its own version of universal values through a national education system.

But the national culture triumphed over human culture in the First World War, as it did in the ill-fated League of Nations after that war. 'Universality' as a concept has a weaker appeal than nationhood in shaping our idea of culture, even to this day.

We are experiencing currently the resurgence of nationalism in reaction to globalization all over the world. In her first speech as Prime Minister to the Conservative Party in the United Kingdom, Theresa May announced, 'To be a citizen of the world is to be a citizen of nowhere'. Did anyone hear Socrates cry out from his residence in heaven?

Now globalization, you may rightly say, is not universality. I too have argued strongly against that view. It covers a broad range of processes that bring people together as much in conflict as in cooperation and it has no intrinsic moral content. Moreover, in its most well-recognized appearance, it is a relatively recent state-supported drive to reduce boundaries between countries. The current rise of nationalism or populism is often cited as one of its consequences.

Nationalism in the rest of the world and now in the West points an accusation at, and finds a justification in the United States's support for globalization. Other countries argue that globalization is only a cover for the national interest of the US and its capitalists and that every nation has the right and need to define its own distinct economic and social policies.

That argument is all the easier to advance since Americans themselves have so often found it difficult to distinguish globalization from Americanization. Thomas Friedman, the highly respected *New York Times* columnist, wrote, 'culturally speaking, globalization is largely, though not entirely, the spread of Americanization'.[1]

Indeed one can argue that the spread of neo-liberal market economics for the majority of its advocates in the US was simply an extension of its commitment to individual rights, freedom of expression and free association supported by a Constitution that created not just the federal union of the original 13 states of America but laid the foundation for modern democracy. In other words the values and interests of the United States can be equated with the values and interests of every country.

---

[1] Friedman 1999, *The Lexus and the Olive Tree*, p. 8,

It is in this sense that the American experience is regarded as the prototype of modernity and opened up a path all should follow. Others too, including Karl Marx, have seen it as the most modern country, and its experience as the whole world in microcosm. Its most famous poet, Walt Whitman, hailed America as the 'globe of globes'.[2]

Our classic founders were well aware of these national limits on world-views. Weber spoke of the world historical mission of Germany precisely because of the difference between its culture and others. Durkheim called on French education to advance universal values, but necessarily from its own standpoint. Sumner, borrowing from the Polish Austrian law professor and theorist of conflict war, Ludwig Gumplowicz, employed a term for this aspect of cultural relations which we have used ever since, ethnocentrism.[3]

> The USA has often regarded globalization as
> a simple extension of its own experience.
> World-views in general are ethnocentric.

The ethnocentrism of world-views is then not confined to the United States. But in recent years the ethnocentrism of American led globalization has become more fully apparent, leading to it being challenged by the rest of world, and even from within the US itself. Its close association with American interests and has prompted other nations to assert alternatives. The most recent is the new Chinese Belt and Road initiative.

Elsewhere I have spoken on Belt and Road in relation to global governance and today I want in effect to focus on one aspect that has an important bearing on its potential success for advancing global social order, namely the extent to which it can rise above the limits of an ethnocentric view of the world and command acceptance for its demonstrable benefits to all humankind.

Many features distinguish Belt and Road from American inspired globalization. In the first place the latter came with an inbuilt theoretical argument, namely that free trade boosted prosperity for all participants, a theory most famously advanced by Adam Smith and critiqued by Marx and Engels. Belt and Road, by contrast, has, at its heart, cooperation between nation-states in investment and building infrastructure. It is not theory-free but bears more similarity to the thinking of the physiocrats, and behind them their Chinese influences, than to Adam Smith.

In this respect, however, it shares with globalization an affinity with a national view of the world, a world of harmony between peoples 'all under heaven', *tianxia*. Here I rely on the extensive elaboration of the concept of *tianxia* by your distinguished academician, Zhao Tinyang.[4] He makes a very persuasive case that

---

[2] Whitman 1993, *Leaves of Grass*, p. 383.
[3] Sumner 1906, *Folkways.*
[4] Zhao 2011, *The Tianxia System.*

the world today needs a concept that provides for a harmonious way of living to-gether and accepting one another and that *tianxia* provides the apex of a structure of Chinese thought that has over centuries provided the solidarity and common purpose that distinguishes contemporary Chinese society.

> *Tianxia* is also based in Chinese experience, a world of harmony contrasting with American tension between individual and community.

I cannot quarrel with Zhao's account of *tianxia*, only wish to draw attention to the equivalent position it occupies to American views of their own social order. Indeed China today is evidently aware of the parallel nature of national values and aspirations when it advances the Chinese Dream to match the American Dream. Those dreams are for domestic consumption; world-views look beyond national boundaries.

Views of the world, world pictures, are built very much on domestic experi-ence. Sociologist Stephen Kalberg has recently pointed to two poles of the Ameri-can spirit of democracy, self-reliance and shared community, allowing us to recog-nize the inherent tension between them. Zhao effectively contrasts the American image of world society, built on individuals, communities and nation-states, with a Chinese view based on families, the state, and all under heaven *jiaguo tianxia*.

Tension is built into the American world-view, harmony into the Chinese, and we can readily, I would say too readily, move to thinking there is an incom-patibility between them too deep to bridge. It is to prevent a precipitate jump to that conclusion that I wish at this point to introduce the concept of transculturality.

Without repeating the argument in my presentation to the Symposium on China Studies earlier this week, I find support for the concept in the work of a Cuban ethnographer, Fernando Ortiz, in the 1950s writing on the creation of new musical forms,[5] in the work of sociologist Margaret Archer since the 1980s and her emphasis on the morphogenetic qualities of culture,[6] and more recently in the work of Hong Kong- and Paris-based anthropologist Shuo Yu.[7] All of them in their different ways emphasize the way that social relations involved in contact between cultures cross their boundaries and are generative of new cultural forms.

Yu cites the inspiration Leibniz drew from Jesuit accounts of Chinese prac-tices for his ideas of a universal language. She also looks forward to a time when a symbiotic dream bridges China-Europe encounters and finds universal accept-ance beyond national boundaries. Professor Xiangqun Chang sees transculturality as a basis and medium for, as well as outcome of the globalization of Chinese

---

[5] Ortiz 1951, *Los Bailes y el Teatro de los Negros en el Folklore de Cuba.*

[6] Archer 1988, *Culture and Agency.*

[7] Yu 2015, 'Universal Dream, National Dreams and Symbiotic Dream: Reflections on Transcultural Generativity in China-Europe Encounters'.

social sciences to which the new journal she has founded, *Journal of China in Comparative Perspective*, is dedicated.

> Transculturality involves not just exchange between cultures but the creation of new culture beyond them.

Perhaps the word 'transculturality' still has an artificial sound, but I think it is useful in enabling us as social scientists to take some of the heat out the culture wars of the past century. For the cultural explorations of younger generations and ideas drawn from foreign cultures (often of course inspiring one another) have often been regarded as threats to national culture.

Internationalism itself, ever since the coining of the word 'international' by Jeremy Bentham, has created alarm, only intensified by its association with the international working men's movement, therefore with communism and, by extension and association with Marx and Engels, then with a cosmopolitan Jewish conspiracy against Western nations. Multiculturalism, the attempt to recognize the integrity of different cultures within the nation-state, has been similarly rejected in the name of national culture.

Transculturality arises out of the very nature of culture. It is a new term for something very old, for culture is a generic human product arising out of aeons of social interaction. We as sociologists treat culture as an elementary concept for our beginning students, quite rightly with definitions like 'culture is the sum of learned behaviour that is transmitted from generation to generation'. Learning and transmission are central to the concept, boundaries are not.

Put another way, all culture is transcultural. Can we find the owners or fix the boundaries of the use of fire or the invention of agriculture or the use of the wheel? 'China's Four Great Inventions – papermaking, gunpowder, printing and the compass,' says Xi Jinping, 'brought drastic changes to the whole world, including the European Renaissance.'[8] He said this during a speech to UNESCO on 27 March 2014 entitled 'Exchanges and Mutual Learning Make Civilizations Richer and More Colourful'.

Xi also cites Buddhism as an example of a religion originating in India and becoming Buddhism with Chinese features as it merged with indigenous Confucianism and Taoism. He mentioned Christianity and Islam in the same text. He might have gone on to speak of Marxism itself and China becoming the most powerful exponent of its ideas in conjunction with Western modernity.

What anthropologists have called enculturation, or sociologists indigenization, has long been acknowledged as a correction to the view that cultures are sealed from outside influences. But the vitality of the host culture is not necessarily diminished as a result. It can respond to the encounter by reasserting an

---

[8] *Xi Jinping: The Governance of China*, 2014. p. 286.

indigenous core, distinct from the new elements. In sociology we explored those processes in the 1980s examining the dialectic between the universal claims of the discipline and indigenous national ways of reframing or indeed challenging its core concepts.

But by transculturality I believe we convey more than exchange between cultures. We are also referring to the development of new culture that has no specific national or local home. This is easy to imagine with the latest revolution in communication technology. The internet is ownerless even if corporations and countries seek to create boundaries around it. Indeed their strenuous efforts to do so only emphasize its transcultural nature. More than that still, arguably all science has that ambition, to speak to the world as a whole, and scientists see themselves as part of a worldwide culture.

If that were the intended target of the concept of transculturality then it might well be dismissed as old wine in new bottles. Its illumination of contemporary issues become more relevant when it is recognized in the processes that govern the relations between the great powers and in the creation of a global social order. For the precepts and principles that the USA and China advance as the basis for world peace have neither the impersonal, universal, technical applicability of digital communications nor the indigenous uniqueness of a god that belongs to no other nation.

> The world-views of the USA and China were each developed originally in a transcultural experience.

Rather, in each case the world-view of the great power has developed out of its own experience of bridging cultural divides within itself. In the United States its historical record of cultural creativity is more recent. The struggles with its individual states to find agreement within communities founded in different religious beliefs and subsequently their reconciliation within a secular constitution concluded with the affirmation of 'self-evident truths'.

In the words of one of their founding fathers, 'Our government is in its theory perfect, and in its operation is perfect also.' The eminent historian Henry Steele Commager described this outlook thus: 'They had solved the problem of imperial organization on which the old British Empire foundered, and constructed a federal system that became the model for the western world.'[9] What I emphasize here is that the process of constructing the United States itself was a transcultural process, the creation of something new. Then, what is projected on to the rest of world is the finished product to which it is expected to conform. Now, while Zhao is a persuasive advocate of the potential of *tianxia* for world order, in its origins it is just as much the outcome of competing claims

---

[9] Commager 1950, *The American Mind*, pp. 311-312.

between political powers as American constitutionalist ideas. When my co-author Zhang Xiaoying and I examined the way Max Weber's concept of 'world empire' was translated as *tianxia* we concluded:

> Yet there are contrasting nuances between 'world empire' and *Tian Xia*. The former is a Western concept which basically sees the world as many different nations in the first place, while the latter first sees it as a whole.[10]

But I would add now, seeing the world as a whole was derived from and constructed out of those original conflicts, and it has been developed over the centuries out of further contact with neighbouring countries and with ethnic groups now known as minorities. Zhao's observation that *tianxia* is close to the Western idea of empire is all the more relevant for our argument. Its use by the Han emperor to impose a client relationship on neighbouring states was based in their acknowledgment of the obligation of the emperor to take responsibility for the harmony of heaven and nature.

Given its origin in China's imperial past, we can envisage *tianxia* and the harmony it requires extending its reach beyond the contemporary boundaries of the nation-state through the conjunction of environmental and infrastructure projects coupled with dependence on the Chinese political centre. And that can be seen to fit very well with the Belt and Road initiative.

I argue, then, that both with American state building and Chinese harmony there is a prior history of the assimilation of the other, a transcultural experience that has come to serve as a parochial universality, a national recipe for the world as a whole. But in claiming universality it has lost a sense of its origins in dialogue, contest and conflict.

The challenge for both the US and China is to recognize the local nature of their own experience, that it was originally transcultural, and to understand that when they encounter one another, transculturality as well as exchange is a necessary outcome. And here I mean necessary, not as inevitable, but in the sense of a necessity for human well-being worldwide.

For what is the alternative? That each should strive to impose itself on the other in a contest ending in outright destruction? Or a productive exchange where new ways of cooperation and new directions for human endeavour enable both cultures to share in a global social order where neither dominates the other, nor any country claims empire over the world?

> When the USA and China reach out to the rest of the world, they are creating a new transcultural space where global governance can grow.

---

[10] Zhang and Albrow 2016, 'Max Weber, China and the World: in Search of Transcultural Communication', p. 39.

It will not surprise you that I see the prospect for this in global governance, precisely because it develops not only out of interaction between almost every country in the world, but also because it represents the outcome of efforts by individuals and collectivities worldwide assuming the responsibility for creating a better world. It is not a government. It is the outcome of the performative citizenship of a world society that faces up to global challenges.

Global governance as transculturality is difficult to convey adequately from within *either* the American *or* the Chinese cultural frame. One might imagine that for Americans the present system of international institutions would have appeal precisely because there is no central government. Yet their conviction that the world needs to be created in their own image makes it difficult for them to accept the equal role of other states within a global system. Individuals yes, even corporations, but not states.

> Americans have a problem with the idea of global governance that depends on equality between nation-states, Chinese have a problem because it lacks a central authority.

The fact too that in a globalized world interaction with other cultures has generated global culture even from within the United States is very difficult to accept. I recall the outrage there was in some quarters about the Oscar-winning film *American Beauty*, a Hollywood product that savaged features of American culture. The anger arose out of impotence in face of the globalization of an iconic institution, for Hollywood's creative industry belongs to global capital, is peopled by actors, producers and teams from all over the world and aims for global audiences.

For Chinese people the opposite probably applies, though they are better qualified to judge than I could possibly be. But if I may allow myself this tentative comment, I suggest in their case the absence of a central world government makes it more difficult to accept that global governance can work. China draws such immense strength from activating its own traditions that the novelty of a cultural sphere beyond the nation-state without a deep cultural heritage may be hard to assimilate. Hence China is likely to be more successful with practical initiatives than with promoting the idea of *tianxia* for global governance.

At the same time, the emphasis in Belt and Road on practical projects provides a better basis for cooperation with others than the institutional imperialism implicit in the Washington consensus.

My conclusion is that, in their relations with one another, China and the United States are most likely to achieve mutual understanding through doing things together. There is much progress here on many fronts where concrete issues face the two nations, whether on climate change, trade relations or even cybersecurity.

> Projects may serve global governance more effectively
> than preconceived ideas. A pragmatic universalism
> may replace the universals of national world-views.

I think understanding one another's world-views is much more complex and this is why I urge engagement in new ideas that do not spring automatically from the past. For me, one of the great innovations of recent years is the rise of the concept of sustainability, a truly transcultural creation of many nations and for which both countries have expressed support. This has emerged out of the need to find a practical answer to an imminent challenge to human life on this earth.

So, please take strength from a new tradition of the last seventy years, that of the United Nations and its agencies, as well as more recently of leaders' summits, such as the one China chaired with such distinction at Hangzhou in 2016. Global culture is generated not just in the film industry, journalism and social media. It is also in constant development in the daily work of people who work in corporations, governments, international governmental and non-governmental organizations and, yes, universities. It is even implicit in movements like Occupy and the World Social Forums.

If I have succeeded in my argument that the concept of transculturality can capture some of the novelty of a global culture and the challenges it poses, not only to your country, but also to the United States and indeed every country in the world today, then the expense of your country in bringing me all this way from the United Kingdom may be justified.

Concepts are validated in use and for human purposes. This pragmatic outlook at least has a philosophical grounding with quite independent roots in both Chinese and American culture. I would urge that in working together for a pragmatic universalism, all sides may find the appropriate spirit for a global age and rise to the challenges that confront all humankind. Human transculturality will once again have proved its creative value.

DOI https://doi.org/10.24103/GCSS.en.2018.13

Chapter Eight
Pragmatic universalism and the quest for global governance

May I first express my gratitude for your generous invitation to speak at this conference on globalization, social change and cultural construction. British scholars, including myself, were among the first to examine the idea of globalization in the West but its historical roots in imperialism put an obligation on any one of us speaking in China on this theme to apologize for the part our country played in your century of humiliation.

> Please accept a personal apology for the British wars of imperialism on China in the nineteenth century.

This is a personal apology. It expresses my sense of belonging to a country with a proud history, having benefited from its protection and culture, and from its past achievements. But to this day, as a result, its citizens benefit from the proceeds of past crimes, against you and others as well as against its own earlier generations.

But I am also a European, a Westerner and a member of our global community. That makes it even more poignant that, as a British citizen, I should be speaking on the theme of global governance. For the United Kingdom has just resolved after a national referendum to leave the European Union of which it has been a member since 1973.

> The recent British referendum result appears to mark a break from progress towards a world of cooperation.

For many of us, this union of like-minded nation-states agreeing to cooperate in their own interest and to speak with one voice was an example of the way ahead in world affairs. Twenty-eight states working together could be effective in regionalizing global governance. They could introduce collective representation into the global summitry otherwise dominated by the superpowers. It seemed to take forward the project of a networked world of cooperation to meet global challenges, finally supplanting the competitive nationalism that had brought the two world wars of the twentieth century.

This also has a very personal meaning. Those who, like me, voted to stay in the European Union have felt a loss, likened by some to a kind of bereavement. On the other side, many of those who voted to leave have expressed elation, a new sense of freedom. The choice then was made out of deep feelings of identity, of cultural identification, much more than from any rational calculation of consequences, on which no expert opinion could offer certainty. The referendum question belonged more to a psychologist's projective test than to a political ballot.

> Brexit reflects the hope to regain control and
> overcome a sense of powerlessness in a
> 'Runaway World' (Giddens).

That the result was a surprise to the British establishment reflected its detachment from popular feeling. The referendum brought together sets of people whose discontent came from quite different sources: nostalgia for the old days; poverty in the midst of plenty; resentment of foreigners; being left behind by new technologies; loss of local control.

Anthony Giddens once summed up the overall impact of contemporary change, in particular of globalization, in the book of the name as *Runaway World* (1999). That expresses the sense of powerlessness over processes and events that individual people feel and their consequent alienation from those who enjoy power and privilege without responsibility. In this respect the British referendum should be recognized as symptom of a much wider global uncertainty, affecting to a greater or lesser extent every country in the world.

But the theme of this conference addresses social change and cultural construction too and I want to propose that we use this local British crisis and the wider confusion it reflects as an occasion for clarification, for finding direction in world affairs, and then to point to the chances that the contribution of Chinese culture, old and new, will make a positive difference to the shaping of global governance.

> We should use the crisis to find a way forward.
> It brings principles into the open.

Crises bring things to the surface, feelings certainly, but also declarations of principle. In the forthcoming negotiations with the UK the leaders of the EU have already asserted it cannot compromise on the principles on which its internal market is founded: the four freedoms of movement of goods, capital, services and people. UK politicians accept the first three, but not the last, the freedom to reside and work in any country of the EU. The EU asserts the four are indivisible and non-negotiable.

Principles are an emergent feature of any system of governance or, to be more precise, the explicit statement of principles is emergent: the principles are themselves already implicit in any established social order. If that appears too sweeping a judgment, let me refer you to the gradual development of codes of behaviour in the great civilizations of the world, that receive ever more sophisticated elaboration over time, or to the grand statements that are foundational for global institutions today, whether declarations of human rights or responsibilities for the environment or shared standards for the global banking system.

When leaders of twenty nations met in London in April 2009, the main outcome was prefaced with a statement of principles. When recently I commented on *Xi Jinping: The Governance of China* (2014), it was to highlight its emphasis on principles and their rootedness in China's history as well as relevance to the present

> Principles are always explored locally.
> The universal is made particular.

As usually stated, principles are unqualified. They appear to apply to all times and places. The right to life is an obvious example. You and I can assert it anywhere in the world, we hope successfully. How about the right to property? That's much more complicated. I have a right to my own, perhaps, but not to yours, and maybe in my own country, but sometimes not elsewhere, and I'm obliged to give up some of it almost everywhere for purposes the state deems right. The right to nationality is enshrined in international law but there is no right to choose one's nationality. Moreover, every national system of law provides different criteria for determining who is a national and who is not, and a huge amount of entitlements flow from that, making it one of the major issues in the UK/EU future negotiations.

The universal is localized, made particular everywhere, even as the local definition appeals to the universality of the principle. The rights of parents over children may be accepted universally, but only over their own children, not anybody else's. The four principles on which the EU insists apply only to its members. When we come to the most abstract principles of all, justice, equality and freedom, then the contextualization of these becomes the standard everyday substance of debate, disagreement, conflict and conflict resolution at every level from the interpersonal to the international.

In the local context, it is the universality of the principle that is relativized, not just in relation to those who are not local but also in relation to other principles. The right to life may or may not extend to the right to take one's own life. In Switzerland it does. The freedoms to drink alcohol or to smoke cannabis are variously restricted worldwide in accord with principles of health or obedience to God's law.

The principles of free movement of capital, goods, services and labour have provided the liberal economic case for globalization. In the EU they operate within the member countries to create an internal market and a trading bloc with the rest of the world. The UK has since the days of Adam Smith seen them as in principle unlimited in application, reluctantly accepting the limit placed on them as a condition for membership of the EU, but then rebelling against the consequences they have for immigration.

> It is the condition of principles to come into contradiction with one another and to be subject to compromise.

The consolidation of frameworks of interlocking and mutually conditioning principles takes place in local contexts that we call cultural and national and the daily task of compromising between them and handling their consequences confronts not just experts but people in their everyday lives. In the end it is the local and personal pressures that push the UK out of the EU.

It was none other than a founder of sociology, Max Weber, who created huge public controversy in his recently created country when he pointed out, in his inaugural lecture at the University of Freiburg in 1895, that liberal economic principles allowed the owners of industry in the west of Germany to recruit agricultural workers from the east, only for them to be replaced by Polish immigrants.[1] It was not possible both to sustain German cultural identity and simultaneously promote free movement of labour.

That same contradiction between principles has been evident again among the advocates of British leaving the EU. Some have applauded the advantages of free trade with the rest of the worlds, others want to preserve British identity and restrict immigration. In the end a pragmatic compromise has to be reached.

> Contact between cultures accelerates the search for compromise between principles

My purpose here in drawing attention to the mutual conditioning of principles and their embeddedness in the local is to emphasize that it is contact between cultures that accelerates the processes of compromise. The development of culture in general is in practice the continual interchange between the universal and the particular. When cultures meet we have the most dynamic context in which to examine the way clashes and contradictions between principles are resolved. Let me then make a few comments about culture in general and culture contact in particular.

> Culture in general knows no boundaries

The most comprehensive consideration of the concept of culture leads us to emphasize it as an evolutionary achievement of the human species as a whole, an

---

[1] Weber 1958, *Gesammelte Politische Schriften*, pp. 1-25.

exponential development of the capacity and resources for communication between individuals and an instrument for the exploration of the nature of existence, on earth and beyond. The pursuit of knowledge, scientific discovery, new technology and creative expression are the collective products of human cooperation beyond boundaries.

At the same time the formation of bonds between human being, for mutual support, reproduction and material and spiritual needs, lead to the selective development and appropriation of cultural resources. 'Culture', in the most general sense, becomes 'cultures', in the sense of being centred on particular societies. In the world as we know it today, in a period of flux, of extraordinary possibilities of communication worldwide, contact between cultures is as much part of everyday experience as is the personal management of the local culture. In social science in recent years the dilemmas in this experience often are labelled as the clash between the cosmopolitan and the local, but that I contend always arises out of culture contact.

> Cultures in particular are always in contact with
> one another, with a diversity of results.

Over the last century any number of outcomes of culture contact have been identified, many highlighted as a result of issues rising to the top of a political agenda. The history of imperialism and the anthropological research it stimulated led to an emphasis on the diffusion of customs and practices. In the United States successive waves of immigration were mirrored in an emphasis on acculturation and assimilation. Ideas of social evolution favoured the ideas of adaptation and syncretism. As the notion of ethnic relations supplanted the idea of race, successively concepts of fusion, multi-culturalism and hybridization have been contrasted. Most recently appropriation has become a critical concept denoting the adoption of membership symbols of the other, usually by the privileged.

These are all concepts that refer to the flow and exchange of ideas and practices expressed as the cultural properties of societies. They reflect the predominant tendency to assume the coincidence of boundaries of society and culture as the starting point for description. Cultural change is then seen as a matter of culture contact between societies and therefore a problem for social order.

> There is no inevitable conflict arising from
> contradictory principles. The EU and the UK
> can agree if the will is there.

In point of fact, the localization of culture is secondary to the features of culture in general, which have always developed across boundaries at the same time as creating local difference. The spread of technologies, from the control of fire through to digital communication, illustrates that well enough. In other words, cultural development takes place irrespective of the shape of particular social boundaries and the possibility of managing conflict between principles is within the capacity of any set of societies. There is no inherent necessity *in principle* for the EU and UK not to agree, and *e fortiori*, for the countries of the world not to develop the social order we call global governance.

Sociological theory has long been occupied with these questions of morality and its embeddedness in society. One classic answer in the West was to point to the universality of moral codes as such and cultural diversity in respect of their content, even as societies claimed universality for their own version of a moral code. Emile Durkheim accepted this diversity, but regarded it as the duty of every national education system to find universality in its own version.

The corollary was that it was only in the dream of a single world society that one could locate a truly universal morality. Short of that unrealizable dream, each culture advanced its claim of its own moral code to be universal. We have mentioned how Durkheim's contemporary, Max Weber, was inclined to see those differing claims as irreconcilable. Durkheim was less pessimistic and also pointed to a lesser form of unity to be found in the worldwide division of labour, in the shared understandings that underpinned what we now call a global economy.

And in this relative optimism we detect what, from the eighteenth century to the present day, has been the central plank in the moral case made by the supporters of the free market, namely that trade and exchange of labour and services generate trust and cooperation that depend not on shared values but on the pursuit of self-interest. In effect, the principles that are developed around free markets are a surer guarantee for future human well-being than any search for common values.

> Huntington's three rules for the avoidance of conflict:
> abstention from intervention; joint mediation;
> seek commonalities.

A century after these sociological classics, the world has changed. But the issue of the potential irreconcilability of cultures is as great a source of profound concern for the future as it was then. The most celebrated recent discussion of potential conflict between cultures is that of Samuel Huntington, whose *Clash of Civilizations and the Remaking of World Order* (1996) aimed to define the shape of international relations after the end of the Cold War. His vision of a multipolar new world in which the main actors are the central powers in great civilizations is often seen as a declaration of the inherent necessity of cultures to come into conflict. Certainly for him pre-modern civilizations were most significantly in contact when one eliminated or subjugated the other.[2] He held too that the West introduced distinctively the idea of a universal civilization.[3] Both are contestable accounts of pre-modern history.

---

[2]   Huntington op. cit., p. 50.
[3]   Ibid. p. 66.

But we may be able to agree with him that, closer to our own time, the process of modernization has strengthened the capacity of every culture to be universal.[4] In face of this development, Huntington asserted that the West needed to preserve its own identity even as it acknowledged the rights of others to keep theirs. In itself, this thesis postulates no inherent necessity for conflict but it does warn against a global Dark Age, a crisis of governance, an assault on the values of any civilization whatsoever.

Huntington concluded that this can only be averted by adherence to three rules: *abstention*, core states must not intervene in the internal conflicts of other civilizations; *joint mediation*, core states must negotiate with one another to halt wars between states of their civilizations; *commonalities*, people everywhere should seek to expand what they have in common with others.[5] Twenty years since his thesis, the current condition of world social order appears to strengthen rather than weaken his argument.

> Culture contact prompts the reformulation of old principles and the rise of new ones, the process of pragmatic universalism.

I have no quarrel with his rules. They illustrate how culture contact prompts the reformulation of old principles (e.g. live and let live) but also the search for new formulae. They are part of an intellectual and political climate that I call *pragmatic universalism*, the recognition that when diverse claims to universality meet they can arrive at mutually acceptable compromises that in turn provide principles. What else is the principle of religious tolerance than a higher order universal?

> Eighteenth century natural religion and twentieth century sustainability are both examples of transculturality where contact between Chinese and Western cultures create something new.

It is not just new principles that emerge out of culture contact. New values may also develop. In recent exchanges between Chinese and Western scholars, this has been called transculturality. Shuo Yu has examined it in the context of Christian and Chinese interaction in the seventeenth and eighteenth centuries, when the philosopher Leibniz and the Jesuits in the Chinese imperial court arrived at a notion of natural religion that extended beyond what was accepted in either cultural setting.[6]

---

[4] Ibid. p. 78.
[5] Ibid. pp. 316-320.
[6] Shuo Yu 2015, 'Universal Dream, National Dreams and Symbiotic Dream: Reflections on Transcultural Generativity in China-Europe Encounters.'

In this case, of course, the implications of this for each were resisted on both sides, though it was not insignificant in inspiring the deistic and spiritual convictions of the Enlightenment philosophers, all too readily and wrongly described as atheistic rationalists by subsequent critics.

Emergent values have become evident too in the last half century in human relations with the environment. The green movement arose across boundaries, generated its own discourse of sustainability and has reshaped both national and global politics. As a globalizing force, it has challenged the main agents of economic globalization and brought the nation-states of the world together in collective action to mitigate the effects of global warming.

Very different cultural traditions of valuing nature with different emphases have transcended their differences in these global agreements, though not without difficulties and with many reservations. Chinese belief in a necessary harmony between human beings and nature and Western ideas of nature as a resource for human development have found a common ground in a new concept of sustainable development. Each view of the human/nature relationship, embedded respectively in Chinese and Western cultures, will be expressed as a universal feature of the human condition.

The contemporary concept of sustainability, to which the nations of the world subscribe, has arisen out of processes of dialogue and negotiation. Dialogue is generative of new principles and values that each party can affirm without relinquishing its core beliefs. This is mirrored in the development of public diplomacy, whereby governments communicate with the publics of other countries, for which Zhao Qizheng has been such a strong advocate.[7]

What globalization and the rising consciousness of issues that require global cooperation have brought to the forefront is the commitment of citizens to transnational codes of behaviour, not just in respect of environmental protection but also in demands for justice, the combatting of poverty worldwide and rights to health and education.

These are negotiated in an ongoing process of debate at all levels within and between societies. The claims to universality give way to the search for common ground, accommodation between different principles and respect for difference. These are characteristic of pragmatic universalism, the development of codes of conduct, institutional arrangements and principles for cooperation that will meet challenges that confront humankind as a whole, but are always under review.

What at this moment remains open is the social grounding of this transculturality. Does it become embedded in the local, national cultures, a process of the acculturation of the global? Or will it be secured in the practices of a cosmopolitan elite, the directors of global corporations, the international civil servants, the owners of capital, the global celebrities who move between their oceangoing

---

[7] Zhao 2012, *The Wisdom of Public Diplomacy: Cross Border Dialogues.*

yachts and fly from land to land in their private jets? And also, mirroring them, the mostly young activists who challenge the WTO, attend the World Social Forums and support the Occupy movement?

> The coming G20 in Hangzhou is a chance for China
> to show how it can contribute to a new global order.

The global society of today is represented by groups that can only demonstrate its profound divisions, reflected in the political disorder of nation-states, above all in the West and the Middle East. It is a turbulent condition in which China and the East's vast experience in managing its own diversity can become the essential new ingredient in shaping the global order of the future.

As it happens, it may be the best of good fortune that it is the People's Republic of China that is to host the next G20 summit of world leaders in Hangzhou in September, for its historical experience demonstrates not only the Chinese ability to assimilate different cultural traditions but also how it can elaborate a system of principles of governance that draw on the West's political experience as well as its own. The result is a unique configuration, the coalescence of Western Marxism with China's ancient values and administrative traditions exemplified especially by the Communist Party of China.

> *Xi Jinping: The Governance of China* shows the
> proven capacity of China to deliver vast projects of
> the scale of the Sustainable Development Goals.

The volume of speeches *Xi Jinping: The Governance of China*, contains an impressive repertoire of theoretical concepts in shaping 'the national governance capacity'.[8] It includes accountability, democracy, human rights, ideals, integrity, soft power, sustainability and values, all part of interconnected systems, 'economic, political, cultural, social and ecological'.

In Xi's words, 'This is a complete set of closely connected and coordinated systems of the state. Our national governance capacity is the ability to use these systems.'[9] These are theoretical statements for practical purpose, a form of political guidance and public philosophy long out of fashion among Western leaders, but well adapted to take on the massive challenge of integrating the new Sustainable Development Goals (SDGs) with global governance.

Take, for example, the current planning for the Sustainable Development Goals (SDGs), 17 of them, with 169 targets, as of 28 May. The Chinese state has long worked with similarly far-reaching lists of ambitions: Xi tells how over 300

---

[8] *Xi Jinping: The Governance of China.* 2014.
[9] Ibid. p. 102.

reform measures in 15 sectors were agreed in November 2013 at the 18th Communist Party of China Central Committee.[10] I would suggest that only China has implemented policies successfully that match the scale required for the SDGs.

> In promoting common and diverse development between states in the Belt and Road initiative, China opens up the possibility of new kinds of global governance.

Xi has set out a strategic vision for China's role in the coming period. His 'One Belt and One Road' evokes both the 2,000-year-old Silk Road and its links with Asia and Europe and the historic maritime links with the neighbouring ASEAN powers. Recently Wang Yiwei has proposed that the offer is an alternative to old-style Western-driven globalization, operating across all sectors and based on a firm communications infrastructure.[11]

> Global governance is more than democracy between countries. It is performed by global citizens of all nationalities in their daily lives.

The Chinese have long rejected the idea of a single development model for all countries. They call both for the acceptance of the right of each country to choose its own model of development and also for the sharing of the fruits of those developments between countries. It is what they call 'common development' in 'the noble cause of promoting democracy in international relations'.[12] In whatever way the reform of the global governance system proceeds, Xi calls for commitment to 'the principles of equality, democracy and inclusiveness'.

Let me conclude by referring back to the deep disappointment in the United Kingdom among all those who voted to remain in the European Union. Like them I see it as a setback for democracy in international relations, but only a temporary one. Global governance is more than democracy between countries: it is the sharing of values and development of principles that bring a global society together. This is cultural construction on a global scale. It happens at all levels, from individuals through communities and associations to states. It is, as I argued in my book, *The Global Age: State and Society beyond Modernity* (1996), performed in their daily lives by global citizens of all nationalities.

---

[10] Ibid. p. 112.
[11] Wang Yiwei 2016, *The Belt and Road Initiative: What Will China Offer the World in its Rise.*
[12] Xi op. cit., p. 355.

DOI https://doi.org/10.24103/GCSS.en.2018.14

Chapter Nine
Can there be a public philosophy for global governance?

Following the horror of the terrorist attacks in Paris, the unanimous resolution 2249 of the United Nations Security Council on 19 November 2015, calling upon member states to 'redouble and coordinate their efforts to prevent and suppress terrorist acts committed by ISIL…' reminds us what global governance is really about. It concerns the creation of unity an order among the diversity of nations.

Governance and diversity are intimately connected. The earliest constitutional treatise in the English language was written in the fifteenth century by the King's Chief Justice Sir John Fortescue. Under the title it acquired a little later, *The Governance of England,* on its very first page, it cites St Thomas Aquinas' account of diversity, using that very word, sounding very contemporary, from lands as different as Scotland, Flanders and, strikingly to us, Egypt and even Libya.[1]

That diversity was the source for a stock of ideas about good governance applied in Fortescue's own country. We in this conference are concerned with the way that governance ideas hold all countries together. Just add the word 'global'. Following the great American writer Walter Lippmann, I am going to call those ideas 'public philosophy'.[2] What he wrote in 1954 is as relevant today as it was then. In face of what he quotes as a 'plurality of incompatible fates', he lays claim to a 'body of positive principles and precepts' which a good citizen cannot deny or ignore. For us just insert 'global' before citizen.

What Professor Shuo Yu has invited us to do is to review these ideas through the lens of culture or, more specifically, transculturality. I think this is a particularly good way of bringing into the open the difficulties of finding principles bridging 'incompatible faiths', especially as a focus on culture confronts us with a particularly modern antithesis of culture versus principle. For we are accustomed to associate culture with difference, imagination and innovation, indeed with the ever-potent source of diversity.

So, when this conference links culture and governance we may feel acute discomfort. Samuel Huntington's *Clash of Civilizations* prompted us to regard culture as the challenge to any kind of ordering of the globe. Social critics have taught us to regard another kind of clash between generations as 'counterculture', social deviance as 'sub-culture' and postmodernism as the cultural subversion of any established culture. Now as we move to 'trans'-culture we can sense all the

---

[1] Fortescue, ed. Charles Plummer 1885, p. 113
[2] Lippmann 1955.

ambiguity and confusion contained in that prefix 'trans', now central to the new discourse of fluid gender and sexuality.

It was not always so. In the mid-nineteenth century, the British civil servant Matthew Arnold wrote a celebrated attack on the progressive ideas of his time. He called it *Culture and Anarchy*.[3] Culture for him meant the realization of the highest values and these were to be located in the citizen's aspiration to the order that would realize these, namely the state, the 'organ of our collective best self'. He claimed not to have a philosophy but in the citizen's culture he was grounding the idea in the people's conscience.

I make no apology for bringing old and even ancient texts to bear on global governance, for they illustrate an essential point for me, namely that governance is an abiding, never-ending issue for human civilization. It is best considered as the active production of the kind of order in society that allows people to live secure, fulfilling and creative lives, a cultural life. It has historically been created in many societies, in different periods with very distinct cultures. Governance is fundamentally a kind of decentred order, in much the same way as a natural language is ordered. As rules arise out of conversations between innumerable multiple partners, any central control that is exercised is very much after the event.

If only for the reason that it contributes so directly to this theme, we should welcome the fact that President Xi Jinping's speeches have been assembled under the title *Xi Jinping: The Governance of China*. In citing the West's ancient texts, I am only imitating him. Xi quotes the ancient Chinese classics: 'The people are the foundation of the state'; 'Everyone is responsible for his country's rise and fall'; 'Govern the country with virtue and educate the people with culture.' These are, he writes, the 'core socialist values' and, I quote him again, 'They carry forward the fine traditional Chinese culture, drawn from the best of world civilizations and reflect the spirit of the times.[4]

Dr Xi (in this context let us give him his correct academic title) is advancing his own sophisticated sociological understanding and effectively carrying forward the significant contributions to steering Chinese society and economy that the doyen of Chinese sociology, Fei Xiaotong, pioneered in the Chinese Academy of Social Sciences when Deng Xiaoping was the Chinese Leader.

Xi's example has particular relevance for transculturality and new global governance. He certainly is not offering an alternative governance model and alternative global governance model. But in the spirit of his book we can draw on the best of world civilizations and reflect the spirit of the times. We can address the potential claims of values, responsibility, principles, rights, etcetera, to universality, but acknowledge their varying interpretation in different countries.

---

[3] Arnold 1869.
[4] Xi, op. cit., p. 188.

The sociologist Daniel Bell called the ideas that occupy a strategic organizing position within the total vocabulary of public order in a society 'axial principles'.[5] Harmony has been central to Chinese reflections on human relations with one another and with nature. The American Dream of aspiration and self-improvement contributed to the rise of the United States and its twentieth-century domination of the global economy. Xi both borrows and adapts from those ideas when he promotes a distinct Chinese dream.

Could any of the national axial principles serve in that position for global society? My own gut feeling is that it's unlikely. The Chinese emphasis on harmony arose in the context of a settled agricultural society, where the well-being of the population was intimately connected with intelligent adaptation to the natural world. The American emphasis on individual aspiration to rise in and contribute to society was the product of a history of migrants finding a new world and creating a new society. When these two cultures encounter one another, misunderstanding as much as understanding arises, especially when the emphasis is placed on distinctive historical experience.

At the beginning of the eighteenth century, Leibniz, the great German philosopher, sought to solve this dilemma by seeking a universal language finding affinities between the *Yijing* and the binary arithmetic he invented. His astonishing insights are, to this day, I believe, better appreciated in China than in the West. Since his time, however, both East and West are coming together in a more sensitive appreciation of the limits of cross-cultural understanding.

Professor Yu's concept of transcultural generativity captures the multiple possible outcomes of encounters between cultures: multiculturalism, adaptation, hybridity, to name just a few current fashionable terms. What she advances is the possibility of a broader cultural sphere that transcends all the others, and one in which they each culture participates. I suggest here that this sphere develops fruitfully from the cultural encounters that arise in undertaking common tasks. Examples might be the cooperation called for in resolution 2249, in the agreement on the Millennium Development Goals and then, we hope, in the coming agreement in Paris to combat the effects of climate change.

It is these very practical issues in relations between cultures that inspired the American philosophical tradition of pragmatism. Its most celebrated representative in the 1920s, John Dewey, detected similar insights in Chinese Daoist thought.[6] The processes involved in cultural encounters are resolved in practice, not in theory, yet out of those practices arise new insights. This is transcultural generativity. It is a process I have called pragmatic universalism, when universality is not achieved by a particular idea, but in accepting that every culture aspires in its own way to discover universality. It is the basis for tolerance, dialogue, for communicative rationality in Jürgen Habermas's sense.

---

[5] Bell 1973, *The Coming of Post-Industrial Society.*
[6] Dewey 1929, *Characters and Events.*

In the recognition that global governance is the ordering of global society we will need to understand that it is conducted through the continuous reappraisal of the concepts that inform that order. The global dialogue is one where a public philosophy is embedded, where ideas of justice, harmony, diversity, rights and respect, regulate cooperation for sustainability, well-being, truth and reconciliation.

These are only a small sift from a harvest of concepts that fill the discourse of leaders in all walks of life. When Obama, Xi, Putin, Merkel, Cameron, Hollande gather at leaders' meetings they speak, as Colin Bradford has observed so closely in this conference, a shared discourse that their officials develop as a continuous narrative between nations. But it is informed by concepts that are shared beyond them by an ever-enlarging global civil society, from the community leader to the cyber activist, from the executive in the global corporation to the environmentally concerned consumer. This is the global public philosophy of our time, belonging to all, commanded by none.

DOI https://doi.org/10.24103/GCSS.en.2018.15

Chapter Ten
How do we discover common values?

Just before the recent meeting of the G20 nations in Hamburg, Germany, the American President Donald Trump addressed the people of Poland and called upon Americans, Poles and Europeans to defend their values 'at any cost'.[1] He cited individual freedom and sovereignty as values defining 'our community of nations', equated in his speech with 'the West'.

An appeal to values as central to a community or society echoes a recurrent theme both in public and academic discourse in the West over the last century. The dominant figure in Western sociology in the 1960s, Talcott Parsons, declared:

> 'That a system of value orientations held in common by the members of a so-cial system can serve as the main point of reference for analysing structure and process in the social system itself may be regarded as a major tenet of modern sociological theory.'[2]

It would be only a slight exaggeration to say that the intensive debates, not just within sociology but even within Western culture itself, from the 1960s on-wards were a prolonged, often bitter conflict between opponents and defenders of the implications of that statement.

What conclusion has been reached? Very broadly, I suggest, until now, noth-ing but confusion about values and scepticism about theory.

Let us be clear at the outset. Common values do not guarantee peace, harmo-ny, cooperation or any of the other goods that make human life tolerable, let alone satisfying. Indeed one can say that President Trump gives the West an impossible task if he expects strength and solidarity to result from a defence of its values 'at any cost'.

Parsons, who was an acute observer of the United States, seeking to steer a path between rival political standpoints, offered a carefully crafted definition of American values. He summed them up as 'instrumental activism' or 'active mastery' towards what he called 'the situation external to the society', and that included both *nature and other societies* (my emphasis). That 'active mastery' might well explain why the rest of the West does not always find American values reassuring.

But it is not just a 'my nation first' attitude that creates conflict. Even the most universal values may have conflict built into them. The prime examples historical-ly must be those of the French Revolution: liberty, equality and fraternity. Am I at

---

[1]   White House Press Office, 'Remarks by President Trump to the People of Poland,' 6 July 2017.
[2]   Parsons 1960, *Structure and Process in Modern Societies*, p. 172.

liberty to oppress you? Can anyone demand we all eat the same amount? Is every stranger to be my brother? When values like these are treated as sacrosanct, is it any wonder that their uncompromising advocates led the French Revolution from jubilation in 1789 to the Reign of Terror in 1793?

Now, it is not my purpose to stigmatize values in general, or even to judge the respective merits of values that different countries revere most. The American Dream and the Chinese Dream have their unique origins and perspectives that are not transferable. But some values do emerge over time that stabilize societies and foster good relations between them.

Consequently, I want to dwell on the processes whereby people and nations find values that help them to live in peace with one another and find fulfilling lives. These may be values that will be held in common, but not necessarily ones they already hold. They will be discovered in the processes of working together. It was in this spirit that President Xi Jinping spoke to UNESCO in March 2014:

> Today we live in a world with different cultures, ethnic groups, skin colors, religions and social systems, and all people on the planet have become members of an intimate community with a shared destiny.
>
> We should encourage different civilizations to respect one another and live in harmony, so as to turn exchanges and mutual learning between civilizations into a bridge promoting friendship between peoples around the world, an engine driving society, and a bond cementing world peace.[3]

This speech was reprinted in Xi's published collection entitled *Xi Jinping: The Governance of China*. It is a volume that draws on Chinese history and culture and especially its recent experience of opening out, as an example of what learning in cooperation with others can achieve. It is also driven by theoretical enthusiasm, a desire to bring ideas for public policy together in a coherent whole.

As such, *Xi Jinping: The Governance of China* offers the kind of leadership, combining ideas and policies in a coherent whole that has no effective Western equivalent. Public policy debates in the West mirror its value conflicts, are confused and lacking in comprehensive theoretical underpinning.

It is a contrast that reminds me of a book famous in the 1970s, also written by a Harvard Professor of Sociology, Daniel Bell. Looking to the future he wrote of the coming of post-industrial society. He correctly recognized the rise of service occupations and, for us today, even more presciently, the future conflict between populist and elitist tendencies.

But Bell was very wide of the mark in predicting that future society would be distinguished by the centrality of theoretical knowledge.[4] Populists today may reject what they see as the power of the experts, but these are technocrats without theory, and the babel of theoretical voices within and across academic disciplines

---

[3] Xi, op. cit., pp. 287-288.
[4] Bell 1974, p. 20.

has little real influence on a public discourse that is led by slogans, tweets and celebrity.

By comparison the serious employment in China of theoretical ideas is a huge strength in its Belt and Road policies, largely unrecognized in the rest of the world. I can do no better than illustrate this by reference to Professor Wang Yiwei's exceptionally useful book *The Belt and Road Initiative: What will China Offer the World in its Rise?*[5]

Wang explicitly points to the deficiencies of Western ideas of globalization and describes current elaborations of the idea of community in Chinese public policy. Based on the report adopted by the 18th Congress of the Communist Party of the People's Republic of China, he points to the ways the idea of a community of common destiny in international affairs transcends the limitations of an older usage of community as conceived in the European Community of 1965.

In Western discourses, the idea of community has often carried strong overtones of exclusion, binding members together and excluding others. Yet it can also express the spontaneous, non-rational basis of shared experience that can reach out to the wider world and it is this that the idea of a community of common human destiny involves as Xi has developed it. For in it there are no outsiders.

This expansive sense of community was explored in the West by the eminent sociologist Amitai Etzioni, who argued for an East-West consensus on values to create a new global order.[6] A compromise between Western individualism and Eastern emphasis on social obligations could extend community to the whole world.

If we might have reservations on this route to shared values for the world, it is that differences on values among different Eastern countries are just as great as, if not greater than the differences between Western countries. To be fair, Etzioni acknowledges this, but we are then on the downward slope to the unresolved debates that followed on from Parsons's doctrine on central values and social integration. If values in general can produce dissensus as much as consensus, by what route can we find those particular ones that bind us together?

Let us take a different starting point. Let us accept there will be irreducible differences between cultures on national values and ask how Belt and Road can work in practice to overcome potential conflicts.

On 18 January this year a crowd of excited residents of the London borough of Barking and Dagenham greeted the first freight train to travel direct the 7,500 miles from the city of Yiwu in China. 'This is great news for the borough and for London,' said the leader of the borough council.

This was win-win cooperation. In the first instance, it offered benefits to both sides. They share, in other words, a community of common interest. How far did this depend on sharing values? Could it be the use-value of the goods? Possibly,

---

[5] Wang 2016.
[6] Etzioni 2004, p. 211.

possibly not. The market for Christmas tree ornaments that are manufactured in China for Western customers is rather limited in the place where they are made. Exchange value, however, is another thing. Exchange in one form or another is, on all anthropological evidence, a universal value, even if it takes many forms. We reaffirm that with every trading deal or purchase.

But the fundamental differences in culture, Western and Eastern, British and Chinese, remain. Do we try then to compromise between them or seek a deeper understanding, an exploration of a profound meaning underlying the differences that we can then all share?

This quest for mutual understanding in all human relations is a recurring theme in Western thought, examined most extensively by the German social philosopher Jürgen Habermas.[7] He finds that the assumption of 'communicative rationality' underlies all human interaction. The speech act in itself presumes the possibility of the other understanding it. Upon that elementary basis it is possible to erect a value system, and on it institutional structures, with dialogue as their pivotal concept.

This is an appealing notion for intellectuals, and I include myself among them, but I would suggest that the strength of Belt and Road does not depend on mutual understanding, however valuable that may be. It may be an outcome. But even if we accept that 'mutual understanding' could well qualify as a universal value, in itself it offers no solution to misunderstandings or deeper conflicts.

Every society begins from the assumption that its own values have a universal applicability. The American Declaration of Independence speaks of self-evident truths, such as 'All men are created equal'. It may be a noble sentiment but manifestly results in paradoxes.

Each person can claim the right to realize his or her own abilities, be different and aspire to be better than others. Equality and competition are then bonded in Parsons's 'instrumental activism' with its outcome of mastery over nature and others.

The West is learning, painfully some would say, to temper its claims to universality for its special historical experience, built as it is so much on the extension of empire and the individual's challenge to authority in the idea of rights. The East, by contrast, has been learning to assimilate and adapt Western notions of markets and legal regulations without undermining its own values of harmony.

But Belt and Road is not offering to amalgamate West and East, still less to diminish the sense of difference between the many cultures along its routes. Belt and Road is based in bringing countries together, and in this way will create new values as well as drawing on old ones. They will belong to no country in particular but become part of a common human heritage.

---

[7] Habermas 1986-7, *The Theory of Communicative Action.*

More important than anything else is the perception of a shared interest in achieving a common goal. This is what Belt and Road offers in abundance. Nothing allows cultures to be bridged more than the recognition of a shared practical interest in results. The four great Chinese inventions, papermaking, gunpowder, printing and the compass, spread worldwide, not through an appreciation of Chinese values but because of their proven usefulness.

The pragmatic demonstration of the importance of a shared goal in overcoming cultural differences, without eliminating them, can be illustrated from anywhere in the world. Let me conclude with an example from the West when in August 2009 I had the privilege to visit the construction site of the Atacama Large Millimeter Array, the ALMA telescope, 5,000 metres high in the Chilean Desert.

This was a joint project of European, American and East Asian consortia in cooperation with Chilean agencies. They shared an aim, to build the world's largest radio telescope by combining 66 radio antennae to work together as a single telescope.

Each individual antenna dish was up to 12 metres in diameter and weighed 115 tonnes. Each of the three international teams assembled its quota of dishes on site. Each did it differently. The Americans proceeded by joining two halves of the dish, the Europeans four quarters. Visitors to the European site could observe this, being allowed to walk round freely and photograph the construction process. But to the American site visitors were allowed a five-minute stay only and photographs were forbidden. On the other hand, access was not permitted at all to the East Asian site.

As we know, all cultures put a value on security, but their norms differ greatly. We may well view those access rules as the inevitable intrusion of cultural norms acting as impediments to international cooperation. Yet in the event the whole project also illustrated the triumph of cooperation around a shared goal over those cultural differences. ALMA proceeded to full operation and was opened officially on 13 March 2013.

Belt and Road will be an immense exercise in discovering shared values and creating common ones. Rooted in practical needs, it can elicit common responses to technology and to wealth creation. The combination of its projects with multiple and diverse national statements of value will stimulate debate and create sites for finding common values. It will reinforce the view that values are not static elements existing in timeless perfection but pragmatic achievements in permanent course of development.

DOI https://doi.org/10.24103/GCSS.en.2018.16

Chapter Eleven
The 'community of shared destiny' under conditions of imperfect understanding

First, on a personal note, let me express my appreciation to Stefan Köngeter and his colleagues in the Trans/Wissen Network for this invitation to Trier. It allows me my second visit to this beautiful city. The first was rather a long time ago, in 1959, to satisfy my curiosity about the birthplace of Karl Marx.

Marx certainly proved ideas travel. Whether they are changed in the journey is a main concern of this conference. Even the simple translation of your network title shows that crossing language boundaries is never straightforward. In English, as spoken in our local British dialect, 'trans-knowledge' is more likely to suggest the politics of gender rather than the spread of scientific ideas.

Marx's ideas travelled to China, in a big way. Today Marxism is a required course in Party schools and institutes of higher learning and, in the words of President Xi, is the guiding ideology in China, a required belief for Party members. I am citing from his book *Xi Jinping: The Governance of China,* a collection of speeches that illuminates the theoretical breadth of thinking behind China's resurgence as a world power.[1] It extends beyond economic and social policy for China to the first outlines of what has become the major Chinese initiative in international relations, 'Belt and Road'.

> We should examine *Xi Jinping: The Governance of China* as a serious theoretical contribution to global governance.

We find in Xi's book approaches to the biggest global issues of our time, to environmental protection, climate change, energy security and nuclear security. At a national level they fit into his conception of the Chinese dream. For their international reception they find expression in his formulation 'a community of shared destiny'.

> A German master of theory, Karl Marx, is required reading in China. We need to draw also on later Neo-Kantian value theory to find common ground between West and East.

---

[1] *Xi Jinping: The Governance of China.* 2014. Foreign Languages Press, p. 171.

The task I have set myself today is to examine that idea as a serious theoretical contribution to global governance, looking at it from a Western perspective. Marx was inspired by a brilliant period of German thought, the idealism of Kant and Hegel.

A time of similar creativity a century later, the so-called neo-Kantian movement, seedbed of Max Weber's ideas, laid much of the foundations of our social sciences. Both periods are equally important in prompting the train of thought that follows.

But it was the neo-Kantians who first brought the issues of common values and mutual understanding into central focus and it is those concerns that preoccupy so many of us today when we seek to imagine the future of global governance.

And those concerns are particularly relevant for the Western reception of Xi's ideas. He draws extensively from older Chinese cultural roots to explain the contribution China today can make to global peace and cooperation.

The ancient wisdom is a vital component of Xi's vision, even though it is absorbed into and explained in terms that are genuinely transnational, focusing on cultural diversity and global issues.

I recently returned from speaking in Beijing at the annual Symposium on China Studies hosted by the Ministry of Culture and the Academy of Social Sciences from 23 to 29 July. Nearly 50 foreign and Chinese scholars met to discuss the contribution of traditional culture to contemporary China, a Chinese solution for global governance, common values and mutual development.

> Paradox: Common values cannot guarantee mutual understanding; they can even promote conflict.

My own contribution was entitled 'How Do We Discover Common Values?' I will spare you a full repetition by summarizing it as follows. Common values have a contested position in Western thought because, though they are held to create solidarity within a society, they also are used to emphasize the differences between cultures and civilizations.

Even more striking and less often mentioned is how shared values can reinforce conflict within society. All may share the values of equality and justice and yet fight one another even as they assert them. Who imagines that the shared value of competitive individualism in the United States has contributed positively to social harmony?

It follows that to meet the challenges of global governance common values *in general* will not be sufficient. Only a specific selection of values, a very particular mix, may deliver a society at ease with itself. It would therefore be wise not to rely exclusively on values to produce social harmony but also to seek alternative bases for peace and cooperation.

Today I want to develop this argument in a particular direction towards those alternative bases, prompted as I am by the interests of the *Trans/Wissen* network and by the opportunity an audience in Germany gives me to make explicit connections to German theoretical traditions.

I said I was in Trier to visit the place where Marx grew up. But that was just a day trip during a year spent in Köln, in Köln-Nippes to be precise, learning your language for the purpose of studying the work of Max Weber.[2] Originally I learned, as every student does, that Weber made understanding (*Verstehen*) one of his most basic concepts for sociology. Sociologists, both aspiring and long-established, ever since have wrestled with his emphasis on understanding motives, a starting point for understanding society that he acknowledged was individualistic, even atomistic.

Every student too learns that Weber was the great defender of value-freedom in science, certainly refusing to judge others' ethics. As he wrote: 'What was ethical or not could only be decided by what was held to be valid within a specific group of people.'[3]

> Max Weber confronts us with the paradox of a
> social science reliant on understanding others, while
> values remain accessible only to their believers.

But then we have to ask how we find a research method to understand values that we do not share. He tried to address this with his famous concept of the ideal type, ignoring the ambiguities of natural language in a term such as 'bureaucracy' by defining it in a unique and precise way for research purposes. (The beginning of a major school of phenomenological sociology can be dated from the famous critique of that position by Alfred Schütz.[4])

But Weber's research expanded into vast comparative studies of religion in civilizations beyond the West, unavoidably leaving his ideal types in the shade as he made judgments about the relative priorities believers gave to certain values. His empirical sociology then went hand in hand with a scientific relativism when it came to studying others' values. But it also allowed for his own or anybody else's value commitments to be held passionately, as in his own case, precisely because they fell outside scientific judgment. He was a German patriot, devoted

---

[2]   That was not a task to be completed in a year, or indeed in a career. I still go back to him for inspiration, most recently to revisit his account of Chinese culture and world-views. See Martin Albrow and Zhang Xiaoying 2014, 'Weber and the Concept of Adaptation: The Case of Confucian Ethics' (Chapter 13 in this volume); Zhang Xiaoying and Martin Albrow 2016, 'Max Weber, China and the World: in Search of Transcultural Communication' (Chapter 12 in this volume).

[3]   Weber 1956, *Wirtschaft und Gesellschaft*, p. 19.

[4]   Schütz 1932, *Der Sinnhafte Aufbau der Sozialen Welt*.

to its culture and as convinced as any of his fellow countrymen of its world significance.

Weber leaves us with dilemmas about understanding and values that force us to go beyond him, even as we try to engage with our own time as he did with his. We can illustrate this today in the way two contemporary civilizations, the United States (as proxy for the West) and China relate to the wider world and one another.

There are many descriptions writers have given to the central values of the United States. Often they are referred to in the words of Thomas Jefferson as the American Creed (a word that conveys beliefs with a religious overtone), in Samuel Huntington's recent listing: 'liberty, equality, democracy, individualism, human rights, the rule of law and private property'.[5]

> American core values embody generations of people building their lives and communities literally from the ground upwards.

Yet the problem with such a list is that it expresses all those universalistic values that are current in societies worldwide and that are subject everywhere to the local debates and open conflicts around their meaning. Each one can mean something different according to cultural context. The set as a whole conveys something specific to the United States, but we only understand that by exploring the way it has been constructed, and that means over time, historically.

By the 1930s it had become common, as it is to this day, to refer to the attitude of mind that upholds those values as the American Dream, every individual empowered and entitled through them to advance in life. An acute observer of America, the German immigrant Hugo Münsterberg, professor of psychology at Harvard wrote in 1904, 'to be an American means to be a partisan of this system [of ideas]… to co-operate in perpetuating the spirit of self-direction throughout the body politic'.[6] Münsterberg enthusiastically disseminated the German ideas of his time, seeking to bring a sense of 'the eternal values' to the New World.[7] (Europeans have never given up hope they can colonize America.)

Later, Talcott Parsons, who dominated American sociology in the mid-twentieth century, summed up those values as 'instrumental activism', 'active mastery towards both nature and other societies'.[8] That is a subtle way to imply the inherent expansionary potential of the American Dream. As I have pointed out elsewhere, American globalization was already foreshadowed in Walt Whitman's poetry and his image of his country as the globe of globes.

---

[5] Huntington 2004, *Who Are We?*, p. 46.
[6] Münsterberg 1904, *The Americans*, 1904, p. 5.
[7] Münsterberg 1909, *The Eternal Values*.
[8] Parsons 1960, *Structure and Process in Modern Societies*, p. 172.

The animating spirit behind the values of the American Creed and the adherents of the American Dream are intelligible only through an understanding of American history, not just the beliefs of the original settlers and wave upon wave of immigrants, but their experience of building lives literally from the ground upwards.

This is what Americans bring to the table in international negotiations, values that are universal in their claims, but to be understood in terms of a local experience, or, if we like, national, because in a global frame the national is local.

Can it be different for China? President Xi has gently, or perhaps not gently enough for some, paid his respects to the American Dream by promoting an equivalent Chinese Dream. It is to rejuvenate a nation with more than 5,000 years of civilization, to build socialism with Chinese characteristics, a 'modern socialist country that is prosperous, strong, democratic, culturally advanced and harmonious', that will 'bring happiness to the people'.[9]

Xi's collection of speeches, published in English as *Xi Jinping: The Governance of China,* provides a comprehensive overview of the ideological thrust behind China's recent advance. The reference to harmony is not incidental. In his words, 'To successfully build a set of core values with strong appeal is connected with a country's social harmony.'[10]

> Chinese values embody centuries of
> experience of compliance with authority.

Travelling in China, it is not uncommon on entering a city to be confronted with an enormous elevated and illuminated display of the core socialist values, modernity in the Chinese version. Harmony, however, connects directly with the 5,000 years reference. In the same speech telling students and teachers of Peking University to practise the core values Xi provides a litany of quotations from the ancient classics, including one from the *Analects* of Confucius on harmony without uniformity.[11] For him, 'To cultivate and disseminate the core socialist values we must take traditional Chinese culture as its base.'[12]

Literally more than a hundred generations of Chinese scholars have explored and elaborated the meaning of core concepts embedded in their cultural experience, concepts such as *dao* (way), *de* (virtue), *li* (ritual), *ren* (humanity), *xin* (heart and mind). In them are stored a unique history, where acceptance of hierarchical authority has grown as the answer to ancient political upheavals. Confucius' own reflections were set against a backcloth of social and political chaos.

---

[9] Xi, op. cit., p. 41.
[10] Ibid. p. 181.
[11] Ibid. p. 190.
[12] Ibid. p. 181.

The unique world-view of the Chinese is one they project on to the wider world, in this sense, that they recognize the contribution their past makes to their present and accept that this must be the same for others. Again in Xi's speech to the young, 'Core values vary in different nations and countries due to different natural conditions and course of development. The core values of nation and country are closely related to its history and culture.'[13]

Now the question I want to pose at this point is, given the respective differences in the formation of core values in the United States and China: What chance is there of mutual understanding? What is 500 hundred years' experience compared with 5,000? Or, to put it more realistically in terms of documented history, 250 years compared with 2,500?

More important than just the timespans involved is the question of what each expects of the other, coming from those very different pasts. Here I want to suggest that Americans begin from a universalistic starting point and the Chinese a relativistic. Most famously, that universalism is enshrined in the American Declaration of Independence: 'We hold these truths to be self-evident, that all men are created equal and endowed by their Creator with certain inalienable rights.' This is a context-free individualism. It owes nothing to government and it encourages Americans to assume it is the universal human condition.

> How then can we expect governance of the globe to be based in mutual understanding between Chinese and Americans when their own national experiences of governance differ so vastly?

It is often equated with the dominant outlook of the West. Let me tell a story against myself here. I was privileged in the 1980s to be taken to a Chinese village to hold interviews with its inhabitants on the impact of the one-child family planning policy. I found myself in a house facing about a dozen women. I wanted an interview with one at a time. The request was put to them. At which they fell about laughing. I asked my interpreter to ask them what made them laugh. The answer was 'Western individualism'.

At this point it dawned on me that my assumption that an individual interview would have more validity than one drawn from the group derived from my own ethnocentrism and even from the sociological methodology of the time. The group response could well be more informative about the normal behaviour of the individual than answers under conditions of privacy and confidentiality.

The relativism of the Chinese and the universalism of the Americans sit uneasily with one another. Their political cultures are equally incongruent. The Chi-

---

[13] Ibid. p. 191.

nese world-view is associated with their respect for authority, the American with a distrust for government.

Now these outlooks in themselves are not an insurmountable impediment to a one to one relationship. There are, at the level of personal relationships, many happy Sino-American couples, there are business relationships to mutual advantage. But my question about mutual understanding extends to the chances of building a better world, of finding forms of global governance that can meet the challenges of our time.

Xi promises that the social harmony of China will contribute to a 'harmonious world of enduring peace and prosperity'.[14] The question that the rest of the world will ask is: How can this work if the United States requires all to share the values it holds to be universal and rejects the idea of world government, while China envisages a world of harmonious societies each organized around different core values?

Each side can only begin understand the other through a deep appreciation of their different historical experience and we may wonder whether even that can be sufficient to provide the community of nations with the tools it requires to meet global challenges. Can either provide the basis for global governance, for a world order without a government and ruled by neither?

At this point let us return to the fountainhead of German if not European social science. The legacy of Kant includes the inescapable requirement that any science of society must be built upon foundational concepts. In the subsequent school of German philosophy known as neo-Kantianism values and understanding became two such concepts.

The most widely known legacy of that school today is, of course, as I mentioned earlier, Max Weber's grounding of sociology in the understanding of human action, with his famous four types of motivation. The concept of values had for him even wider significance, extending beyond sociology into his reflections on methodology, on value freedom and value relevance and on the differentiation of value spheres, in each of which he detected an inner logic driving them apart from one another.

Much of his thinking on values arose out of his reading of Heinrich Rickert (1863-1936), who was recognized widely as the leader of the neo-Kantian movement. Understanding, on the other hand, had been given greater prominence by a scholar from the generation before both Rickert and Weber, Wilhelm Dilthey (1833-1911). Throughout his career he opposed Kant by asserting the priority of experience over concepts (though his own life's experience appears to be as retiring and uneventful as was that of the sage of Königsberg).

Dilthey was notable in making the varieties and limits of understanding other people and their culture his lifelong preoccupation. His oeuvre amounts to a vast

---

[14] Ibid. p. 14.

abundance of reflections around these themes, often as provocative as they are incomplete. But central to his thought was that understanding arose out of experience (*Erleben*) and was prior to the search for transcendental principles. A fine commentator on Dilthey has put this more effectively than I can:

> What Dilthey has done is to show that the principles themselves do not form a single coherent system, that there are alternative sets of them, and that each set represents the way in which a particular type of mind views the world.[15]

In Dilthey's time these ideas were directed towards the debates around European world-views (*Weltanschauungen*). In our time we are more likely to see them as relevant to debates about civilizational divides. In both cases, crucially, the historical deposits of the experience of our ancestors in the language we speak express our experience today. It is both the inexhaustible source of greater understanding of the other and at the same its limit.

When, therefore, President Xi offers us a harmony of civilizations[16] as the direction for human society on this planet, we are obliged to consider what that expression has conveyed first to its Chinese audience, as well as what it may convey when translated for the English speaking world. In that same speech to young people I quoted earlier, he said, 'The core socialist values we advocate today represent the inheritance and upgrading of outstanding traditional Chinese culture.'[17]

When Xi follows his own precepts and combines the classics with core socialist values and refers to harmony (Xi p. 190), he is drawing on the Confucian doctrine of the mean. Together with harmony it provides what the great scholar Lin Yutang (1895-1976) has translated as 'the universal law in the world'.[18] Lin was a great man in many ways, also as a novelist and the inventor of the first Chinese typewriter. About translation he wrote, 'There is no really intelligent translation without the translator's interpretation of the text to be translated.'[19]

Bearing these considerations in mind – that understanding other cultures is a matter of exploring a unique historical experience embedded in today's language – we can never assume that a formula chosen to express the common interests of people on this planet has a plain and simple meaning understood in the same way worldwide. The transnational language for global governance has barely begun, and I include in that the language of the United Nations and all the multilateral bodies.

---

[15] H. A. Hodges 1944, *Wilhelm Dilthey*, p. ix.
[16] Xi op. cit., p. 285.
[17] Ibid. p. 191.
[18] Lin Yutang 2009, *The Wisdom of Confucius*, p. 80.
[19] Ibid. p. 34.

> Xi's formula for global governance, a community of
> common destiny, *mingyun gongtongti*, is embedded in
> Chinese culture. But it invokes more than just understanding
> others. It also depends on exchange and cooperation.

The expression Xi employs for the collective endeavour of human beings (and here of course I am interpreting from the English translation from Mandarin) is 'community of shared destiny'.[20] It sits easily with ideas of Western origin such as 'global village' and 'common development', as in the 2013 speech 'A Better Future for Asia and the World'.[21]

It does connect with some recent uses of 'community of fate' in transnational discussions of climate change as in the public consultation for the UN climate change conference in Copenhagen in 2009 and occasional uses in sociology. But for German readers 'community of fate' translates as *Schicksalsgemeinschaft* and that was used by Weber to refer to those connections between peoples forged by common experience in the past. He alluded in particular to the relations between Alsace and France and the Baltic peoples and Russia for instance. His communities of fate were conceived in conflicts.

But we should note that his translators prefer 'destiny' to 'fate', and in English there is a subtle difference, for fate is something outside human control, while destiny bears with it some sense of a direction in human life. If such overtones are present in English how much more should we be aware of their presence in Chinese?

In over two years, Xi has used the Chinese expression *mingyun gongtongti* on 62 occasions. It has deep roots in Chinese thought. In Mandarin its five characters, all in use in ancient times, are each used in innumerable combinations where meanings of life, social relations, the unpredictable course of events and common interests are involved. Together they convey ordinary daily wisdom more than the English version with its overtones of mystery and prophecy.

The Chinese community of shared destiny is embedded in a centuries-old discourse of commonality and harmony that covers the human life course and relations with nature. The worldwide interactions of human beings with their environment and forces outside their control are woven together to create the future human condition. It is an everyday philosophy for social life.[22]

At the same time, repeatedly Xi emphasizes the cultural diversity of the world and the distinctive ways in which different societies shape their future. As he put it in his speech at the UNESCO headquarters in March 2014, 'Different cultures,

---

[20] Xi op. cit., pp. 287, 362, 387.
[21] Ibid., pp. 360-367.
[22] I am indebted to Professor Jin Wei of Wuhan University for her detailed comments on the origins and meaning of *mingyun gongtongti*.

ethnic groups, skin colours, religions and social systems and all people on the planet have become members of an intimate community with a shared destiny.'[23]

That speech was entitled 'Exchanges and Mutual Learning Make Civilizations Richer and More Colourful'. It explicitly rejects the thesis that different values make a clash of civilizations inevitable. Xi draws on a 2,500-year-old record of praise for harmony without uniformity by a Prime Minister of the State of Qi to make his point that cultural exchange is to everyone's advantage.

Xi puts mutual learning on a par with cultural exchange as a source of harmony and cites the Renaissance reception of the four great Chinese inventions (papermaking, gunpowder, printing and the compass), as well as the introduction of European science and technology into China in the seventeenth century as examples.

This emphasis on learning provides a lead to an alternative to the imperfect understanding that undue emphasis on shared values produces. It strikes me as even more important as I write today, a day after 19 September when President Trump has told the General Assembly of the United Nations that it was based on strong sovereign nations with different cultures and then went on to threaten several of its members. Perhaps that is the most vivid warning yet of where shared values can take us, as with, in this instance, the shared value of sovereignty, even as we assert diversity.

> After a lifetime's thought, Wilhelm Dilthey concluded that understanding took three forms. We can restate them as: a. Logical and scientific; b. Instrumental, or of people's purposes; c. Experiential, or of others' cultures.

Let us return to Dilthey. A lifetime of thought led him to the following general conclusions about understanding human cultural expressions.[24] There were three main types. The first was of concepts and judgments corresponding to logical norms, independent of context, saying little or nothing about the person expressing it. That includes science. The second was of human action, where there is a clear purpose, allowing inferences to the actor's mind that could however be mistaken. The third was of the expression of experience (*Erlebnisausdruck*). Now, there we have to probe behind the veil of ignorance, since we are never party to another person's experience, and with never a conclusive result. In that category, I propose on the basis of my earlier argument we should include others' values.

At the beginning of his career, Dilthey became renowned for emphasizing the difference between the natural sciences and the study of human culture. In the

---

[23] Xi op. cit., p. 287.
[24] Dilthey 1958, *Gesammelte Schriften Vol. VII, Der Aufbau der Geschichtlichen Welt in den Geisteswissenschaften*, pp. 205-209.

end, however, he arrived at a formulation that shows, not an unbridgeable gulf between them, but a spectrum from sciences that can find uniformities across unlimited time and space and that allow mathematical precision, through to ones that produce insightful observation of unique facts.

His conclusion allows for kinds of understanding to achieve Xi's community of shared destiny that are alternatives to understanding other people. One was most famously expressed by a keen observer of human sentiments, Adam Smith, 'It is not from the benevolence of the butcher, the brewer or the baker that we expect our dinner, but from their regard for their own interest.'[25]

On that limited form of understanding, imputing nothing to the other party to an exchange other than his or her interest in what you offer, is erected the whole discipline of economics, and, with the arbitrary exclusion of other motives, the neo-liberal edifice. Smith of course amply appreciated a whole range of other bases for human society, including cooperation in joint projects.

In this respect, the Chinese outlook amply demonstrates the alternative understanding that arises from sharing goals, in particular ones where there is collaboration around shared technologies. The Belt and Road project, which is the major extension of Chinese capital and technological expertise to a hundred or more countries, is based not on shared values but on a common understanding of how ports, railways and air transport work and how it is possible to cooperate on outcomes and for benefits that are understood by all.

> We should expect and work for global governance to develop primarily on the basis of shared technologies and projects rather than relying on understanding one another's culture to deliver peace and human well-being.

It is through the application of science that the world of our time has become one place and it is through the recognition of common threats to humanity from climate change, pollution, disease and nuclear catastrophe that we can share in those projects that will shape the community of shared destiny.

It may be even be the case, and let me add the kind of speculation you expect from an inveterate theorist, that one of the many reasons for the worldwide spread and advance of technology is that it is the bridge over which we clamber to avoid cultural rifts and the pitfalls of imperfect understanding.

This is where I could stop, by concluding my argument that it is not through common values that we can reach the transnational understanding our future on this planet requires, but through cooperation on practical projects with agreed goals. That can allow for diversity on everything else, indeed, requires that diversity, if the energies of us all are to be brought to the essential tasks.

---

[25] Smith 1868 [1776], *The Wealth of Nations*, p. 6.

But I would add a postscript of a self-interested kind, perhaps also appealing to this audience. In the West there has been in recent years a continual loss of recognition for theoretical argument. What I hope to have done is to provide an example of why theory is relevant to the central concerns of global governance. We cannot make advances in a common cause when there is confusion about the relative priorities to be attached to concepts of values, interests, goals, cooperation and motives in their articulation with governance practices.

In that respect, as I have said elsewhere, Western leaders should pay close attention to the example of President Xi's *The Governance of China*. Every speech is a lesson in rhetoric that brings the importance of theoretical ideas not just into the realms of national and international public policy but also into the everyday lives of ordinary citizens.

DOI https://doi.org/10.24103/GCSS.en.2018.17

Part Three
From Max Weber to global society

Max Weber (1864-1920) is sometimes represented as the epitome of bourgeois social science. With Emile Durkheim he shares the reputation of being the founding father of Western sociology.

In the 1960s and 1970s Karl Marx came to rival their influence in the West and in our time the sociology student will find the core ideas of the discipline often presented as a debate between these three giants of social theory.

Weber engaged directly in his career with Marxist ideas, and in particular opposed the economic determinism of some of the cruder interpretations of Marx that were popular in his day. But like all German intellectuals in the nineteenth century both men's early schooling was in the Kantian philosophical tradition.

Marx of course reacted vigorously against its subsequent Hegelian version. Weber's own critical approach to the idealist developments of his own time led him to centre his own work on the issues of understanding other people and other cultures.

While Weber worked with the latest ideas on values and the rational economic actor he fully acknowledged the importance of material factors in social life. As a result his sociological theory has continuing relevance for those who seek to reconcile socialism and markets.

What Western students only learn later (if ever!) is that Weber was fascinated by China. In the last years of his life his intensive study of Confucian and Taoist ideas in relation to economy and society was a major aspect of his developing theory of rationalization and capitalism.

The three essays that follow explore the internal logic of Weber's interpretation of traditional Chinese values and show how he wrestled with the overarching narrative accounts of his time, with materialism, idealism and evolutionism.

In the course of his debates with their advocates he both brought China into his own world historical frame, identifying the forces of change, and developed a rigorous set of concepts with a potential application to any society at any time. He is therefore a major contributor to philosophical social science.

We find in his work concepts and lines of thought that have retained explanatory value through to our own time. The final essay offers an example of what Weberian analysis might illuminate when we attend to the dynamics and direction of contemporary global society.

DOI https://doi.org/10.24103/GCSS.en.2018.18

Chapter Twelve
Max Weber, China and the world: in search of transcultural communication

Co-authored with Zhang Xiaoying[1]

Introduction

A hundred years ago, when Max Weber aimed to find the polar extreme to a spe-cifically Western experience of capitalism, he chose China as a test case. His pur-pose was to test his finding that the ethics of Protestantism in the West had given a unique impetus to capitalist development that was not present elsewhere. Si-multaneously he aimed to demonstrate how a science of culture and society was possible that was both objective and understood the meaning that human beings gave to their actions. The subsequent course of his research was to expose how Western ethnocentrism produced contradictions between these aims, but it also illustrated Weber's intellectual integrity as his growing understanding of China and of Eastern culture and society generally came to influence his formulations of the fundamentals of social science.

He had to deal with a century and more of prejudice about China that was widespread in the West and that initially was also reflected in his writing. In a journal editorial that was to become required reading for generations of sociology students, written a few years before he embarked on his study of China, he had al-ready set out his views on objectivity. He declared it was necessary to disentangle science from personal value commitments and achieve empirical truth and correct logic that had to be accepted as 'correct even by a Chinese'.[2] 'Even' must be un-derstood in relation to his comment in the same paper on 'a Chinese ossification of intellectual life'.[3]

These incidental allusions to China might simply be discounted as typical prejudices of the time, irrelevant to his scientific purposes, if it were not for the fact that he was to proceed to an intensive study of the secondary literature on Chinese culture and society, in particular the ethical systems that the West called

---

[1] Zhang Xiaoying, PhD, Professor of English and International Studies, is the Executive Dean of the School of International Journalism and Communication at Beijing Foreign Studies University. She is Editor of the journal *Global Communication* and author of *The Economist's Construction of Globalization (1985-2010): A Narrative Analysis with a Chinese Perspective.*
[2] Weber 2012a, p. 105.
[3] Ibid. p. 121.

Confucianism and Taoism. Weber's concern to combine scientific objectivity with the understanding of others is paradigmatic for the early stages of professional sociology in the West, but his extension of that interest to understanding other cultures at that time tested deep assumptions of Western superiority to their limits.

In his study of China, he was obliged to use secondary material that reflected the prejudices of Western capitalists and missionaries, but his intellectual integrity and commitment to a science true to human experience led him gradually towards a view that broke with old stereotypes. After this study and subsequent studies of India and ancient Israel, in an introduction to the collection of the resulting essays he elaborated on the multiple achievements of other civilizations, acknowledging both his dependence on secondary literature and the pressing need for ethnographic research, and stressed how the scope of the essays was strictly circumscribed by the aim of explaining the peculiarities of the West. Even if, he concluded, that only in the West had 'science' reached the point where we recognize the 'validity of its empirical findings and reflection on the problems of the world and life', he had to admit he was still a 'son of the modern European cultural world'.[4]

'Problems of the world' and the 'cultural world' appear as terms in the very first page of this introduction to his collected essays. 'World' in English, the translation of *'Welt'* in German, enables the writer to set a frame for a sample of human experience that has a separateness, distinctiveness and self-sustaining, self-referential character that is all-inclusive, yet bounded. In these respects it carries with it the deepest assumptions built into the existence of those cultures. *'Welt'* on its own and in compound words appears prolifically in Weber's studies of religion and is a component of his most general comparisons between Protestantism and Confucianism.

The task we set ourselves in this paper is to examine how far the 'world' can be employed as a basis for comparison between cultures when it has arisen out of and provided a frame for so much of Western experience. Did it help or hinder Weber in his efforts to determine the unique factors accounting for the rise of Western capitalism? Could he find a counterpart concept in Chinese culture? Was he able to create that shared world of science transcending West and East?

Consequently we examine the premises of Weber's study of China by taking understanding of the other seriously, considering the 'world' from a Chinese as well as from a Western viewpoint, and then taking the implications of that inquiry for arriving at judgments on other cultures that will command cross-cultural acceptance. One of our themes will be the way he moved away from the crude stereotypes of China that tend to surface in early work before he began intensive

---

[4] Weber 1976, p. 13. This introduction was originally published quite misleadingly for generations of English speaking students as the introduction to his study of the Protestant Ethic, rather than to the whole set of essays on the economic ethics of the world religions. The Protestant Ethic essay he pointed out was an 'older essay', which looked at only one side of the causal chain (see ibid. p. 27).

studies of the literature, and the other side is the way his studies of China helped him to refine his conceptualization of the influence of ethics and to acknowledge the distinctiveness of different worlds.

To these ends, the next section examines how Weber carried the West's experience and concept of the world into his study of China. In the third section we examine the Chinese translation of Weber's German text and explain the different connotations of the two main Chinese concepts that have been employed to render his concept of world (*Welt* in German), *Tian Xia* (天下) and *Shi Jie* (世界). The fourth section discusses the issues of ethnocentrism that surround critiques of Weber's study. The fifth section engages with Weber's problem setting from a standpoint in Chinese culture. The sixth section proposes that over time he gradually revised both his view of China and his basic concepts in the direction of a deeper appreciation of cultural difference that prepared the way for the later phenomenological and existential ideas of the world in the West. In conclusion, we seek to draw general lessons from this analysis of Weber's study of China that assist towards achieving transcultural communication.

The world in Weber's understanding of China

Reflections on, and images of the world have been pivotal in Western thought from the earliest discussions in ancient Greek philosophy. Anaximander, who died 546 years BC, imagined an infinite, eternal, primal substance that encompassed all worlds. Since then, the 'world' has been a Protean source of speculative accounts of nature, creation, the earth and human existence. Ideas of the world in the West have developed from both classical Greek and Christian sources. Christianity's contribution was to introduce a cleavage between this world and a world after this life, overlaying the older dichotomy between material and ideal realities embedded in Greek thought. The world as experienced in the lives of individual human beings then came variously to be seen as a reflection of, or a testing ground for demands that came from another world, or a preparation for that world. Ideas came to harbour intimations of a spiritual world paralleling a real world.

A highpoint in the Western discussion of the world came with the work of the seventeenth- century German philosopher Gottfried Wilhelm Leibniz (1646–1716).[5] He sought to overcome the tensions between ancient and Christian views of the world by finding multiple worlds possible in logic but one world created from them by a beneficent God, giving rise to his dictum that this world is the best of all possible worlds. What makes Leibniz of particular interest for us is that over nearly twenty years he engaged in intensive conversation with the Jesuit priests who had first-hand experience of the Chinese imperial court and wrote extensively

---

[5]   Bertrand Russell (1945, p. 581) calls Leibniz 'one of the supreme intellects of all time'.

on the possible convergence of primordial ideas of creation, God and the world between Chinese and Christian thought.[6]

These attempts to forge understandings between the Pope, the Chinese emperor and the French king in particular were an early conversation of civilizations.[7] What we call transcultural communication Leibniz sought through finding the equivalent of the universal truths of mathematics in universals in early languages, in particular Chinese. He and the Jesuit Joachim Bouvet saw his binary arithmetic as cognate with the diagrams of the ancient divinatory *I Ching*.[8] It was a line of thought based in cultural comparison and a belief in the universality of human reason as a basis for common understanding. It was effectively cut off for two centuries by the breakdown of the Jesuit efforts to mediate between China and the West, by the assertion of Western superiority in both religion and science that imperial expansion promoted, and by the iconoclasm of the French Enlightenment.

Leibniz became a laughing stock in eighteenth century European salons after Voltaire parodied him in his novel *Candide*. There, Pangloss, the absurd philosopher of unlimited optimism, declares 'Leibniz is incapable of error'.[9] 'The New World is the best of all possible worlds,' says the hero, Candide.[10] But the Jesuit-educated Voltaire's satire both exposed the infinite multiplicity of Western ideas of the world and began the process of shutting down the possibility of reconciling faith and reason. Voltaire was erecting the wall between Leibniz's quest for mutual understanding based in universal ideas and the imperialist assertion of the necessary progress of Western scientific civilization.

After Leibniz and the failure of the Jesuits to achieve accommodation between the Chinese *Tian* and the Christian God, the world in the West became a *topos*, a site where the cosmos, earth, earthly existence, the varieties of human experience, the possibilities of difference and the power of imaginary creation were woven into a tapestry of ideas that defeats all attempts at organization. The idea of the world became an invitation to exploration of both personal experience and of other lands and grew in significance in parallel with the rise of Western individualism. In German thought, the literary genius with a profound influence on Weber, Johann Wilhelm Goethe, expressed this when he wrote:

> The human being only knows himself in so far as he knows the world, which he is aware of only in himself and of himself only in it.[11]

---

[6] See D. E. Mungello 1989, *Curious Land: Jesuits' Accommodation and the Origin of Sinology.*
[7] Yu Shuo (2014) has called this first encounter between China and Europe 'the universal value dream'.
[8] See Li Wenchao and Hans Poser (eds.) 2000, *Das Neueste über China: G.W. Leibnizens Novissima Sinica von 1697.*
[9] François-Marie Arouet Voltaire 2005 [1759], *Candide, or Optimism,* p. 88.
[10] Ibid. p. 24.
[11] Goethe 1949, *Gedenkausgabe,* p. 879.

In Weber's own time, the new discipline of psychology was beginning to examine such insights that had hitherto been the preserve of philosophers and poets. The professor of psychology Hugo Münsterberg contrasted 'subjectivizing' and objectivizing approaches to the social sciences and argued the 'I' of actual life and its 'world' were always ultimately outside the scope of a science that sought explanatory laws.[12]

In early critical essays on methodology, Weber criticized the severe dualism of that view (indeed regarded the task of social science was to provide a bridge between them). For him, the world of facts and the choices of individuals are of the same world when it comes to explaining the course of human action. The key distinction to keep in mind is the one between the scientific quest for laws and the search for historical understanding of human affairs. For the latter, 'no theory of the world can comprehensively include all the constellations of life among its conditions',[13] a formulation that provided Alfred Schütz later with a supportive text for his account of the multiple worlds the individual must negotiate.[14]

Weber's discussion of Münsterberg exhibits an abiding feature of his approach to the world, a recognition of variety coupled with an underlying tendency to imply a shared possession of a single world of human experience, even sometimes referred to as the 'real world'. It is that shared and implicitly objectively recognized real world that comes into play in his studies of religion, for all religion, in his terms, at its root is always in some way external to the real world.

Even as Weber was wrestling with basic methodological problems in the social science he was working towards his first publication in 1904/05 of the essays on religion, which, as *The Protestant Ethic and the Spirit of Capitalism* (1976), with their emphasis on a work ethic specific to capitalism, were to become one of the formative influences on the Western self-understanding in the twentieth century. The core idea was that the 'inner-worldly asceticism' of Puritanism, a self-denying dedication to work as fulfilling God's will, had been crucial for forming an ethic that was particularly suited to the kind of capitalist organization of labour that arose in the West. The thesis generated controversy at the time and has continued unabated to the present day.[15]

'Inner-worldly' was high up as a topic in early debates. In origin it arose from a simple contrast between the Catholic monk's life in a monastery withdrawn from everyday life and the Puritan believer living in the world outside. In response to criticism from Felix Rachfahl in a journal article in 1910, Weber insisted that both the Catholic monk and the Puritan believer shared a parallel asceticism, chas-

---

[12] Münsterberg 1900, *Grundzüge der Psychologie* I.
[13] Weber 2012a, p. 52.
[14] Schütz 1932, *Der Sinnhafter Aufbau der Sozialen Welt*, p. 253
[15] This is not the place to review the resulting vast literature. Stephen Kalberg's new translation, *The Protestant Ethic and the Spirit of Capitalism with Other Writings on the Rise of West* (2009), includes further writing by Weber on modern Western institutions and other religions and provides commentary and scholarly references to subsequent debate.

tity, poverty, independence from the 'world' and a rejection of enjoyment, in sum
the deliberate disciplining of all creaturely desires. But there were differentiating
characteristics, rejection of irrational techniques and of contemplation and

> Finally, and above all: the diversion of asceticism into the inner-worldly, its
> realization in the family and the ascetically defined occupation, from which all
> the differences [between capitalism] and everything else stems.[16]

Immediately after that debate, Weber turned for the first time to study secondary literature on China seriously to test his thesis that elements of capitalism
had existed all over the world but it was Puritanism that made the critical difference in the West. He was particularly interested in Confucianism (so-called, a
term invented in the West) because it too was focused on life on this earth and,
like the Puritans, the Chinese officials educated in the Confucian classics were not
living in monasteries. For Weber, the inner world, conceived in a study of Western
religion could be equated with the world when writing of China:

> Confucianism exclusively represented an inner-worldly morality of laymen.
> Confucianism meant adjustment to the world, to its order and conventions. Ul-
> timately it represented just a tremendous code of political maxims and rules of
> social propriety for cultured men of the world.[17]

> 儒教仅仅是人间的俗人伦理。儒教适应世界及其秩序和习俗。归根
> 结蒂不过是一部对受过教育的世俗人的政治准则与社会利益规则的
> 大法典。(2012b, p. 224)

The idea of the 'inner-worldly', together with the idea he relates to it, adaptation to the world, is central to the contrast Weber draws between Confucianism
and Puritanism. It is the shared base from which to contrast Puritan asceticism
with Confucian acceptance of life's gifts. Asceticism contains another contrast,
between the mundane, everyday world and the spiritual, in Christian thought
equated with earthly power and the kingdom of God respectively. It is a double dualism. Spatial separation, inside and outside, is overlaid with the spiritual/
mundane distinction. The mundane world is also where the non-believer lives. It
was the spiritual world that gave the Puritan the strength to pursue the vocation
and to resist the temptations of everyday life. The Confucian could not have that
advantage:

> The relentlessly and religiously systematized utilitarianism peculiar to rational
> asceticism, to live "in" the world and yet not be "of" it, has helped to produce
> superior rational aptitudes and therewith the spirit of the vocational man, which,
> in the last analysis was denied to Confucianism.[18]

---

[16] Quoted by Baumgarten 1964, *Max Weber, Werk und Person*, p. 183.
[17] Weber 1920, p. 441; 1951, pp. 152-153
[18] Weber 1920, pp. 533-534; 1951, p. 247.

这种宗教系统化了的冷酷的功利主义有任何理性主义文化禁欲所特有的风格：“在”世界中生活，而不是“靠”世界生活，有助于创造职业人阶层的优越的理性能力和“精神”，这些却为儒教及其适应世界的生活方式所不取。(2012b:311)

Arguably, the world is the most important baseline for comparisons that Weber adopts in his study of religion generally, and certainly in respect of China. It receives at least 130 references in the German text if one counts all the terms in which it is combined with another concept. In German the prevalence is more noticeable because of the ease in that language with which compound words are formed.[19] In four cases 'world' appears in quotation marks, Weber's signal that he was alert to the fact he was using it in natural rather than technical language. What is striking in the multiple uses in simple and compound words that Weber makes of the 'world', is that it is overwhelmingly a singular world, the main exception being when he speaks of inner-worldly, thereby implying a world beyond this one (*Aussenwelt*). That distinction had been central in his Protestant Ethic but not in his Confucianism study, the main reason being, as we shall see, that he failed to identify any transcendence in its ethical thinking.

The Chinese translation of Weber's '*Welt*' (world) *tianxia* (天下) and *shijie* (世界)

There are no perfect equivalents in Chinese to 'world' in English or '*Welt*' in German.[20] The differing histories of distinct civilizations ensure that this is not the

---

[19] Chapter VIII *Resultat: Konfuzianismus und Puritanismus* (Weber 1920, pp. 512-536), in the Gerth translation, Chapter VIII Conclusions: Confucianism and Puritanism, pp. 226-249. The translations from German are ours and not Gerth's but they may make it easier to compare with the Chinese. In this chapter, Weber's references to the world, simply or combined with another word, number 60. They include (1920 edition first, then Gerth translation):

Welt; world: 512 (2), 226-227; „513", 227; 513, 227; 514 (4), 227-228; „516", 229; 518, 231; 519 (2), 232-233; „521", 235; 522, 235; 525, 238; 526 (2), 240; 527 (3), 240-241; „530", 244; 531 (2), 244; 532 (2), 245; 534 (6), 247-248; 535, 248; 536, 249

Weltzusammenhang: world connectedness: 513, 227

Überweltlich; world ruling: 515, 229; 516, 229; 522 (2), 235; 523, 236; 526, 240; 527, 240; 534 (2), 247-248

Weltflucht, -ig; world fleeing: 515, 229; 525, 238

Weltbejahung, -end; world affirming: 515, 229; 528, 242

Weltanpassung, -angepassten; adaptation to the world: 515, 229; 534, 248

Weltoptimismus; world optimism: 522, 235

weltoffen; open to the world: 524, 238

Weltbehandlung; handling the world: 524, 238

Weltrationalisierung; rationalization of the world: 524, 238

Weltablehnung; world rejection: 525, 238; 532, 245; 534, 248

innerweltlich; innerworldly: 534 (2), 247

Weltbeherrschung; world ruling: 534, 247

Weltreich; world empire: 536, 249

[20] Karl Jaspers (1932 p. 82) comments on the etymology of *Welt* that it derives from the old German 'weralt', as of course does the English 'world' (cf OED). But of the two elements, *wer* meant man

case: the very origin of the problem Weber faced in comparing them. But if we take the two main sets of meanings in the West, world as the extensive territory of human existence and world as the sum of human experience, there are two Chinese expressions that are roughly equivalent. One is *tianxia* and the other is *shijie*.

Literally, *tianxia* means under the sky, or every place under the sun. *Tian*, a core concept in Chinese culture and belief system, has rich meanings. On oracle bone inscriptions and those on ancient bronze objects, *tian* looks like a small figure with a protruding head. Its original meaning is thus 'head' but has gradually developed to refer to the sky, signifying supremacy. Feng Youlan (1895–1990), a Chinese philosopher, has summarized five meanings of *tian*: the material one, as opposite to the earth; the ruling one as personified by *tiandi*; the will of *tian*, as in Mencius' words, that 'it is the will of *tian* whether one is successful or not'; *tian* as nature, the operation of nature; and *tian* as argumentative philosophy, the supreme principle of the universe.[21]

In ancient China, the Han or Huaxia people, people of a civilized society who lived along the Yellow River in northern China used the term *tianxia*, which emphasized the positive order principle. The emperor was seen as the son of the sky, known as *tianzi*, who governed according to *tianyi*, the will of the universe. In order to maintain the order of *tianxia* for the benefit of all people under the sky, he extended some of his power to other countries. In doing so, the Chinese emperor did not assert his dominance over other countries under the *tianxia* system, and other countries with their own rulers voluntarily recognized the rule of *tianzi*, as they were aware that he would take responsibility for all of them. Otherwise, he would be overthrown. This is what is often called 'the order of *tianxia*'.[22]

The interpretation of the term *tianxia* by Zhao Tingyang, a contemporary Chinese philosopher from the Chinese Academy of Social Sciences, may help us to gain a better understanding. In his book *The Tianxia System: An Introduction to the Philosophy of World Institution* (2011), he explained that the concept of *tianxia* has the connotation of being above the interest or value of a particular nation, and taking responsibility of all people under the universe. He cited the view of Liang Shuming (1893–1988), a Confucian scholar, that *tianxia* is a concept about the 'world' rather than the 'nation'.[23] He likened *tianxia* to the Western concept of 'empire'.[24] But while an empire is a state with politico-military dominion of populations who are culturally and ethnically distinct from the ruling ethnic

---

and *alt* meant age, corresponding to the Latin *saeculum*, an age in human affairs, i,e. something passing, quite the opposite of the dominant modern meaning of something persisting.

[21] Feng 2006, p. 24.

[22] 'The order of *tianxia*' connotes the separation of China and the outside world. Since the end of the eighteenth century the idea of the order of *tianxia* under the rule of the emperor has been under threat. By the end of the nineteenth century, China began to adopt the idea of a connected world in which all nations are equal.

[23] Zhao 2011, *The Tianxia System*, p. 30.

[24] Ibid. p. 27.

group and its culture, usually accompanied by chaos in the process of conquering minority groups, the *tianxia* system goes far beyond that. Zhao summarized three fundamental meanings.[25] First, geographically, it is a system in which humanity and nature coexist harmoniously. Second, psychologically, different countries are interdependent, with smaller ones voluntarily and convincingly following the larger ones. Third, politically or ethically, it is a systemized world, having transformed from chaos to cosmos. All in all, the *tianxia* system is a philosophical concept with a worldview in the full sense of the word.

Tianxia therefore fairly closely renders the occasions when Weber talked of China as a 'world empire':

> 'When China was politically unified into a world empire ...' [26]

> '政治一统天下的中国......' (2012b, p. 165)

Or in:

> 'Since the pacification of the world empire, ...' [27]

> '自从天下太平以来......' (2012b, p. 182)

Yet there are contrasting nuances between 'world empire' and *tianxia*. The former is a Western concept, which basically sees the world as many different nations in the first place, while the latter first sees it as a whole. In Chinese culture, one is many and many is one. Or one is all, and all is one. This is typical Chinese thinking mode called *correlative thinking*, or *tong* (through) *bian* (change) in Chinese.

As Lao Tzu put it, 'Tao begets the one, the one consists of two in opposition (yin-yang); the two begets the three; the three begets all things in the world. All things connote yin-yang. Yin-yang keep acting upon one another and thus things keep changing and unifying themselves.'[28]

The aspiration to represent the world as a whole as expressed in 'world empire' is the outcome of successful imperialism, the imposition of a world-view on many peoples. In contrast, *tianxia* is a pre-existing interdependence. In the words of *Yi Jing –Xu Gua*, the Orderly Sequence of the Hexagrams:

> 'There comes the sky, the earth and then everything; everything is followed by men and women, husband and wife, and father and son; the relationship of father and son brings about the links of king and his officials, thus the class appears and rite is therefore different.'[29]

---

[25] Ibid. pp. 27-28.
[26] Weber 1920, p. 373; 1951, p. 84.
[27] Weber 1920, p. 394; 1951, p. 103.
[28] Lao Tzu 2013, *The Book of Tao*, p. 121.
[29] This is translated by the authors from the original text accessed at http://wenku.baidu.com/view/ad57e57931b765ce05081443.html on 19 January 2015.

Most of the time when Weber writes of the world, he is not, however, thinking in terms of empire or of territory and the earth. He has in mind the other much wider sense of world, one where it is the human experience of existence and possibilities of many worlds. (At the same time he narrowed it down to the inner world of the Puritan dualistic world-view). And this is of course what concerned him most in his study of China. Here, the standard translation is *shijie*, a two-word term originating from Buddhism which was introduced to China from India around the start of the Christian Era. With its Buddhist origins, the term *shijie* is quite capable of expressing a spiritual or, if one prefers, an ideal side to human life. '*Shi*' means 'time' and '*jie*' means 'space'. As a common saying goes, '*shi* refers to all ages from ancient to modern time, and '*jie*' refers to all sides from above and below'.

According to Buddhism, *xiao shi jie* (a small world) is centred around Mount Sumeru, comprising the solar system, planets and satellites. One thousand *xiao shijie* (a small world) make a *xiao qian shijie*. One thousand of *xiao qian shijie* make a *zhong qian shijie*, and one thousand of *zhong qian shijie* make a *da qian shijie* or the *saha* (a big or boundless world). The concept of *shijie* thus implies the entire universe or 'philosophical universe', e.g. 'boundless universe'.[30] The earth on which human beings live is thus a tiny bit of the *da qian shijie*. *Shijie*, in the narrower sense, often refers to the earth inhabited by humans. *Shijie* in the narrower sense is pervasive in the Chinese translation of *The Religion of China*. For example:

> …the good spirits, however, are those who protect order and beauty and harmony in the world.[31]

> 善灵则指那种维护秩序与美、维护世界和谐的精灵。(2012b, p. 206)

Or

> …Confucianism was separated from other systems of Chinese attitudes toward the world.[32]

> 这正是儒家与中国其他世界观体系的区别。(2012b, p. 240)

> But the ethic remained pacifist, inner-worldly…[33]

> 这种伦理成了和平主义的、入世的伦理。(2012b, p. 241)

---

[30] Qiao, Wei and Du 2012, *The Study of the Philosophical Thinking of Tibetan and Han Buddhism*, p. 56.
[31] Weber 1920, p. 420; 1951, p. 131.
[32] Weber 1920, p. 457; 1951, p. 169.
[33] Ibid.

Western ethnocentrism

It is not surprising, given his starting point, given access only to translations and Western commentaries, that Weber's account of Confucianism and Taoism should have been criticized subsequently for its ethnocentrism. As Schluchter pointed out, in seeking to find what differentiated China from the West, Weber began with concepts of specifically Western origin.[34] The question 'Why didn't Western-style capitalism develop anywhere else?' resulted in counterfactual speculation about the absence of Western characteristics for which there was no prior reason to expect their presence, as in: Confucianism 'succeeded in removing the basic pessimistic tension between the world and the supramundane destination of the individual'.[35] Of course it wasn't there to be removed in the first place! Weber to be sure went to enormous lengths to define Western capitalism in a neutral way, as an ideal type, such that it could be applied as a template in any cultural context. It did not occur to him to give 'the world' the same treatment. He was aware of the pitfalls in its use.[36] But in general he adopted the unqualified usage of everyday language, ostensibly equated with 'reality', but overlaid with a Puritan disdain for this world.

Two of the papers in the German volume devoted wholly to reviewing Weber's study of China made a similar point, namely that Weber, in speaking of the ethics of Confucius as 'adaptation to the world', was underestimating its tension with the world and its creative potential.[37] Schmuel Eisenstadt wrote critiques of Weber's account of both China and India, arguing that Weber wrongly excluded the possibility that their religious and ethical orientations played a role in structuring inner-worldly reality.[38] In the case of China he argued there was a tension between the transcendent and the inner-worldly and the idea of cosmic harmony produced standing demands for reform.

Another critic, Thomas Metzger, argued that Weber was mistaken in seeing Confucianism as mere adaptation to the world when there had to be an active engagement to shape human life, which otherwise would be a mere collection of impulses, and that, unlike Mencius, Confucius did not see human beings as naturally good.[39] Weber thus therefore excluded Confucians from the pursuit of a better life and reserved it for the Puritans:

> The world, as promised, fell to Puritanism because the Puritans alone had "striven for God and his justice". In this is vested the basic difference between the two

---

[34] Schluchter 1983, *Max Webers Studie über Konfuzianismus und Taoismus.*

[35] Weber 1920, p. 522; 1951, p. 235.

[36] See above for his critical discussion of Münsterberg's account of objectivizing and subjectivizing the world.

[37] Schluchter (ed.) 1983.

[38] Eisenstadt 1983, 'Innerweltlich Transzendenz und die Stukturierung der Welt'; 1984, 'Die Paradoxie von Zivilizationen mit außerweltlichen Orientierungen'.

[39] Metzger 1983, 'Max Webers Analyse der Konfuzianische Tradition: Eine Kritik'.

kinds of rationalism. Confucian rationalism meant rational adjustment to the world; Puritan rationalism meant rational mastery of the world.[40]

世界属于清教理性伦理，这符合天意，因为只有这种伦理是"为上帝及其正义而奋斗"的。由此，可见两种"理性主义"的区别：儒教理性主义意味着理性对待适应世界；清教理性主义则意味着理性地把握世界。(2012b: 312)

Weber's attachment to the idea of adaptation or adjustment is in part attributable to the then fashionable adherence to the language of evolution. Strangely, elsewhere he conceded it had little explanatory power.[41] 'Adaptation' or 'adjustment' (*Anpassung, Angepasstheit*) to the world combined with its inner worldliness for Weber distinguishes the Confucian ethic from any other religious orientations, and indeed only marginally was he prepared to give it religious status. But the main contrast he aims to draw is with Puritanism, for both were inner worldly and the comparison between the two ethics was the culmination of his enquiries into Chinese society and culture. Typical of some fourteen occasions on which he draws attention to it is:

> [In true prophecy] the "world" is viewed as material to be fashioned ethically according to the norm. Confucianism in contrast meant adjustment to the outside, to the conditions of the "world".[42]

真正的语言按照一种内在的价值尺度制定出生活方式的系统的指南，它把"世界"看成可以按照规范从伦理的角度塑造的物质。儒教则相反，是从外部适应'世界'的条件。(2012b: 301)

In this quotation we can see Weber employing a persuasive contrast between the prophet come to change the world and the class of scholarly officials concerned to maintain it, carrying with it the implication that somehow one ethic adapts and the other does not. Yet the nature of an ethic is counterfactual, existing as a set of standards against which the world is judged, to which people aspire. But it is when the source of those standards is not from a God that Weber is unable to credit them with any coherence. Without God, says Weber, 'life remained a series of occurrences'.[43]

That formula underlies his belief that the Puritan has a unified personality from the inside going out ('*von innen heraus*') while the Confucian can't achieve any inner unity, only able to adapt towards the outside ('*nach außen hin*') and

---

[40] Weber 1920, p. 534; 1951, p. 248.
[41] We examine Weber's uses of the idea of adaptation in a separate paper, 'Weber and the Concept of Adaptation: the Case of Confucian Ethics' (Albrow and Zhang 2014), Chapter Thirteen in this volume. There we point to the way Chinese notions of harmony with nature and Jesuit ideas of accommodation to local customs were conflated and absorbed into the evolutionary vocabulary he used.
[42] Weber 1920, p. 521; 1951, p. 235.
[43] Ibid.

acquire a combination of useful qualities.[44] It is very difficult to square this with a judgement Weber expressed elsewhere about the difference between the characters and abilities of Chinese and Western officials: 'The Confucian basic maxim that the superior man was no tool, its ethic of universal personal self-perfection, was radically opposed to Western ideas of a practical profession.'[45]

Only in respect of the Confucian relating to mass religiosity in the general population does it make some sense to talk of an adaptation to the world. But then it becomes difficult to see the sense of Confucianism as 'inner-worldly'. Though there is a strenuous adherence to an ethic which does not belong to the masses, for Weber it is not unified, because it does not come from the inside, and cannot achieve the unity that 'we' (the Western we) associate with the concept of personality. But where then does it come from? If, as Joachim Radkau suggests, 'world' means the 'everyday world', that was certainly not the cultured world of the Confucian scholar, the *junzi*.[46]

What is surprising about Weber's initial treatment of Confucianism is the difficulty he found in acknowledging the possibility of an ethic that commanded dedication and striving for high achievement that was not underpinned by a belief in God. He recognized the Chinese cosmos as a distinctive and unitary phenomenon.

> The cosmic *orders of the world* were considered fixed and inviolate and *the orders of society* were but a special case of this.[47]

> 世界的宇宙秩序是固定的、不可冒犯的，只有一种特例，这就是社会秩序。(2012b: 224)

But he concluded from the cosmic ordering of the world and society that without a God there could be no transcendent purpose for the individual. However, that only follows from a fundamentally Christian view of the world. He failed to appreciate the place of the human being in the Chinese world-view. It was the difficulty Weber had to recognize China's worldview in its own terms that led to his abortive attempt to use the notion of adaptation to the inner-worldly, when in Chinese thought there is a single world where striving to be perfect in it and to perfect it is the human mission.

The Chinese world image: self-transcendence, consummate person and Ru Shi

From a Chinese viewpoint, the issue is why there is a 'supramundane' or 'supernatural' or 'transcendental' world in the West? Weber, to his credit seeks to answer this. Israel, 'a small nation among the world powers to which it finally suc-

---

[44] Ibid.
[45] Weber 1956a, p. 618; 1978, p. 1049.
[46] Radkau 2009, *Max Weber: A Biography*, p. 387.
[47] Weber 1920, p. 441; 1951, p. 152.

cumbed', needed Jehovah to change the fate of the nation which was at war and faced with many abrupt changes. China, by contrast, was mostly a 'pacified world empire', which did not need an external force to control the fate of the nation.[48]

But to see the absence of God in these geopolitical terms simply drew attention away from alternative kinds of transcendence in Chinese thought – self-transcendence. While recognizing the moral action of *tian* (sky) and *di* (earth), the focus of Chinese thinking was in the first place the human being, i.e. 'self-cultivation', in an effort to become, mostly for Confucianism, *daren* (great man) or *junzi* (consummate or exemplary person) and, mostly for Taoism, *shengren* (sage who takes no credits for his successes) or *zhiren* (sage who has no self and adheres to naturalism).[49] That is why people respectfully called Confucius '*junzi*' or '*shengren*' and Lao Tzu '*zhiren*'.

For a consummate person with a perfect heart, 'integrating into the world' and 'transcending the world' are one thing. Transcending the outside world starts from an inner transcendence. This is a fundamental point on which the West and China divide. The Chinese lived in the world and were of the world without self-denial, regarding the world to be long-lasting and significant, while the Puritans, as Weber pointed out, lived in the world and not of the world, seeing the world as transient and insignificant in comparison with the idea of heaven. The call to the Christian path of self-denial was most important.

To be a *junzi* is a means to self-transcendence. However, it is worth noticing that Weber follows another scholar (Dvorak) in adopting the English word 'gentleman' for the Chinese *junzi*.[50] But 'gentleman' (or a princely man) for *junzi* is misleading. *Junzi* is an exemplary person or a consummate person, not necessarily coming from a family of high social standing. To be a *junzi* is the goal of Confucianism, but for Daoism, it has a higher aim of being a *shengren* (sage, not a saint as is usually translated.) According to *Yi Jing –Wen Yan Zhuan,* the interpretation of the Hexagrams of Qian and Kun, *junzi* has the virtues of *tian* (the sky, the father) and *di* (the earth and mother), e.g. giving birth to myriads of things generously and selflessly, the brightness of the sun and moon, the flexibility to follow the changes of four seasons and the vision of the unpredicted. To be a *junzi* is therefore the goal of the Confucians.

The oneness of this world and the transcendent world featuring Chinese philosophy can also be seen in the relationship between human beings and *shenling.* Unlike the supramundane God in Christianity, Confucianism adopted polytheism. The Chinese equivalent of God is *shenling*, referring to the creators and masters of the universe in legends and mythology such as the sun and moon, or supernatural and immortal beings such as the three *shenlings* of fortune, prosperity and longevity or the spirits of the dead who were widely respected such as Confucius.

---

[48] Weber 2012b, p. 101.
[49] Zhuang Zi 2004, p. 12.
[50] Weber 1920, p. 449; 1951, p. 160.

The Chinese character of *shen* is "神", indicating the shape of thunder in the sky, which the ancient people found changeable and powerful, thus master of the universe. *Ling* is "灵", suggesting the spirits of the dead; *shen,* representing *yang* and *ling*, represents *yin* forming two interlocking parts of one whole.

Polytheism illustrates that the humans are the equals of the *shenling*. The relationship between human beings and *shenling* is close, and people are tolerant of other *shenlings*. When Confucius' student Zi Lu asked him how to offer sacrifices to *shenling*, he replied, 'If you don't understand life, how can you understand death? If you don't know how to serve humans, how can you know how to offer sacrifices to *shenling*?'[51] Confucianism believes that everything begins from this world, but should not end there. Life is limited: it is practical to understand this world. Taking care of this world is not the end, but a means to the other world. It is believed that this world and the other world are correlates. Fu Peirong, professor of philosophy at the National Taiwan University and a renowned scholar of *Yi Jing*, argued that Chinese philosophy does not simply feature humanism, as many people think, but has exhibited 'open humanism – open to the transcendent world' as its predominant feature.[52] What Weber failed to appreciate was the moral striving to be the consummate man. According to Confucianism, the sky, the earth and the human form a unity and the human aspiration to perfection is a constant factor in making a better world. Cosmic order is *tiandao* (natural law, 天道), and social order and family order are *rendao* (humanity仁道). *Tindao* and *rendao* are one, a reflection of the harmony of humanity with nature. The purpose of both is *sheng* (continuity of life, 生). The continuity of the life of *tiandao* is through that of *rendao*, *ren* (仁), meaning the intimacy between two persons or consummate conduct. Thus, self-cultivation is seen as a way to obey *tiandao* and achieve cosmic order. This system adopts the method of beginning from ourselves to others, from the near to the distant, ultimately building the outer world by developing the human's inner world.

The English translation of *ren* in Confucianism also illustrates that the West failed to grasp the Chinese world-view. Although there is no denying that the key concept of *ren* in Confucianism is flexible and open to debate, the conventional English translation of *ren* as 'benevolence' is definitely inaccurate. The word 'benevolence' indicates kindness as shown by God, which is not the case in Confucianism. As Roger T. Ames, professor of philosophy at the University of Hawaii, a widely acclaimed sinologist, explained: 'The word benevolence cannot accurately express the connotation of *ren*, as the concept of benevolence is rather narrow-minded. The concept of *ren* is much broader.'[53]

---

[51] Confucius 2007, *The Analects*, p. 107.
[52] Fu 2010, op. cit. p. 1.
[53] Hu and Ding 2006, 'On China and the West – Interview with Professor Roger T Ames', p. 119.

There are two main reasons why there is no need of salvation by God. First, *Ru Jiao* believes that *tian* helps those who help themselves.[54] In comparison with the Christian transcendent pursuit of God's salvation and the saving of the individual's soul, the transcendent pursuit in Confucianism is to meet the order of *tian*, or answer the call of *tian*, that is, to become a *junzi* who is morally right or just, like *tian* itself. A *junzi* should act morally as *tian* and *di*. Second, Confucianism believes that humans are imperfect yet powerful enough to help themselves. That is why self-cultivation through moral education is made more important. The Confucians are confident of this kind of 'inner power' and 'self-help', because they know that as long as they follow *tiandao* (the will of *tian*), they will become *junzi*.[55] The spirit of *Ru Shi* gives strength and fortitude, making the Chinese nation unyielding in times of difficulties.

Confucius' inner-worldly turn of mind and unreserved participation in the world, or *rushi* (入世), leads some to think there is no transcendence. There is. It is the kind of 'inner transcendence' of oneself from a common human to a consummate being, *junzi* or an immortal person, *shengren,* just like Confucius. The path to it is to have great writings and high moral values and render meritorious service such as pursuing wealth and honour. One can be immortal by doing so, just like a Christian who can enter heaven by working hard to gain wealth and honour to win the favour of God.

However, the pursuit of wealth and honour in Confucianism would not lead to individualism, for the literati in feudal China represent the interest of the masses. Their success has to be recognized by their own people. They must not separate themselves from the people, otherwise, their achievements will not be recognized, and they will not reach the goal of becoming an immortal person. It is thus the ideal personality of the Confucius school of 'internal sagacity and external kingcraft'.

Weber is partially right when he writes:

> As the reward of virtue he expected only long life, health and wealth in this world and beyond death the retention of his good name. Like for truly Hellenic man all transcendental anchorage of ethics, all tensions between the imperatives of a supra-mundane God and a creatural world, all orientation toward a goal in the beyond, all conception of radical evil were absent.[56]

> 他所期待的道德报偿是：今世长寿、健康、富贵，身后留个好名儿。同真正的古希望人一样，儒家也没有任何伦理的先验寄留，没有超凡的神的诫命同被造物现世之间的任何紧张关系，没有对来世目标的任何向往，没有任何元恶概念。(2012b, p. 295)

---

[54] Zhou 2002, op. cit., p. 261. This is the idea that originates from the *Da'you* Hexagram of the *Yi Jing.*

[55] This is an idea that originates from *The Analects*: 'If you do not know *tian*'s will, you cannot be a *junzi*' (Confucius 2007, op. cit., p. 202).

[56] Weber 1920, p. 514; 1951, p. 228.

From a Chinese viewpoint, the Puritans lived in this world according to the demands of the other world, answering God's calling to transform and master this world. The Confucians lived in this world following *tianli* or *tiandao*, the law of nature or the course of nature to transform the world. They don't have to master it, as they have been part of it. There is a famous saying by Zhu Xi, a key figure in Confucianism: keep *tianli* and destroy excessive human desire.[57] In the rationalism of Confucianism, inner-worldly work is to strive for another kind of transcendental goal, an inner one. They want to transform the world from being 'non-reasonable' to 'reasonable', from being 'immoral' to 'moral' based on *tianli*. This attitude towards the world is rather positive, the purpose being to understand it and change it for the better. But the final goal is to go beyond it, to make a thorough examination of the future world so that people can adapt to the changing situation and move forward.

Being inner-worldly, is Confucianism concerned about the other world? Weber thought that Confucianism believes in the life of the world today, instead of that of the past and future world. It is because this world is the best, and human nature is ethically good. This is not exactly right. The Confucians aim to create an ideal society, with the ultimate goal of maintaining a good cosmic order, the origin of everything. Moreover, Confucianism is also concerned about the life after death, the 'nether world' (*yinjie*) or the 'ghosts world' in Chinese, in contrast to the 'mortal world' (*yangjie*) or the 'human world'. However, Confucius believed that only when people understand the mortal world can they understand the nether world. Only when people take good care of the living can they take good care of the dead. So Confucianism cares for the other world by focusing on this world. Confucianism is focused on the affairs of the world, but it does not stop there. It is open to the transcendent world.

From objectivity to transcultural communication

We have emphasized the difficulties of translating the ideas of the world or *Welt* and of *tianxia* and *shijie* into and from English or German and Mandarin Chinese, bringing out the fundamentally different frames of thought that translation seeks to bridge. From a standpoint in the twenty-first century after a hundred years of grappling with cultural relativism, it might seem obvious that a comparative study of religions would need to begin with that issue. Weber did not, because he was engaged in the methodological debates of his time that focused on the possibility of an objective social science, the place of values and the causal explanation of human behaviour. His ideal types were abstract constructions of elements of social processes that had intelligible cause and effect relations built into them, as with ideas of the perfect market or bureaucracy, and it was those concepts, products in his terms of Western rationality, that he took to his studies of non-Western

---

[57] Zhu 2011, *The Analects of Zhu Zi.*

civilizations, to illuminate their differences from the West. They were his constant background reference points in his accounts of the Chinese state and economy. The far-reaching and refined architectonic of sociological concepts that he was crafting in his last years developed from them and was intended to have universal application.

Doubts that he might have had about accessing other cultures were assuaged by his conviction that the rational was a common human property. In the idea of rationality, he felt he had the key to understanding the other, for that had the potential to be a shared possession across cultures, even if took on different colourings in each. 'We can,' he affirmed, 'find rationalism in China too'[58], and his wife recounted how he considered finding the special rationalism of the East to be 'one of his most important discoveries'.[59]

Yet religion was different: it drew on people's deepest feelings about their lives and place on this earth and appealed to higher values at the same time. Whereas with the state and the market Weber could find rational calculation embedded in them, he had to discern another kind of rationality in religion and this he found in the efforts of intellectuals, priests and scholars to find meaning in life, to develop ethical codes and theodicies. Yet these are all expressed in language, not in numbers, and Weber showed very little interest in language or issues of translation. The Chinese, writes Weber, without undue concern, have no special word for religion.[60]

In the context of cross-cultural understanding there is a striking contrast between Weber's and Leibniz's approach to China in their concern for the meaning of its culture.[61] Leibniz and the Jesuits before him saw from the very beginning that issues of translation were key to bringing about an accommodation between the West and China, and that this was not a one-way process. They sought to discover shared and primordial intuitions behind Western ideas of God and the Chinese *tian*.

Nothing is more indicative of the rupture between West and East caused by imperialism than the way Leibniz's name is blanked out in Weber's writing on China. He gave the idea of theodicy, the justification of God's ways in a world of injustice and evil, an important place in his comparative studies of religion without even mentioning Leibniz as the inventor of the term and author of a book with

---

[58] Weber 1951, op. cit. p. 226.

[59] Marianne Weber 1975, *Max Weber: A Biography*, p. 333.

[60] Weber 1920, p. 432; 1951, p. 143.

[61] Adrian Hsia (2000) has highlighted this contrast, much to Weber's disadvantage. In particular, he points to his inappropriate application of the German concept of *Pfründner* (holder of a benefice) to register the social position of the Chinese officials. He points out that the everyday Chinese term for them was *fumuguan*, mother-father-mandarins. Rightly, Hsia points to Weber as writing at the endpoint of the Western denigration of China that began in the eighteenth century, but it would equally be fair to say he also brings the study of China into the mainstream of social science with the aim of achieving a worldwide scientific impartiality.

the same title.[62] He cited the Jesuits and their efforts at accommodation to Chinese ritual without reference to their and Leibniz's quest for the natural religion underlying all religions. With no apparent irony, he attributed to Confucianism an ethic reflecting a belief that this was the best of all possible worlds, when that phrase became famous from the *Candide* travesty of Leibniz's philosophy.[63] There Weber could have read Voltaire's sparkling rendering of the contradictions of the worlds of the philosophers and travellers, abstract reason and experience. Weber's search to reconcile science and understanding began afresh against a background of nineteenth-century Western assumptions of superiority over the East.

With a very different starting point from Leibniz, however, Weber was edging forward on a road that led in the direction of transcultural communication. Signs of a shift towards a greater appreciation of the need for dialogue across cultures appear in his later thinking on values and ethics. In an insertion to the original discussion paper on value judgment,[64] later published as 'On the Meaning of Value Freedom',[65] he advanced the idea of a 'conventional type concept', distinct from his rational ideal type, based in commonly understood ideas among teachers and researchers.[66] It is a step towards accepting the average sense that can be given to an idea rather than a purely rational construction, and that average sense has to be derived from general usage.

But the greatest influence on Weber's own understanding of China was his continuing reading on all aspects of its history, society, economy and culture until the end of his life. As he extended his studies of economic ethics, he became more convinced that ethics came into tension not only with everyday life but with any sphere of life that had its own specialized rationale, such as the economy, the state or art. One of his late amendments to the essays on economic ethics was to include the statement that an economic ethic is not purely religiously determined, and indeed has its own autonomy from religious ideas under economic, geographical and historical conditions. That of course was a necessary qualification, since in his general introduction to his studies of the economic ethics of the world religions he had already said that the status ethic of the literary stratum that influenced Chinese life could equally be said to be religious or irreligious.[67]

---

[62] Christopher Adair-Toteff (2013, '*Sinn der Welt*, Max Weber and the Problem of Theodicy', p. 88) points out that Weber was probably influenced by his friend Ernst Troeltsch, who was writing on theodicy at the same time.

[63] Voltaire's poem 'The Lisbon Earthquake' included the lines:
Leibniz cannot tell me from what secret cause
In a world governed by the wisest laws,
Lasting disorders, woes that never end
With our vain pleasures real sufferings end.
(Voltaire 2005 [1759], *Candide or Optimism*, p. 106).

[64] Weber 1913, Manuscript.

[65] Weber 1917, '*Der Sinn der Wertfreiheit*'.

[66] Weber 1968, p. 533; 2012a, p. 329.

[67] Weber 1920, p. 239; 1948, p. 268.

Weber inserted an essay entitled 'Intermediate Reflections'[68] between his essays on Chinese and Indian economic ethics, where the tension between life spheres and between them and religion became for him the more compelling central concern, rather than the issue of adaptation to the world. When he next turned to Hinduism and Buddhism he continued to refer back to China without reference to adaptation. Tension between the rationalization of religious beliefs and the world could not reasonably exclude Confucian thought, especially as Weber recognized the literati as a status group apart from the masses.[69] But in this respect its conception of the world had as much claim to be a shaping of reality as any other ethic, not merely an adaptation to it.

The unique and autonomous ethical outlook of the Chinese literary stratum gradually led him away from his insistence on its adaptation to the world that had been his first attempt to sum up the character of Chinese ethics. Most instructive was the way he generalized on the quality of Asian religions in the conclusion of his study of Hinduism and Buddhism. Now, Confucian scholars are '(relatively) democratically recruited'.[70] They share with all Asian religions the 'always alert self-control', but the ultimate value of that quest for perfection in lifelong study was hidden from a Westerner.[71] The Confucian protected himself from both spirits and fruitless problems and avoided banal occupations and barbaric indulgence, achieving the dignity of 'personality' in the traditional and sublime mannerisms of the salon.[72]

It is here that Weber turned to the issue of cross-cultural understanding. The Westerner, he said, cannot get hold of a meaning in the ceremonies and rituals of the Asiatics and is tortured by their reserve and apparently highly meaningful silence, but then Westerner and Asiatic alike are often unclear about the original meaning of their own customs. It may be, and here he cites Wilhelm Dilthey, philosopher of meaning, that Nature has no 'ultimate word' to tell us, but Asiatics have dedicated far more unrelenting effort to work on these problems of salvation than the West has done. The Confucian finds inner-worldly fulfilment in the 'charm and dignity of the gesture'.[73] It is a pure 'inner-worldy aesthetic' of self-discipline, bereft of the real forces in life, far from the practical interests of the masses.

---

[68] Weber 1948, pp. 323-359, 1920, '*Zwischenbetrachtung*', pp. 536-573.

[69] Paul Radin, (1957 [1927], *Primitive Man as Philosopher*) arrived independently from Weber at a similar analysis of the relations of thinkers and doers. For Radin the systematization the thinker introduces is a tendency in all human society and one therefore accessible to all in any account of varying views of reality. Reality, as a concept, then is not a Western invention it is the possession of communicating human beings and there are no boundaries to its communicability.

[70] Weber 1921, p. 368; 1958, p. 334.

[71] Weber 1921, p. 373; 1958, p. 338.

[72] Weber 1921, p. 374; 1958, pp. 338-339.

[73] Weber 1921, p. 377; 1958, p, 342.

What is compelling about these final pages of the study of Hinduism and Buddhism is the way Weber absorbed Confucianism into a comparison between the West and Asia, and sought the highest level of generality possible at the level of understanding of meaning that was attainable for the Western observer.[74] He also attended in the same pages to issues of geographical, linguistic and political structures as well as economic interests that were conditions for the rise of Western economic rationalism and helped to explain its absence in the East. In other words, he was now directly concerned with understanding other cultures in the context of a paradigm for social science that provides material explanations in parallel with cultural or meaningful interpretations that reached the limits of understanding the 'other'.

As far as Weber's treatment of the 'world' is concerned, to the end he exploited the open-ended and hermetic nature of the idea and continued to elaborate new orientations towards it.[75] Not once is there mention of an 'adaptation to the world' or of utilitarianism and its implied lack of personality associated with it. Personality now no longer implicitly has to have a core associated with a belief in God, it also belongs to the East even if the core is mysterious, and Weber cannot resist on the very last page a dig at fashionable Western life-style quests to create 'personality'.

In parallel with his studies of religion and economic ethics, Weber was continuously engaged in refining an outline of fundamental concepts in sociology. In a brief comment on ethics he expressed what may be regarded as the culmination of his long engagement with other cultures:

> Whether a widespread idea of what is valid can be regarded as belonging to the sphere of "ethics" or not (therefore not just convention or legal norm) can in an empirical *sociology* not be decided except according to the concept of "ethical" that in *actual fact* has, or had validity among the circle of people in question (Weber's emphases, our translation: 1956, p. 19; cf. 1978, p. 36).

He has moved from 'common understandings among teachers' to the shared ideas of the individuals who are the subject of research. Weber's successors took their cue from the scope of his interest in the meaning of life and the world. Martin Heidegger in his *Sein und Zeit* remarked on the multiple meanings of 'world' in

---

[74] Weber 1921, pp. 363-378; 1958 pp, 329-343.

[75] He writes of the Asian cultural world (1958, p. 329; *Kulturwelt*, 1921, p. 363), things of this world (1958, pp. 330, 338; 1921, pp. 365, 373), 'meaning' of the world (1958, p. 331; 1921, p. 365), world-view (1958, p. 331; *Weltanschauung* 1921, p. 365), a concealed world (1958, p. 331; *Hinterwelt*, 1921, p. 366), a devalued world (1958, p. 332; *entwertete Welt*, 1921, p. 366), world indifference (1958, pp. 332-333; 1921, p. 367), world flight, otherworldly soteriology, worldly nobility (1958, pp. 332-333; 1921, p. 367), rational world direction (1958, p. 335; *Weltlenkung* 1921, p. 370), this antirational world (1958, p. 336; 1921, p. 370), world relationships, world cares, (1958, p. 338; 1921, p. 373), the real world (1958, pp. 342, 343; 1921, pp. 377, 378), the social world (1958, p. 343; 1921, p. 378) and of course inner-worldly ethic (1958, p. 337; 1921, pp. 371, 372) and the inner-worldly asceticism of Protestantism (1958, p. 337; 1921, p. 372).

everyday language.[76] The way was open to the phenomenology of typical everyday conceptions associated with Weber's critic, Alfred Schütz, who dissected Weber's methodology by focusing specifically on his concept of the world.[77]

In the same period, his friend and great admirer Karl Jaspers introduced his three-volume *Philosophy* by placing Weber as the culminating figure in the long history of free thinking in which Kant had the pivotal place, and the line continued through Schelling, Hegel, Kierkegaard, von Humboldt and Nietzsche. Weber, he wrote, 'looked the despair of our time in the eye, diagnosed it with all-embracing knowledge, standing it up on itself in a disintegrating world.'[78] In the same work, Jaspers distinguished world orientation, the world as totality (*Weltall*), the universe) and world picture (*Weltbild*), all of which are to be found in Weber. In a chapter simply entitled simply '*Welt*', Jaspers wrote, 'As little is the world that I can know without the I that knows it, just as little is the I without the world in which I am the I in the first place. There is no world without the I, and no I without the world.'[79]

Carrying forward the position that in the post-Second World War period came to be known as existentialism, Jaspers wrote, 'The world is not an object, we are always in the world, have objects in it, but it never becomes an object.'[80] Approaching the world from a quite different intellectual orientation, contemporary linguistic philosophy comes to no different conclusion. In recent years, Markus Gabriel has gained wide public attention in Germany with his book *Warum es die Welt nicht Gibt* ('Why the World Does not Exist'), making much the same point as Jaspers, the world can no more be an object than the largest number can be a number.[81]

The multiple worlds of the twentieth-century philosophers and the widespread exclusion of God from their accounts of the world point to a convergence between Western and Eastern world pictures. One commentator on neo-Confucian thought, Weiming Tu argues that its world is 'a limitless multiplicity of dynamic interactions through which things come into existence' and points out that this is incompatible with the Christian view of a creator God.[82] Weber too saw the capitalism in his time as having kicked away its old supports in religion and figuratively spoke of the polytheism of conflicting values.

---

[76] Heidegger 1976 [1927], pp. 87-89.
[77] Schütz 1932, op. cit., p. 20.
[78] Jaspers 1932, *Philosophische Weltorientierung*, p. ix.
[79] Ibid. p. 62.
[80] Jaspers 1953, *Einführung in die Philosophie*, p. 75.
[81] Gabriel 2013.
[82] Tu 1983, 'Die Neo-Konfuzianische Ontologie', p. 282.

Conclusion

Through his study of Eastern religions, Weber finally arrived at a cultural rela-tivism that accorded with his perspectival approach to scientific objectivity and the value pluralism in which his ethical theory is embedded. It is expressed at its simplest when he says sociology can only hold to 'a concept of "ethical" that in *actual fact* has or had validity among the circle of people in question'.[83] At a personal level, his own journey is perhaps summed up in a footnote to that last section of the Hinduism and Buddhism study, where he indignantly reproves an American author for calling Asiatic life monotonous.[84] That deserves the astonish-ment of all East Asians, he writes, coming as it does from the authentic homeland of monotony. He has travelled a long way from his view of ossified China. He has anticipated and achieved a vision of the multicultural world that tragically came too late for him to experience.

If the East has acknowledged and successfully adopted the technical and instrumental aspects of Western science, equally the Western recognition that the world is not an object to be controlled and that, on the contrary, reality always ex-tends beyond any present human horizon, brings it close to older Chinese wisdom that human beings are active in that reality, actively seeking to improve their lives as part of it, thinking it through in the spirit of *tongbian*. The rationalistic tendency of Weber's sociology made it difficult for him to escape his own Puritan inher-itance and see the world as any other than something outside the human being to be rejected or mastered – or adapted to. The language of immanence only applied to mystics, not to everyday life.

The linguistic turn in philosophy in the second half of the twentieth century has brought a better understanding of the performative nature of language, and we can convey the spirit of Chinese thought much better if we talk of performing the world. Perhaps it may not be too long before it becomes a standard comment that it is the legacy of centuries of Chinese philosophy which has prepared the Chinese state to think through and chart a successful course through an ever-changing capitalism with more success than Western states have achieved while they are still mired in an old rationalistic modernity. 'Puritanism deformed, Confucianism performs' could become the simplistic slogan of the future.

This paper has been a contribution to dialogue across cultures, Western and Chinese. We two authors each have our own base in one of them and test our understandings of the other in our intellectual exchanges.[85] We try to reach a com-mon view of the issues of cross-cultural understanding that Max Weber's study of Chinese culture raises. In a search for objectivity in accounts of the worlds of others, he arrived at a recognition of the validity of their own definitions of reality,

---

[83] Weber 1956, p. 19; cf. 1978, p. 36.

[84] Weber 1921, p. 371; 1958, p. 336.

[85] Our mother tongues are Mandarin Chinese with English as a second language for Zhang, and English with German as a second language for Albrow.

while believing that through science and rationality common understandings were possible. It was for a later generation of social scientists to go further than he was able to do and recognize that not just rationality but experience of the other and dialogue between cultures can create new definitions of reality, new shared worlds.[86] In that process we may also learn respect for the differences between the cultures into which we were born and those through which we travel.

---

[86] Recently in the *Journal of China in Comparative Perspective* Yu (2015) has described this process as 'transcultural generativity'.

DOI https://doi.org/10.24103/GCSS.en.2018.19

Chapter Thirteen
Weber and the concept of adaptation: the case of Confucian ethics

Co-authored with ZHANG Xiaoying

Introduction

Max Weber was explicit about his reasons for turning to China. He sought to advance his thesis on the influence of Protestantism on the development of capitalism. A hundred years after his study, as China seeks to adapt capitalism to its socialist principles, there are even more reasons to re-examine his evidence and the substance of his argument.[1] Yet such re-examination quickly raises questions extending far beyond contemporary interest in the drivers of capitalism.

For Weber set that study within a broader frame of a comparative sociology of religion, and that in turn was a contribution to a comprehensively conceived and ever more all-embracing study of the interactions of economy and society in recorded human history where rationality was a force for transforming community, law, money and the state, and individuals were confronted with dilemmas for which there were no rational answers.

It is the ever-expanding scope of Weber's inquiries that makes him the representative voice of Western modernity at the outset of the twentieth century, and the anticipation of its coming existential crisis. But he did not reach his conclusions overnight. It was work in progress, always developing and terminated only by an early death. His initial study of China was written in the middle of an intensely creative time in his life, sandwiched between two general reflections on religion and society that are widely seen as pivotal turning points in his work.

Weber was equally concerned both with seeing his own time as a moment in human history and with advancing a science of social reality. The result was persistent iterations between conceptual clarification and examination of cultural contexts. China, even all of Chinese history, provided material therefore for advancing the understanding of factors that could be in play elsewhere at any time: leadership, lifestyle, personality, work ethics, traditionalism, rationalism, ideas and interests.

And those factors were not ones dreamt up in a small study in Heidelberg. Weber's concepts were distilled from the broadest understanding of the intellec-

---

[1] Or adapt socialist principles to capitalism! As we shall see, both are open possibilities for Weber.

tual currents of the West, crafted through engagement with public and academic debates. (Mommsen 1984, Mommsen and Osterhammel 1987). He engaged with materialism, idealism, historicism, nationalism, naturalism, secularism and, largely by proxy through his contemporaries, with Kant, Goethe, Hegel, Marx and Nietzsche (see Löwith 1982, Goldman 1988, Scaff 1989, Albrow 1990, Schroeder 1992, Gonzales Garcia 2011).

One of those broad currents was evolutionism and his study of China was noteworthy for its focal argument, namely that the Confucian mandarin status group adhered to an ethic of 'adaptation to the world' (*Weltanpassung*). Adaptation was and remains a concept central to evolutionary theory and Weber attended closely to its possible applications in historical and social research, which were as controversial in his time as they remain to this day. The grand narratives of his time were Weber's ongoing targets. Natural selection, scientific progress and materialism combined in the Monist movement and its prominent academic representatives such as Wilhelm Ostwald, were to be the targets of some of Weber's most vehement polemics. Weber was committed to research and not to a worldview.[2] The widespread popular acceptance of concepts from the sciences could not immunize them from critical scrutiny.

Equally, however, it was also still a concept with strong ethical associations, antedating Darwin, that have now largely been lost to our time. We devote this paper to examining the roots of Weber's interest in this concept, why he applies it to China, and, in particular we explore and seek to explain the apparent paradox that he declared of little scientific use while continuing to employ it when writing of ethics. His account of China is then more than it normally is held up to be, namely a test case for his Protestant ethic thesis.[3] It is also a prime example of the duality of Weber's ambition. He strove to develop explanatory concepts with the widest historical and comparative utility, a paradigmatic struggle for the professional discipline of sociology. Paralleling his conception of science, however, he was always drawn to what lay beyond it, the ethics of choice in the modern world.

The writing sequence

One of the difficulties in tracking the development of Weber's thinking is that the dating of versions of published texts tests the best of archivists and this is compounded by way the process of fragmentary translation into English has obscured

---

[2] In a critique of Ostwald written in 1909 he wrote, 'Nowadays, of course, it is quite customary to turn the "image of the world" [*Weltbild*] in a discipline upside down and transform it into a "world view" [*Weltanschauung*], and it is common knowledge how this usually happens in Darwinian biology (1968: 401; 2012: 253).

[3] Cross-cultural comparisons, even with China, are within Weber's sights as early as 1904. He sharply distinguishes the Protestant work ethic from acquisitiveness, something that has existed in pre-capitalist eras, 'among the Chinese mandarins, Roman aristocrats and modern farmers' (1904/5, 20.1: 20; 1920: 41; 1976: 56).

any temporal ordering of what so often appear as entirely distinct fields of enquiry. It also distracts attention from the interlocking features of those texts. Weber worked simultaneously on methodology, religion, law, the city, political order,
ethics, and music, to name only some of his fields of interest. He alluded copious-
ly throughout his career to adaptation (*Anpassung*), together with its twinned concept, selection (*Auslese*). They belonged both to the mainstream scientific culture
and to the public sphere of his time. He employed ideas drawn from evolutionary
theory most controversially in his 1895 Freiburg inaugural lecture; they guided his
research on the working conditions and practices of textile workers; his political
thought revolved around issues of the selection of leaders and in his final lecture
series on economic history he contrasted worktools adapted for human use with
the apparatus to which human beings had to adapt themselves (Weber 1923: 9).

It is well known that Weber turned to the study of China to identify a system of thought at first glance as far as possible from the Western experience, in
particular of Protestantism. Precise origins for his study of China are impossible
to pin down. According to Wolfgang Schluchter (2014: 11) Weber's last lecture
course in Heidelberg in 1897/98 'alluded to the "entry of East Asia into the orbit
of the occidental culture sphere"'. He had already read about the activities of
Protestant missionaries in China in 1904 (1904/5: 20.1:16; 1920:100; 1976: 225)
and he was content to convey in early PE some of the stereotypes about China
that he shared with contemporaries, like 'Chinese petrifaction' (Weber 1904/5:
21.1:109).[4] He could well have been stimulated by a lecture on Chinese religion
to the Eranos circle in 1906 by the sinologist and Austrian diplomat Arthur von
Rosthorn, with whom he corresponded in 1918 (1989: 41-3).[5]

We have his wife's testimony (Marianne Weber 1975: 331) that he began
work on China in 1911 and his own (1915a: 1; 1920: 237) that in 1913 he read to
colleagues his Introduction (1915a), Early Confucianism Studies (1915b-e) and
the Intermediate Reflections (1915f), later to be published as a series of journal
articles, entitled 'The Economic Ethics of World Religions. Sociology of Religion
Sketches' in the *Archiv für Sozialwissenschaft und Sozialpolitik*, Volume 41, 1916.
These were accompanied by more theoretical work on religion written for inclu-
sion in the grandly conceived publishing project *Grundriss der Sozialökonomik*
(Outline of Social Economics) that he was editing for Paul Siebeck that eventu-

---

[4] A reflection of Weber's later sophisticated knowledge of China is that he amended this reference
to petrifaction (*Versteinerung*) from 'Chinese' to 'mechanized' in GARS1 (1920: 204; 1976: 182).

[5] Radkau (2005: 454) regards his joining the informal discussion group Eranos as the spur to
expanding his interests in religion beyond Christianity. His long-standing friend Georg Jellinek
was one of the group, whose death in 1911 prompted Weber to say he had that 'delicate fragrance
which comes to us from the gentle and pure world of the Orient' (Marianne Weber 1975: 477). But
a striking thing about Weber's continuing and intense interest in China until the end of his life was
that he seemed to have no academic or Chinese interlocutors. Honigsheim's (1963) immensely
detailed memoir of Weber contains no reference to China.

ally became part of *Wirtschaft und Gesellschaft* (1956b) translated as Chapter VI 'Religious Groups (The Sociology of Religion)' of *Economy and Society* (1978).[6]

We share Friedrich Tenbruck's (1980: 329) view that Weber's series of studies of religion represents a continuous effort, beginning with his study of the Protestant ethic, to find a general solution to the problem of the relation of ideas and interests and to explain the impact of rationality in creating a distinctive Western civilization. Tenbruck highlights the two theoretical essays in that series, the Introduction (1915a) and the Intermediate Reflections (1915f), as reaching a higher level of thinking not attained either in the empirical studies or in the massive *Economy and Society* (1978). Sandwiched between them were the early Confucianism Studies (1915b-e). In particular the Conclusion (1915e) of those studies offered a general interpretation of Confucianism as an ethic of 'adaptation to the world' while the Puritan ethic by contrast was in a 'pathetic tension' with the world. What could be more reasonable than to expect a continuous development of ideas?

To explore that expectation we need to attend to his substantial revisions of the original publications that were incorporated in the final published version of the collected essays on the Sociology of Religion (1920, GARS1).[7] Included in it were the much expanded early PE (1904/05) essays, the early Confucianism Studies with their Conclusion (1915b-d), also with copious footnotes and insertions in the original text, and the Introduction (1915a) and Intermediate Reflections (1915f) with minor additions.[8] In toto these amplifications and amendments provide a fascinating insight into Weber's ongoing process of conceptual clarification. China and Puritanism remained the dominant comparative focus but ethics and the explanation of human action were preoccupations through to the end of his life.

We can regard the conclusion to the early Confucianism studies as the culmination of a train of thought that is gathering steam throughout the two articles that contained them, but it develops in tandem with his comparative studies of the world religions in general, in India and ancient Israel particularly, but also mediaeval Christianity and Islam. We know from his own testimony that the systematic sociology of religion that was intended for *Economy and Society* was being written at the same time, probably preceding the Intermediate Reflections since, as Schluchter pointed out, it contains a section `Religious Ethics and "World"' that reads like its first draft and the materials for the planned Outline of Social Economics were ready by the end of 1913 (Roth and Schluchter 1979: 61).

The dating of the completion of the first phase of Weber's work on China to the year of 1913 gives an added interest to the forerunner of his famous article

---

[6] The complex origins and development of what for English readers eventually became *Economy and Society* (Weber, 1979) are described in Radkau (2009: 405-426).

[7] Schluchter has given a detailed account of the revision process (Roth and Schluchter 1979: 59-64).

[8] For a detailed analysis of the effects of these changes see Schluchter (1984).

on the meaning of value freedom, published in 1917, but originally prepared as a paper for an internal discussion in the *Verein für Sozialpolitik* (Association for Social Policy) in 1913.[9] It includes references to China in the context of a lengthy analysis of the ethical and scientific problems involved in the use of the concept of adaptation and casts light therefore on development of his understanding of China and Confucianism and of economic ethics and religion generally. For an easier overview of this development see Table 1 Max Weber on Adaptation and Confucian Ethics.

1.	1895 'Freiburg inaugural' (Weber 1958, 2012).
2.	1904/5 Protestant ethic essays in their first edition ['early PE'] (Weber 1904/5).
3.	1907/8 Karl 'Fischer dispute' on adaptation and religious belief (Weber 1907/8, 1972).
4.	1908/9 Industrial 'Workforce Studies' (Weber 1908, 1909, 1924).
5.	1911-13 Essays on the Economic Ethics of World Religions [WeWr].
	(i) 'Introduction' to the economic ethics of world religions (Weber 1915a).
	(ii) 'Early Confucianism Studies' (Weber 1915b-e).
	(iii) 'Intermediate Reflections' (Weber 1915f).
6.	1911-13 'Sociology of Religion' section of *Economy and Society* (Weber 1956b, 1978).
7.	1913 'Value Judgment paper' for the Verein für Sozialpolitik. (Baumgarten 1964).
8.	1917 'Value Freedom article' (Weber 2012).
9.	1919 Economic History lectures (Weber 1923).
10.	1919 Legitimacy and conflict sections in *Economy and Society*. (Weber 1956a, 1978).
11.	1919 Revised versions of early PE and WeWr included in Volume 1 of the collected essays on the sociology of religion [GARS1] (Weber 1920, 1948, 1951, 1976).

Table 1 Max Weber on adaptation and Confucian ethics.

Date sequence may refer to original period of writing/delivery or of publication as will be clear from this paper. Quotation marks indicate referencing convention here. Bracketed references are to the texts used for this paper.

The early development of his idea of adaptation

For the adaptation side of this paper clearly the Freiburg inaugural lecture provides a benchmark. It singled Weber out, even then, as a thinker with huge intellectual ambition intent on contributing to the core political issues of his time. His merciless exposition of the self-deceptions of those who imagined free markets and national power were ultimately consistent with one another remains relevant to this day. What now appears more than just dated, but seriously politically incorrect, is his use of ideas of selection and adaptation to argue that the then greater

---

[9] Baumgarten (1964: 403) includes an extract from Franz Boese's (1939: 145-148) history of the Verein that shows Weber would have submitted this draft for the exclusive sight of members by 1 April, 1913 and how later in its General Assembly in 1920, he was credited both with having founded the scientific study of work and having initiated the great debates on value judgments.

adaptation to market conditions of Polish peasants, and hence superiority to local German populations, was their lower cultural level 'whether it arose from qualities of social organization or race' (1958: 9). At the same time he entered strong reservations about equating age-old concepts of 'selection' *(Auslese)* and breeding *(Züchtung*, 'going back to Plato') with Darwinian ideas and thinking they could be used to refute socialism.

Reservations surface again in an explicit way in 1904. He declared the capitalist market was a cosmos of norms eliminating manufacturers who did not conform, and putting workers who could or would not adapt on the street. The capitalism that then dominated economic life educated, and in the course of economic *selection* created for itself, the kinds of economic subjects, employers or workers, it needed. But this was the point where you could see the limitations of the "selection" concept for historical explanation purposes. The adapted way of life and occupational outlook that beat other ways and was "selected" must have arisen somehow, not in isolated individuals, but as the property of human groups and that was what had to be explained. Any talk of it being a reflection or superstructure of economic conditions was naïve historical materialism (1904/5, 20.1: 17; 1920: 37; 1976: 55). He picks this up later by saying that this 'spirit' of capitalism could indeed in his own time be seen as a product of adaptation to current institutional arrangements, but that was only after capitalism had emancipated itself from the old conditions.[10]

The strongest indication of the future direction his research was to take came in a footnote towards the end of the early PE essays when he addressed head on the question of the class basis of religious movements. He says to satisfy those who are never content without an economic interpretation of religious ideas he will indeed examine the 'reciprocal adaptation processes and relations of both' but the ideas can't be deduced from the economy and remain 'the most powerful and plastic elements of 'national character' and contain their autonomy *(Eigengesetzlichkeit)* and compelling force purely in themselves' (1904/5, 21.1: 101; 1920: 192; cf 1976: 277-278). This is the earliest and most succinct formulation there is of the elective affinities Weber assumed between historical materialism, evolutionism and the development of ideas that he was to elaborate later into his own theory of rationalization processes.

It was this nexus of ideas that the economic historian H. Karl Fischer (1907: 236; 1972:16) picked up and criticized as reminiscent of Hegel's belief in the immanent force of reason when in fact the most straightforward interpretation

---

[10] Isobel Darmon (2011: 206) rightly highlights this passage as expressing Weber's view of the way contemporary capitalism had dispensed with the old Puritan spirit and how it now just created the agents it required. Weber goes on to say that indeed religious norms are even felt as hindrances, and he deems it necessary in 1920 in GARS1 to strengthen his point about adaptation by adding 'Whoever does not adapt his way of life to the conditions of capitalistic success goes under and doesn't come up again' (1904/5, 20.1: 31; 1920: 56; 1976: 72).

of the retreat of the Baptist movement from radical theology was 'adaptation to tough reality'. Weber (1907/8a: 244; 1972: 35) indignantly rejected the Hegelian slur: 'adaptation to the world' was his own expression for the transformation of Baptist ethics but that was decidedly not 'adaptation to capitalism' since it occurred in places like Friesland, much less developed than in neighbouring areas. Fischer (1908: 272: 1972: 40) responded that the Protestant elevation of work to be the highest moral duty could just as easily be interpreted as the adaptation (*Anpassung*) of religious ideas to economic conditions as the reverse, and that all Weber's accumulation of religious texts could show was the co-existence of both.

In the main text of his rejoinder Weber said that any expression imputing something like the 'adaptation' of religious ideas to economic conditions raised matters of fact, and that was his concern in his articles (1907/8b: 276; 1972: 45), and in the footnote that followed he declared that to say anything was adapted to anything else meant everything or nothing if the concept of adaptation were not precisely elucidated.[11] He continued, 'I could directly formulate the theme of my inquiries as: '*in what sense* [Weber's emphasis] could one speak at all of "adaptation" [of the various cultural elements to one another] in these contexts' (Ibid: 53).

Why did each of his replies to Fischer contain substantial footnotes on 'adaptation' rather than 'determination' or 'causation' when it was causal explanation that was the core concern in the Protestant Ethic essays? The answer is to be found in the popularity of Darwinian and Marxist ideas that had seized the narrative of human development in the late nineteenth century. There has been no shortage of commentary, in Weber's time and to this day, on the underlying dialogue with Marxism in the Protestant Ethic, less however to its Darwinian themes, even though they were intricately bound up with one another. Not just Marxism, but the grand narratives of his time in general were Weber's ongoing targets.[12] He rejected biological determinism, not because he disregarded the possibility of biological influences on human behaviour but because he aimed to introduce scientific rigour into the analysis of culture. Weber had availed himself of the popular imagery of a struggle for existence in his strident Freiburg inaugural, but his commitment to science led him later to regret its tone.[13]

In that spirit he took his first step into big science, prompted in part by the arrival in Heidelberg of his brother Alfred, who was convinced of the value of Darwinian ideas for social sciences. Between them they devised an ambitious programme of Workforce Studies (1908/9a,b) that simultaneously paid regard to the

---

[11] In one of the earliest synoptic accounts of Weber's work Reinhard Bendix (1960: 270) drew our attention to the significance of this obscure footnote in Weber's last response to Fischer.

[12] David Beetham (1974: 39-44) pointed to Weber's persisting use of this vocabulary and rightly distinguished it from a crude Social Darwinism.

[13] Weber's Value Judgment paper to the Verein für Sozialpolitik in 1913 referred to his concern for the quality of human resources that he had raised in his Freiburg inaugural and spoke of its immature form and how 'in several other important points he could no longer identify with it' (Baumgarten 1964: 127). He omitted these remarks in the 1918 Value Freedom article.

interests in profit of owners of capital, to the concerns of critics of the dehumanising effects of factory work and to theories of natural and cultural inheritance. Max completed an exhaustive commentary on the methods of such an enquiry (1908/9a). He proposed it could employ a whole range of concepts recently developed in experimental psychology and establish the way in which the adaptation of particular psychophysical elements advanced with practice in complex tasks. Following up with an independent book-length report on the Psychophysics of Industrial Work (1908/9b) he speculated on what kind of longer-term adaptations would arise if textile workers took full account of the impact on earnings of switching between looms (1924: 215). His conclusion expressed great scepticism in respect of widely held assumptions about biological, especially inherited, determinants of workforce capacities. 'Other moments play so strong a selective and adaptive role that singling out an "inheritance" factor appears utterly problematical' (1924: 251).

In 1911 in a plenary address about workers' psychology to the Verein für Sozialpolitk (Association for Social Policy) in Nuremberg (1924: 424-430), Weber drew attention to a theme that would occupy their attention in future, namely 'selection', in this case the selection of leaders in the dominant professions, their social origins and the conditions which were most favourable to their achievement of their positions (1924: 228).[14] At the October 1912 meeting in Berlin Weber displayed a dazzling command of illustrative material to make the case against asserting race as a factor in historical, political and cultural development. We couldn't even do it, he exclaimed, when our field was as narrow as explaining workers' industrial output, so how can we use it to explain the fall of the Roman Empire? The development of music (in which Weber had recently formed an intense interest) could not stand up as evidence of racial difference, he said, when music from the Far East was close to the ancient Greek and China's music was closer to that than to modern German (1924: 490).[15] All the elements we have discussed in connection with the concept of adaptation were then in place and alive even as Weber began his essays on the world religions.

Adaptation in the early Confucianism studies

Weber's intellectual commitments and interests in 1913 are signalled by the way he introduced his early Confucianism studies. He established sociological foun-

---

[14] What Radkau (2009: 250) has called Weber's 'seven-year fight with naturalism against naturalism' involved an intense interest in the natural foundations of human behaviour, but concepts like 'adaptation' had to be emptied of biological content where the facts were more consistent with a cultural explanation and that meant establishing the place of values in a science of social reality.

[15] In the same month as the Berlin gathering, Marianne and Max enjoyed the unusual event of a four-day house visit. Hermann Graf Keyserling was a magnetic, guru-type figure, who had returned from a world trip and bombarded them with impressions of the East. For Radkau the impact he made on Weber can be detected in his idea of 'intellectualist ecstasy' (Ibid: 426).

dations and institutions, pointing to the long history of Chinese cities, the development of currency, the position of the Emperor, officialdom and legal institutions, declaring the institutional prerequisites for Western style rational industrial capitalism were lacking, but the main handicap was the 'ethos' of the officials, a distinct status group in China and 'to speak of that is our real theme, which we have now finally reached' (1920: 395; 1951: 104). They possessed 'a rational social ethical system' (1920: 411; 1951: 122), based on classic texts, but directed to ritual/ceremonial or traditional ethical concerns (1920: 415; 1951: 126) that was also influential for middle status lifestyles in general. The system bore the mark of a religious-utilitarian welfare-state (1920: 424-425; 1951: 136).[16]

Yet there was no rationalization of popular worship of ancestors. The Chinese had no word for religion, and their word for Confucianism was 'Doctrine of the scholars', focused on everyday (*diesseitig*) concerns with no interest in eschatology or transcendental values (1920: 432-434; 1951: 144-145). This 'social ethic' allowed any person to lead a good life and leave behind a good name to be revered after their death (Weber 1920: 435; 1951: 146-147). It was an ethic of material justice that avoided the Western tension with formal law, natural rights and individualism (1920: 436; 1951:148). Indeed an ethic dictated by office holders allowed no competition from elements specific to the West like rational science, theology, law or technology (1920: 440; 1951: 151).

> Confucianism, like Buddhism, consisted only of ethics and in this Tao (the term is ambiguous as we shall see below) corresponds to the Indian Dharma. However, in sharp contrast to Buddhism, Confucianism exclusively represented an innerworldy morality of laymen. Confucianism meant adjustment (*Anpassung*) to the world, to its orders and conventions. Ultimately it represented just a tremendous code of political maxims and rules of social propriety for cultured men of the world. This was in still greater contrast to Buddhism. The cosmic orders of the world were considered fixed and inviolate, and the orders of society were but a special case of this. (1920: 441; 1951:152-153).

Buddhism represented a turning away from the world, the quest for salvation from the world (1920: 445; 1951: 156), a rejection of worldly goods and women (Weber 1920: 450; 1951: 161). By contrast the world was as good as it could be for Confucian thinking (1920: 442; 1951: 153). The cultured or superior man was not a tool but an end in himself aiming for fulfilment (*Selbstvollendung*) (1920: 449; 1951:160-161) but always within the bounds of propriety, and in this ethic of social adaptation perfection (*Vervollkommnung*) was achieved through continuous study of the classics. (1920: 452; 1951: 163). It contrasted with the mystical direction that following the way ('Tao') took with Lao Tsu's who 'demanded the "great" virtue as opposed to the "little" virtue of Confucianism, i.e. accommo-

---

[16] The utilitarian nature of Confucianism is a repeated theme for Weber (see e.g. 1920: 447, 528; 1951: 159, 241), an illustration of his recognition that Chinese ethics were a genuine contribution to understanding ethics in general, East and West.

dation to the world,' (1920: 468; 1951: 183) which Weber goes on to elaborate as 'guided by the yardstick of cultivation and accommodation to the world and society as they happen to be' (1920: 469; 1951: 184).

A striking feature of the early Confucianism Studies is that they are already peppered with comparative references to the ancient world, India, the West and other religions. This is maintained even as it concludes with a comparison of Puritanism and Confucianism (1915e), where Weber seeks to characterise the distinctive core of their respective ethics.[17] Both exhibited a rational relation to the world, both arrived at utilitarian conclusions, but Puritanism was embroiled in a 'pathetic tension' (*pathetische Spannung*) with the world as it sought to fulfil God's commands, while Confucianism almost eliminated tension with the world. This for Weber is a general point: 'Every religion which opposes the world with rational, ethical imperatives finds itself at some point in a state of tension with the irrationalities of the world' (1920: 513; 1952: 227). He elaborates this arguing that the points and strength of tension will vary from religion to religion, depending very much on the type of metaphysical promises in their quest for salvation. This type of general statement about all religions anticipates then the transition to the Intermediate Reflections and in its stress on tension points to what will be the focus of that paper.

In the case of Confucianism, it sought self-perfection in a philosophical literary culture that prescribed adaptation to the eternal orders of the world, beyond any god, with a pious compliance to mundane powers (Weber 1920: 513-514; 1951: 228). This was not rational in the scientific sense. 'The inner premise of this ethic of unconditional affirmation of and adaptation to the world was the uninterrupted continuity of purely magical religiosity' (Weber 1920: 515; 1951: 229). Puritanism excluded magic entirely in its systematic orientation to the world.

> By contrast Confucianism was adaptation towards the outside, to the conditions of the 'world'. An optimally adapted person, just to the extent that their way of life requires adaptation, is no systematic unity, only a combination of useful qualities ... that striving for the unity coming from the inside that we associate with the concept 'personality' could not emerge. Life remained a series of occurrences, not a unity methodically set under a transcendent goal.' (1920: 521; own translation cf. 1951: 235)

This social ethic, declared Weber, while it might have superficial similarities to the patriarchal sides of Thomist and Lutheran ethics, was completely different from them in terms of its fundamentally optimistic outlook on the world. It had no otherworldly reference point that created a tension between godhead and nature; it was bound up in tradition and convention (Weber 1920: 522: 1951: 236). The religious duty of the pious Chinese was directed towards self-expression in or-

---

[17] Schmidt-Glintzer (1989: 53) confirms that this section was originally conceived by Weber as a conclusion to the study and contains a reaffirmation of the purpose of the study.

ganically given personal relationships. (Weber 1920: 523; 1951: 236). Puritanism was diametrically opposed. 'Adaptation to the world's customary vanities was a sign of damnation, self-perfection in the Confucian sense a blasphemous, idolatrous ideal' (1920: 525; 1951: 238). The Puritan's self-affirmation was demonstrated in fulfilling material purposes and occupational duty, while the Confucian saw world-adapted self-perfection as an end in itself. The famous summation of Weber's argument was: 'Confucian rationalism meant rational adaptation to the world, Puritan rationalism was rational mastery of the world' (Weber 1920: 534; 1951: 248).

In this conclusion to the early Confucianism Studies we can detect the beginnings of the gradual crystallization of Weber's later thinking on adaptation, causality and culture. Pivotal points are his generalization of the concept of tension from the case of Puritanism to religious ethics and the association with them of inner autonomy (*Eigengesetzlichkeit*) in the first instance tentatively as a feature of political authority structures (1920: 528; 1951: 241), but then in the concluding sentence: `In view of their autonomous laws, one can hardly fail to ascribe to these attitudes effects strongly counteractive to capitalist development.' These autonomies belonged to the fundamental properties of the *Gesinnung*, the practical attitude to the world (1920: 536: 1951: 249).

The frame of the early Confucianism studies

The early work on China was already conceived within the frame of a comparative historical study of economic ethics of world religions. He therefore wrote the Introduction (1915a) to the planned project to be published before the first article on Confucianism. At the very beginning he stressed that there could be no question of an economic ethic being a mere 'function' of economic organizational form or the reverse (1920: 238; 1948: 268). One determinant was certainly a religiously defined way of life but this was deeply influenced by a whole range of other political economic determinants within geographical, political, social and national boundaries. But, he cautions, it would be a voyage into a shoreless sea to attempt to follow all these interconnections and so he is going only to focus on the elements of the way of life of those social groups that exercised a determining influence on their economic ethic. For example, he said, taking Confucianism first, this was the ethic of a literary educated and worldly-wise rational place-holding class, but, he repeats, it was not a simple function of that social position, neither in the sense of historical materialism nor in the Nietzschean sense (1920: 241; 1948: 270). His concern for the all-embracing explanatory doctrines of his time that was uppermost in early PE remained a prime consideration.

The Introduction contains some of Weber's most characteristic and celebrated formulations of causal relations between material and ideal factors. The age old idea of salvation gained a specific meaning once a systematically rationalized world image (*Weltbild*) had been developed by a stratum of intellectuals, with the result that religion was pushed into the sphere of the irrational. That stratum's idea of salvation was strongly influenced by its own character and position in the wider culture and society (1920: 253; 1948: 281).

Also notable is his application of the idea of autonomy (*Eigengesetzlichkeit*) to the central doctrine of a religion having far-reaching consequences in shaping a way of life (1920: 258-259; 1948: 286). Later it becomes a central idea for him in developing a general theory of rationalization processes and the differentiation of separate spheres of life to which his parallel studies of religion, law, and economic organization were leading and which he elaborated in the Intermediate Reflections (1915f). That leads him to examine multiple orientations to the world between the polar opposites of rationalized practice in the world of the West and the escape from the meaninglessness of the world in the religions of Asia. There he addresses the difficulties in defining religious attitudes to the world. The inner-worldly asceticism of Protestant was world rejecting (*weltablehnend*) in denying pleasure, did not flee the world as did contemplation, but it was oriented to the world (*weltzugewendet*) in a more penetrating way than in the world affirming (*Weltbejahung*) attitudes of the ancient world or lay Catholicism (1920: 263; 1948: 291).[18]

Then via characteristic comments on typologies and history he turns to an assessment of what rationalism might mean, and distinguishes the rationalism of a systematic view of the world from ends-means thinking, and immediately as his first case he instances Confucianism, suggesting it was at the outer extreme of what one could call a religious ethic, more utilitarian than any system except Benthamism (1920: 266; 1948: 293). This is a theme of his Value Judgment paper (Baumgarten 1964; 1913b) he was preparing at around the same time (see later).

The linkage between adaptation or accommodation to the world and cultivation is repeated in Weber's account of tensions between ethics and the world in the Sociology of Religion (1978: 594) where in Confucianism 'ethics is no more than a prudent accommodation to the world on the part of the educated man' which, however, regarded 'irregular sexual expression' with disdain as falling below such a man's standards (Ibid: 604). Since inner- worldly asceticism was marked particularly by the rejection of sexual pleasure, one might think that in this respect at least Confucianism's adaptation to the world was limited. And yet, as Weber

---

[18] Weber experiments throughout his studies of religious ethics with ways of expressing an orientation to the 'world' but never settles on a final formulation. Other variations in the final chapter of the early Confucianism Studies include: 'flight from the world' (*Weltflucht*) (1920: 515, 525; 1951: 229, 238); 'dealing with the world' (*Weltbehandlung*) (1920: 524; 1951: 238); 'mastery of the world' (*Weltbeherrschung*) (1920: 534; 1951: 248); as well as 'adaptation to the world' (*Weltanpassung*) (1920: 515, 534; 1951: 229, 248). Schluchter (1984: 39-40) draws out an implicit classification of religions that can be derived from Weber and points out that Weber explicitly aimed to contribute to sociological typology while emphasizing its always inadequate reflection of reality.

wrote several times, it was the purest case of an ethic of adaptation (Ibid: 582, 604).

The section that includes these comments is entitled 'Religious Ethics and the "World"', where the key concept is in fact tension, *Spannung* (1956b: 348; 1978: 576). It is part of a tentative developmental scheme in which early stages of religion are indistinguishable from magic and law, enshrined in magic books as with Hindus, Muslims, Parsee, Jews and with the Chinese classical prescriptions on ceremonies, rituals and law. Then ethical prophecy breaks through and leads to a transformation of everyday, and in particular economic life, though it has to compete with powerful economic interests. Weber writes: One can't give a general formula for the relative substantive weight of the various developmental components and of their kind of *"adaptation"* (our emphasis) to one another. (1956b: 349; cf 1978: 577) This is when religion can develop in a variety of directions, and the way a religious norm is applied in practice is quite unpredictable. He goes on to say that economic life might have a variety of meanings: reinterpreting sacred commandments, bypassing them, dispensing with them, or simply producing areas on which the religious laws were silent. In other words all these are forms of 'adaptation' (recall the 'all or nothing' formula of the ethical neutrality essay).

But one direction is fundamentally different. It may be the production of a religion of salvation: life may be systematically organized around the goal of salvation, knowing no holy law, only a holy sentiment (*Gesinnung*), which can produce 'situationally varied maxims of conduct, and thus is elastic and has the *capacity to be adaptable* (*anpassungsfähig*, our emphasis)' (1956b: 349; cf 1978: 578). But this capacity is achieved at the expense of an enhanced and 'internalized problematic'. Inner tension with the "world" actually increases. 'The increasing rationalization of social relations and their contents increases conflicts with the autonomy of the different life spheres'. Then the more rational the cosmos the religious viewpoint establishes so the ethical tensions with inner worldly orders increases. A new world rejecting ethic arises and becomes a powerful force for development 'which by its very nature completely lacks any of that stereotyping character which has been associated with sacred laws' (1956b: 349-50; 1978: 579).

This densely written and pivotal passage in Weber's thought is summarized here to bring out the ambiguities in the notion of adaptation that he was alluding to, possibly at the same time, in his Value Judgment paper. For a 'world rejecting' ethic appears also as a kind of adaptation, the conflict relations of one life sphere to another also can be adaptation. Up to now it has been Confucianism that is the prime example of an ethic of adaptation to the world, but religious prophecy now has that characteristic too. It would even allow for 'mastery of the world' to be a kind of adaptation. We note the reference to the Chinese classical prescriptions. Imbued with magic they have minimum tension with the world. But where does this leave the Confucian ethic, a later development? What is it to which any religion, or indeed any ethic, since Confucianism is hardly a religion, adapts?

There follows the first version of the famous division of life spheres that Weber later elaborates in the Intermediate Reflections including the economy, politics, law, sexuality, art, before a final brief review of each of Judaism, Islam, Buddhism and Christianity in their relations to the world. They were as he explicitly stated to be read along with his studies of the economic ethics of the world religions. In the sections on the separate spheres references to Confucianism appear throughout. It supported charity to the poor (1956b: 349-50; 1978: 581), accepted usury (1956b: 351; 1978: 583), lauded heroic death (1956b: 356; 1978: 590), easily accommodated magic (1956b: 357; 1978: 594), treated power relations as personal (1956b: 361; 1978: 600), disdained casual sex (1956b: 363; 1978: 604), valued children (1956b: 364; 1978: 606).[19] Each ethic has a different emphasis and in the case of Confucianism it was upon family piety. Ritual correctness was valued above honesty.

As Schluchter has pointed out the Sociology of Religion section of *Economy and Society* contains effectively a first draft of the 'Intermediate Reflections' and, opposed to Baumgarten, (1964: 473) he detects changes in the direction of greater emphasis on the rationalization of value-spheres and beginnings of an interest in science (Roth and Schluchter 1979: 63) We would add another and in some ways more striking difference. The theme of adaptation so strong in the first draft has now made way entirely to "*Spannung*", tension. On just one occasion Weber declares that the pursuit of values can only adapt to the requirement of fraternity through self-deception. Apart from the first sentence contrasting China and India the one place in the Intermediate Reflections (1915f) where he explicitly alludes to Confucianism relates to its great pedagogical system and that of the Western ancient world and its escape from priestly control (Weber 1920: 565; 1951: 352).

There is however a covert allusion at the very end of those reflections when he asserts that religious thinking can only see the 'meaninglessness of the inner-worldly self-perfection (*Selbstvervollkommnung*) of the man of culture'. (Weber 1920: 569; 1951: 356). Weber characterized the Chinese official with precisely that form of words. Significantly however it referred to the Confucian control of education as an example of intellectualism in tension with religion. Paradoxically 'inner-worldly self-perfection' is precisely the formula Weber used to describe Confucianism earlier, and now this is in no way to be described as an 'adaptation to the world'. It is instead a site of tension. The inference we draw is that Weber now has severe reservations about the usefulness of describing Confucianism as an ethic of adaptation and he is arriving at the idea that it is in the nature of any ethic to involve tension with the world. Only by stressing its tolerance and encouragement of magic and popular religiosity is Weber able to maintain the difference

---

[19] The concluding sphere of art (Ibid: 607-610) has no reference to China or Confucianism, an omission that has some significance in the train of Weber's thinking.

between the West and East that originally he had sought to sustain through the contrast of world mastery in Puritanism and adaptation to the world in Confucianism. In so far as it was rational, it too was in tension with the world, not just adapted to it.

An important transition is underway. The idea of adaptation, a staple resource for Weber's work up to and including the essay of Confucianism, has in the Intermediate Reflections been almost eliminated, with the concepts of autonomy and tension occupying strategic positions in his argument. It becomes clear the moment Weber turns to India, that the relation of the individual to the world that he has honed in the comparison of Puritanism and Confucianism is to be the focus of his comparisons of religious ethics in general. In *Economy and Society* his formula is 'Jainism and Buddhism, the radical antithesis of Confucian world adaptation – were the tangible expression of a radical anti-political, pacifist and world-denying kind of intellectual conviction' (Weber 1956: 306; 1978: 504). In the Intermediate Reflections it becomes 'Indian religiosity is in strongest contrast to China, the cradle in theory and practice of the most world-denying forms of religious ethic that the earth has brought forth' (Weber, 1920: 536; cf. 1948: 323). In his study of India in the second volume of GARS there are many comparative references to China, yet 'adaptation' only applies to Islam, retaining its beliefs in a superficial acceptance of the Indian caste system (1921: 132).

Given other conditions of Weber's intellectual development, for instance in his relations with his brother and with Mina Tobler, there appears to be convincing evidence of a major shift in outlook occurring around 1913 and this can be indexed by reference to his reservations on adaptation and an enhanced sophistication about evolutionary concepts. We arrive then at an aporia in Weber's thought. Confucianism at one time the social utilitarian ethic, at another the ethic of self-perfection, even despising useful trades. And these were even combined:

For the Confucian the specialist could not be accorded any positive esteem because of his social utilitarian value. For – this was decisive – the 'superior man' (gentleman) was 'no tool', that is he was in his world-adapted self-perfection an ultimate value in himself. (Weber 1920; 532: 1956: 246)

The difficulty into which the idea of adaptation to the world has brought Weber is glaringly apparent here for it raises exactly what is the relation to the world of an ethic that is almost non-religious, even utilitarian. Given that Weber was engaged in heated exchanges with colleagues about keeping value judgments out of science, he could hardly avoid making the connection between that issue and his studies of economic ethics in the world religions.

China and adaptation in the Value Judgment paper of 1913

Weber drew attention to the similarity between Benthamite thought and Confucianism in the Value Judgment paper, speaking of them both as ethics of adaptation. There he took to task colleagues who imagined that purely technical recipes for policy flow from concepts like development or progress. They contain implicit value positions quite distinct from any factual conditions to which they might at any one time refer. In the discussion of the idea of developmental trends Weber refers to an ultimate objective, say national power interests and the necessary means for its achievement, where changing circumstances might bring either the end or the means into question. He pointed to the German glorifiers of 'Realpolitik' who were prepared to adapt both their ends and their means to the likelihood of success, but he held no empirical science could prove that success was the ultimate value, or indeed that there was any value in 'adaptation' to a developmental trend. These were matters for individual conscience. There follows a passage, exemplified by China, that would have been transparent to his academic audience familiar with his work at the time, but may lose the reader a hundred years later:

> In a sense, it is true that successful political action is always 'the art of the possible'. However, it is equally true that, very often, the possible has only been attained by reaching for the impossible that lay beyond it. After all, it was not the only really consistent ethic of 'adaptation' to the possible – the bureaucratic morals of Confucianism, that created those specific features of our culture to which all of us probably, in spite of all [our] other differences of opinion, subjectively attach a (more or less) positive value' (Baumgarten 1964: 124; Weber 1968: 514; translation in Weber 2012: 318).

'Politics is the art of the possible' was a saying attributed to Bismarck who had launched the policy known as the *Kulturkampf* with the purpose of eliminating the influence of Roman Catholics from public life. In particular this involved banning the Jesuit order from Prussia. Yet it was the Jesuits who historically were most associated with the idea of adaptation to the culture of the countries to which they sent missions, and most famously to China. Is there an unspoken premise here is that the Chinese were consistent in their ethics whereas the Jesuits were not? He continues by taking the example of a convinced syndicalist who cannot be dissuaded from a course of action just by showing it is unrealizable. Summing up the pros and cons of say, strike action, as in old fashioned administrative science or 'maybe still in modern Chinese policy papers' had no scientific basis. The achievement of a valuation-free science is limited to the most rational and consistent statement of the syndicalist position, the conditions for its origin, likelihood of success and the attendant consequences. The professor can not praise quixotic conduct, but also not its opposite either, and ask the student to adapt ideals to developmental trends.

At this point Weber says that his context has made clear how he has been using the concept of adaptation, but it has had two meanings, adaptation of means to ends according to differing circumstances, or adaptation of ends to the likelihood of their success. It can give rise to misunderstanding whether it is used to explain the presence of ethical standpoints among particular groups at particular times, or to show the value of those positions because they 'fit' and it would be best excluded from any of their discussions. It belongs to biology and to show that a way of life is 'adapted' to the reproduction of those who follow it says nothing about its value. Actually the introduction of 'adaptedness' into such discussion adds nothing. '"Adapted" in the field of "culture", whatever one means with the concept, is either everything or nothing. For "conflict" cannot be excluded from any cultural life' (Baumgarten 1964: 127; cf. Weber 2012: 319). Peace is only another kind of conflict in that selection takes place still and no empirical investigation solves the ethical dilemmas, save that establishing what kind of human being becomes dominant is bound to be relevant to one's choices.

Weber's allusions to China at this point were preceded by a reference to Chinese astronomy, and coupled with his linking of the notion of adaptation to Chinese ethics they point to his contemporaneous work on China. Even more important, he employs in this section of the Value Judgment paper concepts that are central to the Intermediate Reflections (1915f) with its theme of the irreconcilable conflict of value spheres (Baumgarten 1964: 117; cf. 2012: 314-5): 'ethic of conviction' (*Gesinnungsethik*) (Baumgarten 1964: 124; cf. 2012: 319), rationalization (*Rationalisierung*) (Baumgarten 1964: 128; cf. 2012: 321): tension (*Spannung*) (Ibid). Weber was sceptical about the usefulness of the concept of adaptation in the Value Judgment paper even as he was using it to characterise Chinese ethics. It was, we contend, precisely the difficulty of applying the self-denying rule on value judgments in the empirical study of ethics and the conflicts that arose with others in that connection that forced him to take steps back from the concept of adaptation in the Intermediate Reflections.

Towards a transcultural ethics of adaptation

Some of the best clues to the developing directions in Weber's thought come from the amendments he made between early drafts and publications and their later appearance. This also applies to the Value Judgment paper that was modified and expanded to become the Value Freedom journal article of 1917. In both places he raised the question of the attitude of empirical disciplines to the idea of progress. They had no answer to the question of whether one should treat current new 'possibilities of feeling' with their attendant 'tensions' and 'problems' as 'values'; but with the idea of progress there were passionate disagreements. That much is more or less common to both documents. But in 1917 he has inserted several pages that examine art and music as spheres of value rationalization, in other words he is developing the value spheres arguments of the Intermediate Reflections.

When reworking the Introduction (1915a) for publication in GARS1 Weber's main concern seems to have been to strengthen the emphasis on rationality and to provide a more nuanced account of its relation to religion. Thus his celebrated formula for the relation of ideas and the material world is a late insertion:

> Interests (material and ideal), not ideas, directly dominate the actions of human beings. But 'world images', which were created through 'ideas', have often act-

ed as points switchers, determining the tracks on which the dynamic of interests took action forward.' (Weber 1920: 252; 1948: 280)

In the same vein he elaborates a passage on the meaning of rationalism that revolves around Confucianism, compared again with utilitarianism. He had originally declared it was so remote from any metaphysic and so rationalistic that it could hardly be called a 'religious' ethic. Now he adds nuanced distinctions that allow for the differing rationalities of artistic doctrine, or in programmes of contemplation, or, in practical ethics (and this is of the greatest interest to us in this paper):

> All types of practical ethics oriented systematically and unambiguously to firm salvation objectives were 'rational', *partly in that same sense of formal method, partly in their distinction between the normatively 'valid' and the empirically given* (Author's translation, Weber's insertion in italics). (Weber 1920: 266; 1948: 293-294.)

These are continuous ethical concerns that are carried through into the great lectures on the professions of science and politics and China was at the back of his mind all the time. No longer is adaptation to the world the main concern, rather China's peculiar rationalism. As if he realizes 'Chinese rationalism' will have raised eyebrows, he inserts at the beginning of his Conclusion, (renamed *Resultat,* 'outcome'), 'for it deserves this name' (1920: 512; cf. 1948: 226).[20]

His expansion of the early Confucianism studies includes lengthier treatment of Taoism and that prompts him to a general proposition about rationalization of empirical knowledge in China being always directed towards a magical world picture (1920: 481: 1951: 196). And now he compensates for the earlier neglect of China in the Intermediate Reflections by inserting references to its magical world picture and anti-religious scepticism, (1920: 564-565: 1948: 350), all part of placing further emphasis on the kinds of tension existing between value spheres under rationalizing conditions. Under these circumstances Confucian rationalism sustained political rationalization while the magical world picture kept the masses in thrall.[21]

When he uses the idea of a utilitarian adaptation to the world once more, it is in a new passage in the later PE, but this time to refer to Jesuit theology and

---

[20] A critic of our thesis could point out that Weber retained the idea of adaptation to the world in the final publication of the Conclusion to the Confucianism study. There are two points to make in this connection. The first is that there is evidence he was running out of time and energy to make revisions (see Schmidt-Glintzer and Kolonko 1989: 53). The other is that the comparison with Puritanism remained valid for him at the ethical level. The system was intentionally adaptive, in practice however, as any ethical system must be, in tension with reality, hence the turn to the value spheres where tension was generated.

[21] The idea of the world in a Chinese sense was something quite different, an issue we will turn to in a separate paper.

ethics. One of the revisions most relevant to our argument occurs in the following paragraph. In the original it stood as:

> There is in point of fact no doubt, and it can count as a commonplace, that this moral enhancement of mundane occupational life was one of the most consequence laden achievements of the Reformation and, especially therefore, of Luther. But how in particular the practical significance of that achievement should be viewed is in general more of a dim intimation than a clear recognition. (1904/5, 20.1: 44)

Weber inserts two footnotes and a new passage in this text (Weber 1920: 72; 1976: 81). The first footnote, after 'Luther', says it is astonishing and he just could not understand how that any researcher could imagine that such an innovation would have no effect on human action. Then at the same place he inserts this passage:

> This is an outlook that stands miles apart from the deep hatred in Pascal's contemplative mood, born of his deepest conviction, which rejected as explicable only by vanity or cunning the attachment of value to practical activity in the world. To be sure, it is further still from the open-hearted utilitarian *adaptation* to the world that the probabilism of the Jesuits accomplished.[22]

In that new passage he inserted another new footnote referencing the outstanding thesis (1914) of Dr Paul Honigsheim on the antecedents of the French Enlightenment and linking Pascal to the Jansenists, who were indeed only the most prominent of the many opponents of the Jesuits in the Catholic Church.[23] Weber mentioned the Jesuits at several points in passing but here he thinks them important enough to deserve special mention in the context of an emphasis on the practical significance of ethics. This context and the insertion allude to a complex history that Weber felt no need to elaborate, but it needs to be made explicit to aid our understanding now of his continuing engagement with religious thought in his time.

The idea of adaptation or (what was often a synonym) 'accommodation' went back at least to Aquinas and Augustine in Christian thought.[24] The point of these

---

[22] 'Probabilism' was the doctrine that a course of action was justified if on balance it was likely to turn out favourably. Weber mentions it again in his 'Religious Ethics and the "World"' essay as the expression of the extremely lax principles of the Jesuits (1956b: 354; 1978: 587). Elsewhere he speaks of the Jesuits as the supreme exponents of rational asceticism that could be put into the service of hierocratic power (1956a: 707: 1978: 1172). The combination of internal discipline and adaptability to cultures and circumstances made the Jesuits regular targets for criticism from other orders in the Catholic Church.

[23] Honigsheim's (1963: 250-252) extensive reminiscences of Weber remark on his deep interest in the Catholic Counter-Reformation, his opposition to Bismarck's *Kulturkampf* in line with his fervent support for minorities, and his intimate knowledge of the many currents within Catholic post-Enlightenment thought, especially of an anti-Jesuit and romantic kind.

[24] Louis Caruana (2008: 243-262) cites Augustine: 'God knows much better than man what pertains by accommodation (*accommodate*) to each period of time' and Aquinas' 'Scripture speaks

additions to the original text of early PE is that they refer forward to the different orientations to the world that Weber had developed in the comparative sociology of religion GARS1, where he works around contrasting ideas of retreat into mysticism and pragmatic accommodation to the world's requirements, preferred respectively by the opposing camps of Jansenists and the Jesuits. Both for Weber had to be distinguished from the innerworldly asceticism of the Puritan.

But the Jesuits were not only the outstanding proponents of the idea of adaptation in ethics, through it they were also famously associated with China. They developed their own 'adaptation to the world' in the sixteenth century through their mission to China that became the main route for the reception of Chinese, especially Confucian, ideas into Europe (He 2008, Zhang 2009). The controversy in the Catholic Church around this issue became so intense that it led eventually to the dissolution of the Jesuit order, and the breach between the Pope and the Chinese Emperor over their respective claims to supremacy represents one of the key turning points in East/West relations with far reaching consequences.[25] Weber was well aware of this, wrote in passing in a discussion of sect formation in China that he would not discuss the Chinese persecution of the "European worship of the Lord of Heaven' and mentioned how the Jesuits had been tolerated originally for their astronomical knowledge. (1920: 504; 1951: 219)

The key figure in the Jesuits' adaptation, known usually as the policy of accommodation, was Matteo Ricci (1552-1610) who became a permanent resident and died in China. He adopted the dress and rituals of the official class, acquainting them and the imperial court with Western science and emphasising the age-old values of Chinese civilization and their consistency with Christianity (Mungello 1989). This became what has been described as the corporate culture of the Jesuits in China, and was shaped indeed as much by the Other that was China as by themselves. Had they not adapted to the dominant Confucian ideology of the time they would have been treated as a subversive sect (Standaert 2008: 174).[26]

'Adaptation to the world' then was not in the first instance a theoretical construct for Weber.[27] It was his preferred name for an ethic, as he understood

---

according to the opinion of the people' as authorities the Jesuits employed to enable them to engage with doctrines that were otherwise unorthodox.

[25] Shuo Yu (2014) points to the China-Europe encounter of the 16th-18th centuries as the first in a series of transcultural generativity in which the universalism of each was the mirror of the other.

[26] Nicolas Standaert (2008) points out that Ricci through his successor, Joachim Bouvet (1656-1730) influenced in turn, Leibniz, Montesquieu, Voltaire and Rousseau to find in Chinese thought an anticipation of enlightenment values. The scholar who was responsible for compiling the Chong Zhen Calendar, Xu Guangqi (1562-1633) stressed the cultural similarities between the West and China but the Emperor Kangxi (1662-1722) aimed to overcome opposition to Western ideas by asserting that their origin was Chinese, an idea effectively endorsed by the Jesuit Bouvet whose accommodation strategy involved finding ideas in the Chinese classics that were common to the West (Han 1998).

[27] The sinologist Herbert Franke (1966: 129-130) argues that Chinese historiography's predominantly conceptual and ethical discourse was well fitted to Weber's own generalising and

it to be practised by the Chinese, for which his familiarity with both Protestant and Catholic, in particular Jesuit, ethics prepared the ground. Traditional Chinese thought could be construed as revolving around an idea of adaptation.[28] Weber relied for his main authority for Chinese religion on J.J.M de Groot (1910: 93), who in numerous publications emphasized the requirement for the Chinese to follow Tao, the way, the direction of the world and all that was in it: 'Indeed there is only one means for ensuring life and prosperity to mankind, and this means consists in making all acts conform to nature itself.' But we may observe that adaptation to 'nature' in Confucianism and to the 'world' in Puritanism were very different.[29]

All this was a very far cry from evolutionary theory. 'Adaptation to the world' was not what it might at first sight seem, the popular nineteenth century assimilation of a term from science, almost the reverse was the case. Science, in the biological theory of evolution, had borrowed a term arising in the time when science was natural philosophy and intimately connected with ethics and theology. Weber was well versed in that older religious discourse. He might well have read about adaptation in William Channing, his mother's favourite religious writer, about whom they corresponded in his younger years. Channing described how a man of faith 'perceives more of the harmonies or mutual adaptations of the world without or the world within him' (Channing [1824] 1870: 21). He wrote of the demands that a new enlightened age made upon the Christian ministry, of the resulting diversity of opinion, and the need of a special adaptation to it. The Christian minister had to 'accommodate his ministry to its wants and demands' (Ibid: 174). Pure Jesuitical thinking in Unitarian clothing.[30]

Darwin himself was at pains to point out that the principle of selection for breeding animals or improving plant species was known and applied from ancient times. He even found 'it distinctly given in an ancient Chinese encyclopaedia' (Darwin 1859 [1928: 41]). The big discovery was to be called Natural Selection 'in order to mark its relation to man's power of selection', though he added 'the expression often used by Mr. Hebert Spencer of the Survival of the Fittest is more accurate, and is sometimes equally convenient … man by selection can certainly

---

sociological approach and enabled him to take the study of China out of its disciplinary isolation.

[28] We are indebted here to conversations with sinologist Professor Li Xuetao of the Beijing Foreign Studies University

[29] De Groot (1918: 312) observing how the Emperor was required to follow the instructions of the calendar or almanac in minute detail translates *Shixian shu* as `Weisungen für die (Anpassung an die) Zeiten)`, `instructions for the (adaptation to the) times'. This was the later name for the Chong Zhen calendar adopted by the Qing dynasty in 1645 after revision by the Jesuit Johann Adam Schall von Bell:
(www1.chineseculture.org/library/2008-02/01/content_26234.htm). For this reference we are grateful to Dr Joy Zhang, University of Kent, who suggests adaptation may refer here to the assimilation of Western calendars.

[30] We have no direct evidence that he read Nathaniel Hawthorne's *The Scarlet Letter*, but this celebrated novel, written in 1850, set in a New England Puritan community, refers to the failure in 'adaptation to the world' of the child of the outcast fallen woman (Hawthorne 2000: 81).

produce great results, and can adapt organic beings to his own uses' (ibid: 67). In Spencer there was certainly a paradigm case of the mixing of scientific and value judgments that Weber deplored, though Darwin was usually more circumspect.[31]

But Weber's concept of adaptation to the world was unwittingly over de-termined by the history of the intercultural politics of Catholicism and Confu-cianism.[32] The Chinese concept of adaptation is very different from the kind of enculturation the Jesuits practised. In the Chinese translation of Konfuzianismus und Taoismus 'inner-worldly' is rendered as '*ru shi*' (Weber: 2003).[33] Confucian-ism's *ru shi* is reflected in its idea of cultivating good thoughts, self-cultivation, managing families, governing the country and making peace in Tian Xia. Then it carries the sense of active participation, rather than either acquiescence in, or mastery of an alien environment, the opposition Weber wanted to set up between Confucianism and Puritanism. Adjustment or adaptation is *shi ying* in Chinese (Li 2009). The original meaning of *shi* is to 'go somewhere', indicating a direction. The old writing of *shi* contains the root of a tree, meaning following the basic principle, or the law of nature. Put together, *shi ying* is not doing nothing, but doing it appropriately, not coercively. To Confucian rationalism, inner-worldly work was to strive for another kind of transcendental goal, an inner one.[34] The aim is to transform the world from being 'non-reasonable' to 'reasonable', from being 'immoral' to 'moral' based on '*tian li*', the law of nature. Confucian adjustment to the world is rather positive, the purpose of which was to understand it and change for the better (Yu 1987; Ye 2003).

As his study of China deepened over the year Weber became more sensitive to these nuances and the shift we detect between the Conclusion of the Confu-cianism essay and the Intermediate Reflections, in both the original versions and in the amplifications to them and to the early PE articles as he allowed them to go to press in 1919 is best interpreted as a twin recognition – namely that 'adaptation to the world' was indeed a Western formulation and the only way to write empir-ically on Confucian ethics was to recognize them as ethics, with all the varying degrees of tension with reality that is the defining and universal feature of ethics.[35]

---

[31] J. D. Y. Peel (1971: 155) points out, in terms identical to Weber's, that Spencer used adaptation to explain everything, therefore, in practice, nothing.

[32] Jack Barbalet (2014) has examined the ways in which the idea of Confucian orthodoxy is itself a Western projection.

[33] Possibly ameliorating the dualism of Weber's account and understating its Western ethnocentrism.

[34] Thomas Metzger (1983: 235-236) argues that the sweeping nature of Weber's judgment on the lack of a transcendent anchorage and tension with the world in Confucianism is at odds with his interpretative methodology and does not allow for the diversity of opinion among the Confucian scholars. Similarly Schmuel Eisenstadt (1983) argued that Weber considered transcendence exclu-sively in terms of an orientation to a world beyond inhabited by a personal God when Chinese thought offers an inner transcendence.

[35] One of Weber's most eloquent insertions in the later PE emphasizes Catholic ethics as an 'ethic of conscience', *Entzauberung*, the elimination of magic, and the immense tension which was the fate of the Calvinist living an ethic without the props of confession and forgiveness. To strengthen

Conclusion: the theoretical direction of Weber's study of China

We conclude with some remarks on the direction we believe we can take from Weber's uses and critiques of evolutionary ideas that stemmed from his engagement with Confucian ethics. It has often been remarked how his account of a general process of rationalization appears at odds with his emphasis on multi-factor causality, especially in the light of his rejection of the idea of a deterministic biological account of social evolution. But it can be inferred from the central place that the study of China had for him, sandwiched as it was between two papers that show how quickly his ideas were developing, that standard evolutionary ideas, where successful adaptation to underlying natural forces and to competitor organisms guaranteed survival, had to give way to a more complex interactive account where human beings were as much shapers of their destiny as they were determined by forces outside their control.

Very broadly his critique of the grand narratives began with a stress on multi-factor causation in which ideas had equal importance to material factors but matured to a position where processes of adaptation were situated in a real world where ideas had an internal autonomy and dynamic as against material factors. Stephen Kalberg's (2012: 43-72) intensive explorations of Weber's conceptual thought and comparative method have rightly identified the centrality for Weber of dynamic autonomy (*Eigengesetzlichkeit*) and rationalization in precisely defining the nature of the impact of ideas in history. Mediated as they were by interests, ideas still had their internal dynamic that gave them a direction over and beyond any merely reactive adaptive process. That dynamic was provided by rationality but rationalization was not some overarching historical development.[36] As Kalberg (ibid: 13-42) emphasizes, it was a process that could only be set in train by the interests of powerful groups independently in different cultures at different times Weber moved beyond multi-factor impersonal forces and centred historical narrative on the interests and ideas of human beings as they are carried forward in their collective lives.

Our account of the development of Weber's understanding of Confucian ethics suggests that his persistent critique of the uses of the concept of adaptation introduced tension (Spannung) as an indispensable component of any explanation of historical change and an essential complement to dynamic autonomy and rationalization. This takes us beyond the proposal that W. G. Runciman (2001) makes that an idea like predestination could be regarded as a mutant meme able to cross cultures. In Weber's terms only in a bundle of ideal and material interests held together by ethical rationality could it have such an impact. It means for in-

---

this he adds a footnote: 'The absolute central significance of this moment, is, as already once mentioned, gradually advanced in the Economic Ethics of the World Religions'. There is no better instance of Weber's own recognition of the continuous development of his own ideas (1920: 114).

[36] Martin Albrow (1987) provides as example of contemporary rationalizations in a Weberian sense in legislation on artificial human reproduction and on data protection.

stance, in contemporary terms, neo-liberalism and market choice develop along the lines of their intrinsic rationality as long as they serve the interests of the global elite, but their ethic, in so far as one exists at all, need not be religious, at least not for those who enjoy the wealth that accrues.

Weber's turn to China was not then a personal whim. It was a field for enquiry into the universality or otherwise of Western experience. While his questions about motivations to work, as he acknowledged, were clearly Eurocentric in origin, nonetheless he made himself as open as he could be to the novelty and difference of a different route in human development.[37] The special character of Eastern rationalism and the role it could play for the West he regarded, on his wife's account, as 'one of his most important discoveries' (Marianne Weber 1975: 333). The theory of multiple developments in rationality rather than a single direction or determinant in history must be regarded as an equally important contribution to the self-understanding both of his time and ours.

The conceptual shift is firmly established and can be documented in Weber's last version of the fundamental concepts of sociology where he locates a discussion of selection and adaptation under the general heading of struggle or conflict *(Kampf)* and makes fine distinctions between competition, social selection, biological selection, between planned and unplanned selection of individuals, and of social relationships. He says it is open to anyone to talk of the selection and the greater 'adaptedness' of social relations, but that has nothing to do with human types or biology. To remove any possible doubt about his own value commitments he concludes the passage by declaring that recent years have brought far too many value judgments into empirical work about the general 'adaptedness' of a particular social relation (1956: 21; 1978: 40).

A little earlier than the section on conflict Weber embedded in an analysis of legitimacy some remarks on the nature of ethical standards. They were normative conceptions about the 'morally good' and as such could influence action without any external guarantee, though they often had religious backing, and had a varying relation to convention or law. But what was 'ethical' depended entirely on what claimed validity in a specific human group (1956: 19; 1978: 36). There we have the distillation of years of thinking about ethics, the autonomy of ideas and the varieties of human experience. He had arrived at this position through a persistent critique of the lazy use of Darwinian and Marxist ideas, summed up in the concept of adaptation. But in that prodigious effort he wrestled with two problems that remained unresolved to the end.

The first was that in the empirical study of ethics, an exercise in the science of reality, judgements on the degree to which ethical prescriptions are observed by human beings are unavoidable and those are value judgments, that is an inter-

---

[37] In Stephen Molloy's (1980: 395) effective summing up, 'Weber was concerned, not with a Chinese social system analogous to the social system of pre-capitalist Europe, but with a unique and immensely lengthy historical process: the rationalization of Chinese culture'.

pretation of the meaning of a norm and a judgment whether it has been observed or not.[38] Of course one hastens to add the Weberian point that this is not a commitment to the value. In doing so the observer social scientist cannot avoid assessing the rationality or otherwise of the ethical prescription. That means non-empirical science. Weber did not evade the issue; he tried to meet it head on in his Value Judgment paper, and it raised questions he wrestled with in the China studies.

The second and related issue is the question of transcultural methodology, or more simply, translation. Weber found it difficult to consider China from its own point of view and thus projected on to it initially an idea of adaptation to the world that owed more to Western ideas of a sinful life on this earth than to Chinese ideas of a harmony between human beings and nature. But from a universal viewpoint, rationality, appearing in many forms and places, was a quality that provided a dynamic impetus, as in capitalism, or rigidity and strength, as in bureaucracy, or a coherence of lifestyle, as in Protestantism. Overall it added survival value to anything to which it attached. This was neither inevitable, nor foreordained, but it was an identifiable and repeated phenomenon in history. In this sense we can understand the introductory paragraph of Weber's preface to the three volumes of the sociology of religion, paraphrased: what is the chain of events that have led us in Europe to think we have found developments that have a universal significance? (1920: 1; 19; 1976: 13).

We should leave Weber to have the last word on adaptation and explanation, as he expressed it in *Economy and Society*. In the conflict between different types of social relations, all kinds of natural and cultural conditions play a part. 'The explanation of these processes involves so many factors it does not seem expedient to employ a single term for them' (1956: 21; 1978: 40).

And on China: 'As soon as the mandarins realized there was profit to be made they overcame all the difficulties [with geomancy]. They are now the chief executives of the railways' (1923: 308).

---

[38] This same issue arises in relation to Weber's sociology of law and is examined in Albrow (1975).

DOI https://doi.org/10.24103/GCSS.en.2018.20

Chapter Fourteen
Max Weber, China and the future of global society

No social scientist has ever been more aware than Max Weber that we work on the cusp of the past and the future. We can call it the history of the present and he was first of all a historian, only later in his career devoting himself to the profession-alization of sociology. For good measure he was also lawyer, economist, political theorist, profoundly interested in psychology and widely read in theology. The fruit of his personal trans-disciplinarity was a deep understanding of public issues extending far into the future.

For the future he looked to the past. He fearlessly breached disciplinary boundaries seeking truths relevant for the human future. He turned to the East in order to unlock the secrets of the West, in particular to understand the unique nature of its capitalism that was on course to dominate the world.

In his classic essays on China published originally a century ago he gave full recognition to the work of distinguished sinologists of his time. But his greatest tribute to them was to show the significance of their work, not just for China, but for shared human understanding.[1] And he learnt from them.

Contrast this quaint remark in 1904 before he began his studies of China:

> A correct proof in the field of social science must, in order to have reached its goal, also be accepted as correct even by a Chinese.[2]

With this of 1916 after years of research on China:

> In respect of his dogma about "the monotony" of Asiatic life, coming from an American, that has to evoke the justified astonishment of all East Asian people.[3]

His first remark betrays the legacy of more than a century of Western stere-otyping; the second expresses modern multiculturalism, voicing incredulity that an American, living in his words in 'the heartland of monotony' could believe that life in Asia was monotonous. From 1905, China became a site for both for his personal enlightenment and the development of his social scientific method.[4]

---

[1] In an insightful evaluation of Weber's contribution to research on China, Herbert Francke (1966, 'Max Weber's Soziologie der Ostasiatischen Religionen', p. 129) commented that he led sinology out of the ghetto of oriental philology and showed how Chinese society and history could be understood through the methods of a universal science.

[2] Weber 2012, *Collected Methodological Writings,* p. 105.

[3] Weber 1967, *The Religion of India,* p. 341.

[4] See Martin Albrow and Zhang Xiaoying 2014, 'Weber and the Concept of Adaptation: the Case of Confucian Ethics', for an account of the way Weber's thinking on evolution and ethics developed through his China studies.

Many have called Weber the voice of modernity, some of postmodernity. I would see him on the cusp of both, able to look far into the past, but also into the postmodern distance ahead, towards the increasing rationalization of every life sphere and the varied reactions to it, the quest for identity and the clash of values in a world both of many faiths and none. Weber tracked the changes of his times, a period that covered Bismarck's triumphant unification of Germany in 1870 to the humiliation of the Versailles treaty of 1919. Weber died in 1920.

I was born in 1937. I was closer to him in my twenties than I am now to my first studies of Weber. My lifespan includes the atomic bombs dropped on Hiroshima and Nagaski through to the fall of the Berlin Wall, a period of transition to the age through which we have been passing and which gives the title to my book *The Global Age*.[5]

The fact that in my book I declared a rupture with the period before 1945, an epochal shift such that we can say a plague on both modern and postmodern houses, allowing us to engage with the issues of our own time, has led to the suspicion that I want to consign Max Weber to the dusty pages of 1960s text books.[6] The suspicion becomes accusation when I go on to talk of global society, given that Weber himself was notably reluctant even to use the word society. Nothing can be further from the truth.

Let me then say a few words about the concept of global society. The idea of society has been much contested in recent years, especially by those who see it as irredeemably associated with modernity, even a modern invention. Weber's reluctance to speak of society in a collective sense was part and parcel of his rejection of the use of collective concepts in sociology if they could not in principle be registered in the actions of individual human beings. This so-called 'methodological individualism' carried with it the necessity of being very precise about the use of the term 'social' too, another word that loses purchase on reality through overuse.

But such difficulties did not prevent Weber from making all possible use of collective concepts in his broader diagnoses of the human condition in his time. Society, state, nation, class all figure in his public discourse and in his reflections on the future. One of his familiar ways of signposting popular usage of terms was to put them in quotation marks, highlighting both their imprecision and equally their indispensable function in communication.

He did not speak of 'global society' or indeed of 'global' anything. Why not? Because the world has changed fundamentally since his time. But I am going to argue that his own method for analysing the reality of his own day, offering so

---

[5] Albrow 1996.
[6] George Ritzer 2007 in 'A New "Global Age", but Are there New Perspectives on It'? demands from me new concepts for a new age. To which the response is that the age has produced the new concepts, and my small contributions only reinforce the novelty of our time. At the same time we should not discard those concepts modern and older, even with universal application, that still have purchase on current issues.

much for understanding the direction the world would take in the future, has just as much relevance for seeing into our own futures. His study of China, and more generally religious ethics, was a primary testing ground for that method.

Weber and China's readiness for capitalism

As far as we know, unlike his learning of Russian and Hebrew, he never attempted to learn Chinese, but his interest in China was not a passing fad. It began almost as soon as he returned to work in 1904 after his nervous breakdown. His interest was sustained through to the end of his life in 1920, often delving deeply into the literature even during the dark years of the First World War.[7]

The length of his commitment is sometimes forgotten, overshadowed as it is by the publication of his study of Confucianism and Taoism as a separate book, but his later work is peppered with references to China, matched only by his parallel study of the religions of India.

I want to emphasize this interweaving of China into the full corpus of Weber's later work. He was engaged in writing what at the time was called universal history.[8] He studied China to understand the world of his time and its direction, in particular why Western capitalism was rampant worldwide. The method he adopted for China he employed everywhere else.

He considered the main social entities involved in perpetuating or changing their parent society. He analysed their agency, their influence on that wider society in terms of their interests, knowledge, values and ethics.[9] And he pointed to processes that arose out of and even constrained their freedom of action, without ever forgetting the causal relevance of material factors in the environment and human natural capacities.

In what he called the sociological foundations of imperial China, he highlighted the village-based extended families, the city guilds, the society-wide class of officials or mandarins, the monks and the imperial court. He emphasized too certain absences: no churches, no city corporations, no business enterprises.

It's the kind of counterfactual history that has attracted criticism, similar to his contemporary Werner Sombart who explained in 1906 why there was no socialism in the United States.[10] But Weber's overriding purpose was to explain why Western-type capitalism had not arisen anywhere else in the world.

---

[7] He heard sinologist and Austrian diplomat von Rosthorn in the Eranos Circle in 1907, and visited him in 1918 (Weber 1989, *Die Wirtschaftsethik der Weltreligionen Konfuzianismus und Taoismus: Schriften 1915-20*, pp. 41-43).

[8] According to Bernhard Pfister 1966, 'Max Weber: Persönlichkeit und Werk', Weber placed exceptional value on the world historical reflections of the great Swiss scholar Jacob Burckhardt.

[9] I am much indebted to the series of publications in which Stephen Kalberg (see especially 1994, *Max Weber's Comparative-Historical Sociology* and 2012, *Max Weber's Comparative-Historical Sociology Today*) has demonstrated the importance of Weber's interest in agency and causation for his comparative-historical sociology.

[10] Werner Sombart 1976 [1906], *Why Is There No Socialism in the United States?*

For him, the key precipitating factor in the West was the rise of a new Puritan work ethic, fulfilling the purposes of an omnipotent God. It introduced a revolutionary type of rationalism into economic life, dedication to work in this world for the sake of life in the next.

Nothing equivalent existed in China. For Weber, China had its own ethical rationalism, but directed towards different ends altogether, to the Confucian-inspired perfection of the ideal person in this life. This ethic of adaptation to the world served the interests of the mandarins but supplied none of the motivational force for capitalist development that Puritanism provided.[11]

The subsequent criticisms of Weber's account of Chinese economic ethics are exceeded only by those for the Protestant ethic thesis.[12] Perhaps the most telling is the accusation that he underestimated those parts of Confucian ethics that promoted reform and the betterment of the human condition. Less justified, however, is the idea that he denied the possibility of capitalism developing in China.

Undoubtedly his account fitted with a nineteenth-century Western stereotype of a society mired in tradition, but its elaborate specification of the interplay of the effective factors allowed ample scope for subsequent transformation. Based on the European experience, he found a whole array of factors in Chinese history favourable to capitalistic development, including the early development of money, unprecedented population growth, legendary acquisitiveness, industriousness and capacity for work,[13] economic theory, money interest, pursuit of profit,[14] the unbelievable parsimony of the masses.[15]

Weber also noted the 'not inconsiderable' technical inventiveness of the Chinese,[16] including their invention of the compass, printing and gunpowder.[17] Yet these were empirical achievements, underpinned not by rational science but by a different kind of rationalization altogether, an alignment with magic and superstition that shrouded every aspect of the daily life of the masses.

He called the complex interwoven beliefs in geomancy, calendar ritual, astrology and traditional medicine 'a superstructure of magical "rational" learning', a 'rationalization' in which the mandarins participated.[18] And when it came to the twentieth century it was this prevalence of belief in magic rather than the absence

---

[11] Albrow and Zhang 2014, op. cit.
[12] Eisenstadt 1983, 'Innerweltlich Transzendenz und die Stukturierung der Welt. Metzger 1983, 'Max Webers Analyse der Konfuzianische Tradition: Eine Kritik'. Tu 1983, `Die Neo-Konfuzianische Ontologie`.
[13] Weber 1951, *The Religion of China: Confucianism and Taoism,* p. 63.
[14] Ibid. p.159.
[15] Ibid. p. 209.
[16] Ibid. p. 200.
[17] Ibid. p. 142.
[18] Ibid. p. 200.

of a religious ethic that he regarded as the biggest obstacle to economic rationality.[19]

In the West, on the other hand, Puritanism and science had demystified the world. The more he read and wrote on China, the more Weber emphasized what he called this 'magic garden' and its influence on everyday life, including economic activity.[20] But even this pervasive influence could not in the end stave off the impact of Western capitalism. When it was allied with the substantial wealth of the mandarins, the railways came to China and overcame the traditional obstacles.[21] As he put it in his *General Economic History*:

> As soon as the Mandarins realized the chances for gain open to them, these difficulties suddenly ceased to be insuperable; today they are the leading stockholders in the railways. In the long run no religious-ethical conviction is capable of barring the way to the entry of capitalism … but the fact that it is able to leap over magical barriers does not prove that genuine capitalism could have originated in circumstances where magic played such a role.[22]

This comment is entirely consistent with his appreciation of the development of capitalism in both West and East. Puritanism initially had given an ethical foundation to capitalism, but, by rejecting popular superstition, belief in miracles and the Church as God's creation, had also contributed to the disenchantment of the West. By Weber's own time, capitalism had kicked away the ethical basis that Puritanism had given it and in China had overcome resistance from traditional codes and practices. It was then able to draw on all those other elements in Chinese culture favourable to capitalism that he had enumerated.

In the course of studies of China his reflections on the differences between West and East shifted their focus from religion to rationality and it was the peculiar quality of Western rationalism that reclaimed his attention. It extended into law, art, music, architecture, the state and of course, capitalism. Rationalization was the advance of rationalism bringing together elements of precise calculation, logical argument, observance of rules, taking account of the facts and careful planning, each reinforcing the other.

Only in the West had rationalization taken on such a comprehensive coverage of people's lives that it had come to be seen as a threat, a dark future and a shackling of individual freedom. The peculiarities of Western rationalism, sub-

---

[19] Weber 1961, 276.

[20] Weber was heavily reliant on J.J.M de Groot's (1910, *The Religion of the Chinese*; 1918, *Universismus*) characterization of the Chinese world picture as 'universism'.

[21] Günther Roth 1999, 'Max Weber und der globale Kapitalismus damals und heute,' p. 33, tells how social connections between Weber's family and the railway tycoon Henry Villard accounted for his particular interest in railway speculation.

[22] Weber 1961, *General Economic History*, p. 276.

sequently equated in the West to modernity, Weber regarded as one of his most important discoveries.[23]

In his comments on the 'disenchantment of the world', Weber joined the ranks of those who saw in modernity bleak prospects for individual self-expression. Social unrest and mass democracy were, he believed direct outcomes of capitalism's dependence on free labour, combined with mass manufacturing and urbanization.

Parliamentary democracy was a possible solution but Weber had little confidence in it without inspired leadership and he was more inclined to foresee mass irrationality and charismatic leaders as a result. Socialism as a doctrine was also a product of Western rationalism but Weber insisted that, as a potential alternative social order, its necessary connection with bureaucracy would be fatal to its prospects for survival when confronted with capitalism.

Bureaucracy, capitalism, religious ethics: these were the great structures that framed individual lives and shaped the future of nation-states, but rationality was a force inhabiting each, cumulative, bringing them into alliance with one another, also breaking them apart, while creating ever more powerful entities that dominated the course of history. Summed up as rationalization, this for Weber was the course that the world was taking in his time.

In all of these developments, Weber glimpsed futures that came to pass, and his insights depended, I would argue, on the sophistication of his analytical method, both for the long term and the short term. The most fateful prediction he made for the short term was of course his insistence that the terms the allied powers imposed on Germany in the Versailles treaty at the end of the first World War were bound to result in a backlash, out of a sense of national dignity as well as impoverishment.

The nation-state of the time was for him the bearer of the culture and values of a people, the period's most powerful agency. The bonds that tied people to it were the source of its power in the competition between nations that dominated the international order.

The pertinence of these observations for his time and their prescience for the time to come have impressed subsequent commentators to the extent that the messenger has been blamed for the outcome. Certainly Weber's account fits the rise of Hitler, but to see him as preparing the way for it, and to blame him for the evils of Nazism, is absurd. He rejected anti-Semitism, racism and territorial ambitions for Germany. His main concern was for the preservation of a political order strong enough to sustain German culture and ensure a world-historical role for Germany on the international stage.

For Weber it was collective political power that set the direction of world history and this was exercised by the nation-state, the reason why he wrote in 1916:

---

[23] Marianne Weber 1926, *Max Weber: Ein Lebensbild*, p. 348.

> Germany had to be a power state and we had to let it come to this war, to have a voice in the decision on the future of the earth.[24]

This was not a question of power for its own sake, but to realize the values that German culture contained. The state had a responsibility before history, and those who led the state took that responsibility on their shoulders. Weber insisted that responsible leadership on the part of individuals and whole classes was essential if the state was to fulfil its historic role. This combination of state mission and personal duty is the clearest example of how he built collective agency on an individualistic method.

A method for the diagnosis of the time

Universal history, comparative sociology and diagnosis of his time were intimately linked in Weber's programme for social science. They required in-depth discussion of method. Weber is known throughout the social sciences for two tags applied to his methodology that are equally celebrated and controversial, namely methodological individualism and the ideal type of concept formation.

There is another 'understanding', not so controversial perhaps, because it is often referred to by its German name '*Verstehen*'. We have to understand what people mean. Be reassured I am not going to elaborate on themes that are done to death in the scholarly literature. Rather, I want to highlight two features of his explanatory strategy, namely his concern for collective agency on the one hand and for impersonal forces on the other, both of which are fundamental to finding directions in history.

So much attention has been directed towards his axiom that individuals are the basic atom in a science of society that the fact that he focused his work overwhelmingly on the molecules, the ways in which people are grouped together, has been neglected. Sometimes they may be treated as aggregates of individuals with shared characteristics, as with classes or castes, sometimes as organized entities such as states or churches.[25]

He did not in either case hesitate to impute common agency to the individuals involved. He found no difficulty in combining collective consciousness with individual action. Each mandarin had his share in reproducing at least some of the ethos of Confucianism and as a mandarin class or status group ensuring the perpetuation of its economic ethic. He could not have put it more clearly when he excused himself from using ethnographic data:

> This omission has also seemed to be permissible because we are here necessarily dealing with the religious ethics of the classes which were the culture bearers

---

[24] Weber 1958, *Gesammelte Politische Schriften*, p. 171.

[25] Kalberg's (1994, op. cit., pp. 58-62, 71-78; 2012, op. cit., pp. 83-84, 255-56) valuable examinations of the explanatory strategies Weber adopted have stressed the importance of social groups as carriers of patterns of social action.

of their respective countries. We are concerned with the influence which their conduct has had.[26]

People collectively moved events, though of course the contribution each individual made to collective agency was different. He recognized that it was only in the modern age that the nation-state became the prime collective actor, but his individualistic research principle entailed that all such collective human agencies were constituted over time in and through the lives of individuals and could equally be disassembled into smaller units right down to their individual members. Even when Weber was at his most 'individualistic' emphasizing individual aspiration in the Protestant Ethic, he was still alluding to what Jack Barbalet has neatly called 'communal incorporation'.[27]

Historically, both city-states and empires had moved events, while guilds, churches and corporations could also command allegiance and act as a unit. In his day, he highlighted the role of political parties and the Mafia, corporations and trade unions and in his commentaries and interventions in the politics of the day it was to classes and constituted agencies he appealed and in terms of whose interests and values he sketched possible futures. It was the interests and avarice of the mandarins as a class that enmeshed them in the advance of Western capitalism.

The other element I am emphasizing is impersonal forces, and in this case those intimately connected with agency, for Weber made Marx's dictum, that people make their own history but not under conditions of their own choosing, even more stringent; their choices are constrained by the logic of their own ideas.

I refer to all he wrote around the theme of rationalism, rationality and rationalization, perhaps even more contentious than his so called individualism. Collective agency is both implemented through and constrained by frameworks of action that are aspects of rationalization. The most famous example is of course, Weber's ideal type of bureaucracy, developed to further the state's goals and to provide the law and order that capitalism requires. Rationalization operated in numerous spheres of modern life, in science, art, the mass media, but historically was evident in religious doctrine and in ethical systems such as had existed for millennia in China.

The rationalism of the Confucian teachings, of ancient Israel or of the early Christians exemplified the drive of intellectuals to systematize. *Ratio* was a compelling force and a vital element in the development of ideas. Of course, the assembled body of intellectuals themselves developed interests in their prestige, position and income and at any moment of time those were uppermost, but interests are ephemeral, dependent on power.

Rationalization, on the other hand, delivers ever more refined and powerful instruments, ever more elaborate and extensive cultural products. But it is not a

---

[26] Weber 1976, *The Protestant Ethic and the Spirit of Capitalism*, p. 30.
[27] Barbalet 2008, *Weber, Passion and Profits: The Protestant Ethic and the Spirit of Capitalism in Context*, p. 216.

single movement through time: it appears independently in different cultures and in different combinations. There are many rationalizations, both obsolete and actual, and the particular Western configuration was penetrating the whole world in Weber's time.

Scholars have taken widely different attitudes to the overwhelming number of references Weber makes to rationality and its cognate terms. My old boss Stanislav Andreski called it his weakest point, profoundly unclear and a semantic ragbag.[28] The outstanding contemporary commentator on Max Weber, Wolfgang Schluchter, finds in it a viable approach to directional analysis in history.[29] Both, however, agree that Weber is not using rationalization as a name for a single direction of development. On the contrary, it could apply to different times and cultures and involve contradictory directions. It was not a single process, but one that repeated itself in different contexts.

He employed it to highlight the independence of spheres of life or values from one another and to point to inherent tendencies in their development. One technical advance would lead to another, e.g. the Gothic vault could set in train a whole style of architecture and art, double entry bookkeeping enabled capital and profit to be calculated, facilitated investment and the business enterprise. The development of economic theory was a pure case of extension of an inner logic, so was the rational bureaucracy of the modern state.[30]

As each value sphere or style or method gained strength, so clearly its durability and capacity to resist destructive forces became greater. That meant tensions could easily develop with other spheres and this consideration came to preoccupy Weber in the course of his comparative studies of religion.

Equally, however a process of transfer and collaboration could develop and this was fundamental in the development of Western capitalism. This great structure was the outcome of the coalescence of the rationalization of many spheres of life, state, science, citizenship, bourgeois lifestyle and not just economic activity combining to constitute a world transforming force.[31]

The sheer complexity of Weber's reflections around the theme of concept construction and historical explanation can detract from the obvious success he has had in persuading the community of social scientists that his accounts had a hold on the reality of his time, and command respect for their relevance to us even today. Who can write about the modern state without taking account of his concepts of bureaucracy, legitimacy and charisma while recognizing that the flaws he

---

[28] Andreski 1984, *Max Weber's Insights and Errors*, pp. 58-82.

[29] Schluchter 1985, *The Rise of Western Rationalism: Max Weber's Developmental History*, p. 174.

[30] Weber favourite term for this inner development is '*Eigengesetzlichkeit*', literally 'its own lawfulness' or in English something like 'internal dynamics' or 'inner logic'. Kalberg (2012, op. cit. p. 43) prefers 'dynamic autonomy'.

[31] Niklas Luhmann's (1998, *Die Gesellschaft der Gesellschaft*, pp. 92-120) concepts of 'structural coupling' and 'operative closure' effectively revisit Weber's account of consolidation, conflict and reconstitution of value spheres.

found in democracy have been demonstrated time and again, even though, rather like a later British statesman, he reluctantly acknowledged its necessity for the modern age?

If we talk of Weber's intuition of the future development of human society then it is rationalization rather than capitalism that holds the centre stage and often this has been held to be the weakest point in his work, a lapse into a historical determinism akin to his predecessor Hegel's belief in the necessary advance of reason or even the modern belief in progress and the superiority of Western civilization.

A rejoinder to that criticism can make two points. The first is that Weber, far from celebrating rationalization, was inclined to decry the limits it placed on personal freedom. The second is that he recognized countervailing factors including, above all, the potential for mass reaction led by charismatic personalities, the idea of charisma becoming one of his most lasting contributions to political sociology. In sum, we can expect rationalization in any sphere of life, but we cannot anticipate it carrying all before it, and human beings have the capacity to imagine all kinds of alternatives and to commit to contradictory values.

That this was a diagnosis of his time that speculated far into the future he and others realized. It led him to reject, for instance, the likelihood of a future socialist utopia. He foresaw, rather than the advance of freedom, an all embracing bureaucratization of everyday life. Unlike others on left and right, he understood that the advance of capitalism depended on democratization, that this undermined traditional status orders and required leaders who could command mass appeal if a modern state was to promote its own culture in a competitive international order.

The world was the frame for his thought and research, which means that, although, like his contemporaries in the imperialist era he was a fervent national patriot, he was fully alert to the shifting balance of power in the world as a whole and the ephemeral nature of states. There was no basis in scientific knowledge for attributing ethnic differences to underlying racial characteristics and one could not pin the idea of society to any particular local configuration of territory and culture. Those for Weber are independent elements in the continual reorganization of structures of social relations.

That was an added reason for appealing to national values and for asserting the role of Germany in the world. It meant also keeping close watch on trends that could be to the advantage or detriment of his own country. He always had an eye to the future and in this respect the future of capitalism was a lifelong concern of his, predating even his interest in China.

Global society

Is this an account that recommends itself for our own time? So much has changed that we can easily doubt it. I have argued that the shift of focus to global issues in world affairs constitutes a move from the modern to the global age. Rather than bureaucracy, we talk of network organization, neo-liberalism overshadows capitalism, states are enmeshed in global governance, civil society crosses boundaries and the interconnectedness of our time makes it easy to speak of global society. Globalization rather than rationalization became the watchword in the 1990s.

Since Weber's time, capitalism has become global, and the West only exists in the anachronism of military alliances. A consciousness of the planet under threat and a sense of the precariousness of the continuation of the human species are shared among people in all parts of the earth. So fundamental is this change, I proposed to call it the Global Age, and used the language of epochs exactly to highlight the rupture with older modern ideas of progress and advancing civilization. I was using the language of historical change for the broader shift in human practice that Ulrich Beck had signalled in his risk society, the globe becoming the bearer of the fate of the species as a whole, effectively generalizing the risk to extend to human existence as such.[32] In each case, the direction and focus of human agency is in question and both address a fundamental change in orientation.

I do not equate world society and global society. World society has always existed in the sense of the network of social relations that extends at any one time to include all people on this earth. It is human society in its geographical configuration.

Global society, on the other hand, is a particular kind of society, on analogy with modern society or Western society, society orientated to the globe, finding its momentum through ignoring or at least overcoming national and other boundaries. On Weberian principles, it exists in and through individual actions, but those individuals equally may be members of national societies, of local communities or of voluntary associations. Global society is not exclusive, equally it does not include everybody, even if no one is excluded from its impact.

Who are the people who belong to global society? It is an immensely diverse population often conflicting with one another. Leaders of countries, their diplomats and officials are obliged to consider global issues and consult across borders. Those employed in multilateral organizations but also those in global corporations are globally oriented. The activists of Friends of the Earth or *Médecins sans Frontiéres*, for example, represent wider global concerns that vast numbers outside their membership share. Those who enjoy Hollywood or Bollywood or who follow the Olympics or the World Cup are sharing in a wider global culture.

In general, then, I paint a picture of a world of 7 or 8 billion individuals, all of whom have multiple allegiances, or identities, as it is more popularly expressed, existing in a multiplicity of social relations that constitute the vast network that we can call world society. Global society emerged as consciousness of a common fate grew after the Second World War, first in awareness of the risk of a nuclear holocaust and next in the recognition that the ever-increasing growth in the release

---

[32] Beck 1992 [1986], *Risk Society: Towards a New Modernity.*

of carbon gases would, unless stopped, eventually result in the incineration of our natural habitat.

In our time, we note the rise of new nations, international agencies, transnational corporations and the proliferation of non-governmental agencies, crossing boundaries, advocating causes, often led by charismatic leaders, that we call global civil society. The complexity and intensity of the interconnections between such collective agencies and the people out of which they are composed constitute what sociologist Manuel Castells has called network society.[33] When we consider the technologies of communication between these social units or entities, the possibilities of speaking and exchanging information in real time with anyone, anywhere in the world, then we may speak of digital society.

Steadily over time, as its economy has developed China has become enmeshed in this worldwide digitalized system, member of the United Nations, the IMF, the World Trade Organization, signatory to numerous international conventions and the second most important trading country in the world. Already there is the prospect of the renminbi becoming a global reserve currency, competing with the dollar. But, as every trading country learns, as Weber tried to tell the new Germany of his time, trade increases wealth but it also disperses power and reduces national autonomy.

Applied science and internet technology developed originally for national purposes, know no boundaries, and the largest and most rapidly growing global corporations are the ones that provide communication possibilities for all people and for any purpose, regardless of boundaries. The rise of China in recent decades that Martin Jacques so ably portrays is paralleled by, and to a degree overshadowed by the rise of network society, itself the latest self-transformation of global capital.[34]

Global society has been both top down and bottom up, the expression of a globalized public opinion, translated into a vast diversity of programmes, projects and governmental and civil society groups of actors of all kinds. A decentred yet focused human agency has been the characteristic of the global age, analysable precisely through the kind of sociology of social relations that Weber advanced in his fundamental concepts. He could not foresee either nuclear weapons or global warming, yet his methods did enable him to track at least some trends of his time into a more distant future.

We live at a crisis point in the Global Age, when the high hopes that were cherished in the early 1990s of a new world order and the worldwide glow of

---

[33] Castells 1996, *The Rise of the Network Society.*

[34] Interestingly Jacques (1993, *When China Rules the World*) was one of the earliest commentators on globalization to point to the consequential decline in the autonomy of the nation-state. In his thinking on new modernities they bear national identities and China becomes the dominant agent in the world. In global society, however, there is no single agency that has that role. There are many agencies, among them nation-states.

collective celebration with the new Millennium have passed away into history. My characterization of the Global Age was that its signature theme, its defining characteristic, was the collective sense of the need to address global challenges. It was and remains, albeit much damaged, an unprecedented mobilization of people worldwide around a practical programme of measures, of which the Millennium Development Goals are only the most prominent, to save the planet and secure the future of humankind.

Yet that very centrality of global issues for human endeavour is in acute danger of being displaced both by negative and destructive forces and by the relentless advance of the technologies for connectedness. When we join together simply for its own sake and not for any other purpose, and pursue the enjoyment of advancing technology regardless, then we may clearly recognize the advance of a new age, the Digital Age, where technology has advanced beyond human control.[35] The Global Age then may begin to signify a commitment to an ethic of saving the world, the rubric of a cause, as much as a period of human history.

There is a crisis in our time. We may identify it thus, as the threat to the Global Age from the Digital Age. But that is just headlining, not diagnosis. This is where we need deeper analysis and here I am going to propose turning to Max Weber and to suggest that from him we can gain deeper insights to help us in that task. His enquiries into the foundations of a science of society lead us to address questions of collective and individual agency that are at the heart of this crisis. For if we give up on globality and fail to recognize the way the fate of humankind depends on collective agency for global ends then no amount of advance in communication technology will save the planet or indeed satisfy individual aspirations and well-being.

Bringing Weber into the Global Age

Weber's sense of historical continuity and change enabled him to see rationalization as a potential in human society in widely separated times and places. The evidence for its worldwide advance since his time and into the Global Age is overwhelming wherever we look: communications, construction, medicine, applications of science for peace and war.

George Ritzer's examination of the methods of the McDonald's franchise is perhaps the most well-known application of Weber's rationalization thesis, seventy years after Weber's death, for a consumer capitalism far beyond the industrial capitalism of the time.[36] Ulrich Beck's chosen rubric for our time, second moder-

---

[35] For data on digital and global age usage see Albrow 2014, *Global Age Essays on Social and Cultural Change,* pp. 13, 83.

[36] Ritzer 1993, *The McDonaldization of Society.* For an example of research applied to the regulation of human reproduction and data protection, see Albrow 1987, 'The Application of the Weberian Concept of Rationalization to Contemporary Conditions'. In relation to journalism, see Aeron Davis 2013, 'Applying a Weberian Perspective to the Analysis of UK Journalism'.

nity, draws attention precisely to the continuities of Weber's rationalization in the reflexivity of technologies that handle risk.[37]

In Weber's time, bureaucracy was the latest stage of rationalization. He likened it to an animated machine, but, echoing a persistent theme of the industrial age, he recognized its double-edged nature:

> An inanimate machine is objectified mind. Only this provides it with the power to force men into its service and to dominate their everyday working life as completely as is actually the case in the factory.[38]

The rationalization of communication that Weber recognized in rational bureaucracy was clearly linked to the purposes of state and business enterprise. But the rationalization of the means of everyday communication goes far beyond the old bureaucratic systems in standardizing the most mundane activities, from sending a message to accessing money.

And just as with bureaucracy, there is widespread recognition that, however effective the new media, there are always unwanted side-effects. If rationalization is the driver of change, it is the agents, whether steering or opposing, who compose the narrative for our time.

He would have pointed to the ambivalent relationship between the rationalized structure and the realization of human purpose. He would have had the same fears for individual freedom in the potential of the internet for mass surveillance as he had in the dehumanization of mass production processes. His famous inaugural lecture on the contradiction between free trade and national culture is precisely paralleled in the contradictions between economic globalization and the sovereignty of the nation-state.[39]

Above all, his method points to the revolution in individual and collective agency in our world today, the multiple agencies of state, business and civil society. And he would have recognized charismatic responses to rationalization from Geoffrey Pleyers's evidence on civil society agency and resistance to globalization.[40] He would have perceived the new information and communication technology as a global resource for the proliferation of new social entities, for friendships, business enterprises and civil society organizations as well as countries and corporations.

Geopolitics was the big frame for his history of the present. The existence of the United Nations and the complex network of global governance institutions today are in vast contrast to his time. The agency of the nation-state is both pooled with and limited by others. But on my reading, Weber's sense of the mutability of state and national agency was so deeply historical he would have had no dif-

---

[37] Beck 2000, *What is Globalization?* p. 12. He chooses it for a book series with the publisher Suhrkamp.

[38] Weber 1978, *Economy and Society*, p. 1402.

[39] Weber 1958, op. cit., pp. 1-25.

[40] Pleyers 2010, *Alter-Globalization: Becoming Actors in the Global Age.*

ficulty in recognizing the new international order.[41] China in his terms is a world historical actor or, in the more limited understanding of our day, a 'great power', or 'superpower'.

Projecting its rise further forward some even argue that the world is going to be ruled by China. Advancing that view, Martin Jacques believes that a culture that sees the state more as an extension of the family than an alien system is likely to become dominant over a West with its declining living standards and dysfunctional political systems.[42] One could add, in support of that view, Weber's lack of commitment to parliamentary democracy except as a way of satisfying the masses and selecting leaders. He would have had no difficulty in recognizing a symbiotic relationship between a one-party state and capitalist institutions.

But does the world of today allow the great power the same position Weber gave to the Britain or Germany of his own time? Is the balance between the power of the nation-state and the empowering and constraining force of rationalization the same as then? I think he would be less than impressed with the capacity of any nation-state, whether the United States or China or any other, to dominate the world.

Rather he would have recognized the way globalization took a new phase of the rationalization process forward and he would have recognized the new global economy together with neo-liberal ideology based on the collusion of transnational corporations and the nation-state. That collusion has led to the vast expansion of what is now called global governance, built upon institutions established at the end of the Second World War to create peace between nations. In the international agencies Weber would see the successors of his national bureaucracies and question the responsibilities of their staff.

In sustaining the agency of the state, the legitimacy of its rulers in the eyes of the ruled was a crucial component, a legitimacy that both the German Emperor and the national bourgeoisie had lost in Weber's eyes.[43] In support of rulers, bureaucrats played a key role. But in our world where states are so interconnected that we can talk of a global state the commitment of national officials is no longer so clear-cut. The quality and ethos of national leadership for him determined the fate of the nation, which was why he deplored Germany's conduct of the Great War even as he supported his own country. In the decentred world of today, leadership is no longer national.

---

[41] Wolfgang Mommsen believes his fervent nationalism would have impeded any recognition of the kind of order the League of Nations would represent, but this is not confirmed by the hopes he placed on it as a guarantor of the kind of peace treaty he wanted at the end of the First World War (Mommsen 1984, *Max Weber and German Politics 1890-1920*, pp. 48, 319).

[42] Jacques 2012, op. cit.

[43] Inspired in part by Weber's theoretical position, Randall Collins predicted the decline of the Russian Soviet Empire as early as 1986 (Collins 1986, *Weberian Sociological Theory*, pp. 186-209).

I think we can find the direction of Weber's thinking for our time in the extraordinary lecture he gave, not long before his death, on politics as a vocation.[44] As with his account of the rise of capitalism in the West and in the East the ethics of those in power, and hence their quality as people, provided the key to determining the future. He contrasted the social strata from which leaders arose in different times and cultures, the clergy in historic empires, the Chinese mandarins, the English gentry, the European lawyers, very significantly with the new strata of journalists and the professionals of the political parties, all with their special interests.

But, once in power, facing all these strata was a choice between two kinds of ethic, to follow their values regardless of consequences or to take responsibility for the outcomes of their actions. The starkness of the contrast he drew is what has attracted most comment. But, to my mind, the very fact of Weber's assumption that politics involves ethical decisions is more important. The path to the future is determined in part by what we think we ought to do and he left the content of those commitments open.

The 'we' now in global society involves multiple agencies, international, national, transnational, local, trans-local, regional, trans-regional. It involves churches, mosques, temples and synagogues. It employs social workers and soldiers, police and paramedics. It galvanizes the energies of individuals. It is directed towards a huge diversity of governance objects: [45] ending the use of fossil fuels, eliminating nuclear weapons, establishing social justice, stabilizing the world's population, providing sustainable food supplies, removing terrorist threats and controlling disease, to name only the top priorities for global action.

The collaboration and effectiveness of those agencies cannot be guaranteed either by force or by markets. What is required is what Weber called a legitimate order, to underpin genuine global governance with democratic participation and oversight, institutions that secure orderly relations in this vast web of interconnected, overlapping and often competing agencies. One might add that global public opinion would be a necessary component, if it were not for the fact that Weber regarded public opinion on the national level as too amorphous an idea for scientific analysis.

The scope for further rationalization of this scale of global governance is clearly enormous but, both from past experience and from what Weber has taught us, it will not be long before the digital economy becomes digital global citizenship, the rights and duties of every person in the world's population will be guaranteed through their unique identity number and those multiple agencies will be registered and regulated.

Such an order, even though based in the vast capabilities of digital technology will still depend on the belief in its legitimacy and, under conditions of globality, only a common commitment to human life on this planet will be able

---

[44] Weber 1948, *From Max Weber*, pp. 77-128.
[45] Olaf Corry 2013, *Constructing the Global Polity.*

to deliver that legitimacy. Without that, the Global Age will be the last but one in human history.

These are intimations of the future, giving myself the same licence Weber allowed himself. Let me end on an even more speculative note. Weber's explorations of the idea of rationality and rationalization are themselves fraught and often end up in contradictions, as for instance that between formal rationality, that is, procedures for right decisions, and material rationality, the delivery of value, often public goods.

It is an opposition expressed simply in the conflict between law and justice. He also showed the uses of rationality in forming his ideal type concepts, as in the idea of economic man. But he never examined the concept of rationality in a critical way. He made no attempt at philosophical or logical enquiry, only repeated applications of the concept in historical contexts.

Yet there have been advances in rationalization since his time that bring us face to face with the most basic principles of logic. The pervasive use of the term and the idea of the 'digital', the referencing of one or zero, existence or non-existence, the basis of binary arithmetic, hence the computing programming and technology, takes us all the way back to its inventor Gottfried Leibniz, the intellectual giant who can look down even on Weber. As is well known in China, Leibniz took his enquiries into the fundamentals of existence, into comparative linguistics and the Yi Ching.

Digitalization in our time is the extension of the programme of mapping reality, natural and human, onto the mathematics he initiated as the necessary partner to the modern revolution in experimental science. Weber's commitment to scientific rationality is a stage on that journey of rationalization running from his time to ours. It runs relentlessly towards the further quantification of the practice and control of everyday life.

Weber's instincts about the direction of world history were basically correct, including his identification of the conflicts that rationality throws up. Advances in rationality fail to reduce conflict, only transform the value spheres of a differentiated society. The unification of state and economy proceeds apace while the new site for conflict is over the control of digitalized information, a battle between two ever more sharply distinguished spheres, security on the one hand and creativity on the other.

Meanwhile, the future of the planet depends on the agency of individuals and groups seeking to influence public policy while resisting the collateral damage to their privacy and autonomy resulting from the conflict between the new spheres. In this new configuration, those who despair of their lost past, visit destruction on the present and seek fulfilment in life after death. Only an ethic of collective salvation on this planet holds out a promise for future generations. The question waiting for an answer is: Will the carriers of that ethic be able to deliver?

DOI https://doi.org/10.24103/GCSS.en.2018.21

Postscript
A Chinese episode in the globalization of sociology

A volume celebrating Fei Xiaotong's immense achievements may well empha-size his understanding of China, but in the framework of a global sociology that is bound to lead towards an understanding of a wider and a better world. It has indeed already done so. Writing a short book introducing sociology to a general public, I cited Fei as the sociologist whose work has produced the greatest effect on the greatest number of people anywhere.[1]

My reasoning was based on the cumulative influence that his research had exercised over the years on the introduction of the responsibility system in Chi-nese agriculture. He was a creative co-author at the outset of the long story of the massive release of personal and collective energies that continues to be told in China today and is now spreading its influence worldwide. 'For China today, for the world tomorrow': that has to be the direction of those energies in the social sciences too. The brief memoir that follows will relate an early episode in such a story as it happened in sociology from the standpoint of a participant.

As a graduate student at the London School of Economics working on Max Weber, I was familiar with his seminal study of the religion of China.[2] But my first acquaintance with contemporary Chinese scholarship and with Fei's work was in-spired in 1960 by that fine anthropologist Maurice Freedman. Because, as a rather green student in his graduate seminar, I rashly admitted a schoolboy enthusiasm for Arthur Waley's translations of Chinese poetry, he asked me to prepare a paper on Chinese social institutions. He thus led me into the mysteries (for a Westerner) of *li* via his student Sybille van der Sprenkel's thesis on Chinese law.[3]

It was a big ask of someone whose first degree was in Western history, and an entry in my diary for 20 January 1960 reads, 'Desperation over this paper on China – contemplate giving up – why must every little setback appear a cosmic is-sue?' But a day later Maurice changed it all. The diary continues, 'Paper delivered – generous praise, excessive pleasure.' His kind treatment of the resulting paper was an important ingredient in my later confident belief that sociology could build a firm bridge across the West–East cultural divides – and, yes, the youthful diary writer was right, bridging those divides will determine the human future and, in that anthropocentric sense, is 'cosmic'.[4]

---

[1] Albrow 1999a, *Sociology; The Basics*, p. 64.
[2] Weber 1951, *The Religion of China*.
[3] van der Sprenkel 1954, 'A Sociological Analysis of Chinese Legal Institutions'.
[4] An extended autobiographical account of the atmosphere of the LSE at that time and the stages of a journey through global sociology back to it again in the Global Governance Centre can be found in Mathieu Deflem's volume *Sociologists in a Global Age* (Albrow 2007).

A fuller test of that confidence came in the 1980s after I was asked to become the founding editor of a new journal for the International Sociological Association (ISA), *International Sociology*. This was part of a renewed drive by the ISA to strengthen bridges between the 'three worlds', capitalist, socialist and developing. It reflected, and took advantage of the lowering of international barriers at that time to the free exchange of information and ideas. Liberalization of communist regimes was being promoted in the Soviet Union by President Mikhail Gorbachev through *perestroika*.

In China, reform was being led by senior leader Deng Xiaoping, Chairman and General Secretary Hu Yaobang and Premier Zhao Ziyang through the responsibility system in agriculture. This was the geopolitical and cultural climate in which the Executive Committee of the ISA, first under its president, Fernando Cardoso, subsequently President of Brazil, and then under his successor, Margaret Archer of the University of Warwick, determined to realize sociology's potential as a universalizing agency for creating one world.

The journal aimed, in Cardoso's words, 'to offer the reader a more global and comprehensive view of contemporary sociology' but to do that 'by showing pluralistic paths of concern in sociology rooted in different historical and cultural traditions'.[5] It was therefore my privilege as its editor to follow the discipline wherever in the world it led. One direction was China, partly because of the happy accident that I was already working in partnership with a significant player in China's drive to modernize, the State Family Planning Commission.

In 1979, the Chinese Government and the United Nations Fund for Population Activities had signed a Memorandum of Understanding which led to in-country assistance for family planning programmes and cooperation with multilateral agencies including the International Planned Parenthood Federation and with training centres overseas.[6] Within that framework, the Population Centre of University College Cardiff provided courses for mid-career officials in the population programmes of developing countries and the State Family Planning Commission of China was one of the agencies that each year sent us two or three of their staff for a Diploma or Master's Degree in Population Policies. Such was the strategic significance of their work for the direction of China's population policies that we were honoured by the visit to Cardiff of the minister in charge of the Commission, Wang Wei, in February 1987.[7]

---

[5] Cardoso 1986, Foreword.

[6] Government of China 1987, Leaflet: 'Family Planning Program in China 1987'.

[7] In the newspaper *Western Mail* (26 February 1987) Charles Hymas, under the headline 'Experts of birth control on visit', wrote, 'A Chinese leader with the toughest family planning job in the world got the chance of some on-the-spot population analysis on a visit to South Wales yesterday.' Wang Wei was pictured viewing computer population projections and the story told how sixteen officials from the State Family Planning Commission had studied at the Cardiff Population Centre over the previous five years.

In November 1987, accompanied by our former student, friend and translator, Li Yong, my wife, Sue Owen, who lectured at the Centre on the economics of aging, and I, as Director of the Centre, had the privilege of being conducted on visits to offices and sites of the Commission's work in Beijing, Nanjing and Hangzhou and neighbouring villages. We lectured in Nanjing College for Family Planning Administrators on 'The Education of Population Programme Professionals: The Cardiff Philosophy' (Albrow) and on 'Fertility Decline and Female Labour Force participation in the West' (Owen). In Hangzhou University we gave a joint lecture on 'The Old and the Young: the Contemporary Western Crisis'.[8]

At the same time, my visit to China provided a wonderful opportunity to renew an invitation to Chinese sociologists to join in the ISA's efforts to internationalize the discipline. I was deputed by Margaret Archer to represent the Association on my visit and met with Ding Weizhi, Deputy Secretary of the Chinese Academy of Social Sciences, and Professor Lu Xueyi, Deputy Director of the Academy's Institute of Sociology, to discuss Chinese membership of the Association.

There was a history to these talks. The ISA had for some time been seeking to bring the Chinese Sociological Research Society, of which Professor Fei Xiaotong was president, into full membership, and therefore to represent sociology for the People's Republic of China. A formal invitation was sent in August 1985 and repeated in February 1986 and Fei came to the World Congress in Delhi that year and discussed the matter with the ISA's president, Fernando Cardoso.

The talks came to nothing because of the sensitive issue of concurrent membership of the Chinese Sociological Association of Taiwan. That was still the situation in November 1987, and in explaining it Professor Margaret Archer, the new President of the ISA, wished me well in my discussions with the Chinese sociologists, writing, 'If you could somehow find your way through this wood you will have accomplished a major geo-political miracle in sociological terms'.[9]

It was clear to me that such a miracle was beyond my powers, but equally my experience of working relations with Chinese officials in the population field showed there was always the possibility of finding areas of cooperation across political boundaries if we sought to find areas of common interest and values.

Sociology had been suspended in 1952, politically prohibited in 1959 and re-established in China in 1979 when Deng declared that 'we neglected the study of political science, law, sociology and international politics, and it is now essential for us to catch up' (Dai 1993a, p. 92).

The Chinese Sociological Research Association was founded in 1979 and there was a growing enthusiasm for the subject in official circles and rapid expansion in its provision in the 1980s. The State Education Commission commissioned

---

[8] An unpublished account of the tour was circulated as 'Report of an Observational Tour of the Family Planning Programme of the People's Republic of China' by Martin Albrow and Susan Owen, 25 November 1987.

[9] Private communication from Margaret Archer, 13 October 1987.

a report in 1986 on the future demand for sociologists from the Departments of Sociology of Nankai University and of the Shanghai College of Liberal Arts. It was published in the new journal *Shehuixue Yanjiu* (*Sociological Studies*) in July 1987, concluding that 798 postgraduates and 1,423 first-degree holders were urgently needed across government, the Party, in journalism and publishing, in large enterprises and in education.[10] The climate was therefore favourable to an approach in 1987 that invited collaborative work rather than the formal institutional agreements that the ISA had previously been seeking.

The fortunate basis for that collaboration was the new journal I edited and, with the enthusiastic support of Lu Xueyi, who visited us in Cardiff with his colleague Dai Kejing, we were able to establish a productive publication arrangement which included Dai becoming an Associate Editor for *International Sociology*. She and I, with the generous agreement of its editor, Wang Yuming, worked together to publish five papers in English from *Shehuixue Yanjiu* in 1989 and 1990 including the report on the demand for sociology graduates. *Shehuixue Yanjiu* started publication in January 1986 appeared every two months and usually included about 20 articles in each issue, so choosing just five to appear in *International Sociology* was an invidious task. What we tried to do was to find a balance between papers reporting research on Chinese society, such as market towns[11] and social security[12], and ones that reflected on China's place in the contemporary world, social modernization [13]and the dual structure of Chinese society.[14]

A further three papers by Dai on rural women,[15] Li Lulu, Yang Xiao and Wang Fengyu on stratification,[16] and Lu Jianjua (1991) on workers' expectations of management,[17] appeared in the last issue of *International Sociology* that I edited. These gave me particular pleasure because the latter two papers had been selected by a Chinese jury for the ISA's Competition for Young Sociologists and Lu's was one of the five eventual winners from the worldwide field of 335 entries.[18]

Under Dai's careful editorial scrutiny, the journal was able over the years to publish a series of academic papers from Chinese sociologists working in China. I stress 'Chinese working in China' because the philosophy underlying the journal was that there should be no political, cultural or linguistic barriers to publication.

---

[10] Investigation Group of Nankai University, 1989.
[11] Ye et al. 1989, 'The Establishment of Market Town Sociology with Chinese Characteristics'.
[12] Chen 1990, 'Social Developmental Mechanisms and Social Security Functions'.
[13] Li 1989, 'Theoretical Theses on "Social Modernization"'.
[14] Pan 1990, 'The Dual Structure of Chinese Society and its Influence on Modern Chinese Society'.
[15] Dai 1991, 'The Life Experience and Status of Chinese Rural Women from Observation of Three Age Groups'.
[16] Li, Yang and Wang 1991, 'The Structure of Social Stratification and the Modernization Process in Contemporary China'.
[17] Lu 1991, 'Chinese Worker's High Expectations of Enterprise Managers'.
[18] Bertaux 1990, 'Designing the Worldwide Competition'.

This may well appear to be the policy for so many Western so-called 'internation-al' academic journals, but in practice those barriers exist, especially the linguistic one that requires authors to write in perfect English.

Our policy was that no paper would be rejected on language grounds, which meant that we had to assess papers in the language of their origin first.[19] Dai's bi-lingualism was invaluable for the journal, as it was when she translated Fei's LSE doctorate into Chinese in 1986, a volume which had previously been regarded as 'criminal evidence' of 'a widespread pernicious influence' in the Cultural Revo-lution when he was detained in the 'cowshed' or sent for 'retraining' in the 'cadre school'.[20]

But bridging the language barrier was only one aspect of the way we con-ceived of the sociological mission at the time. A culminating moment came in 1990 with the World Congress of Sociology in Bielefeld, advertised with the theme 'Sociology for One World: Unity and Diversity'. Archer used that title for her presidential address,[21] in which she argued for the universality of human reason, rejecting both a false unitary perspective on the world, whether as modernization or postmodernism, and a relativism that postulated unbridgeable gulfs between cultures. Sociology, she argued, showed how global mechanisms combined with regional circumstances to create a diversity of novel configurations. Globalization was then not the effect of a new world on the old but part of the interaction of new and old to create a different world.

'Sociology for One World' had been the title of an editorial article I wrote earlier for the second volume of *International Sociology*, in which I argued that the drive for indigenous sociologies was not a retreat from the programme of a universal science.[22] I also touched on the practical consequences of such a vision for selecting papers for the journal. One of the more contentious conclusions I drew in effect was that intellectual excellence alone was not the sole criterion for publication. Stated so baldly, this caused considerable debate. My position was, and remains, that the universalizing mission of sociology requires knowledge to be grown from multiple viewpoints. 'The corpus of sociological knowledge is enriched by contributions from representatives of groups with distinctive social experience'[23]

Let me illustrate the implications of this policy in practical terms, with a necessarily invented example. Let us suppose there are 20 papers, all rated good, competing for space in one issue of a journal that can publish only ten. The 'best' 15 papers are by Western men and women on features of industrialized societies: there are three by women on women's issues in the West and two by non-Western-

---

[19] A fuller account of that policy appears in Albrow 1991.
[20] Dai 1993b, Portrait: 'Fei Xiaotong 1910 –'.
[21] Archer 1991, Presidential Address.
[22] Albrow 1987b, 'Sociology for One World'.
[23] Ibid. p. 7.

ers, one by a man, one by a woman, in each case on issues from their own cultures. What do I choose for publication? On the basis of my principle of representing diversity, I choose six of the 15, two of the three on women's issues, and both the non-Western papers. Nine of the best papers will have to go elsewhere. Now, of course, you can query the premise of this example as follows: Why would the best papers all be by Westerners? To which my reply is that this simply represents the subterranean, often subliminal processes, judgments made on language, networks, reputations and orthodox paradigms of research, which time and again will bias the judgment of what is 'best' and will lead to the exclusion of whole areas that sociology needs to take into account.

Diversity as a policy promotes the intellectual comprehensiveness and innovative excellence of the discipline as a whole, as opposed to what happens when we work as if seeking the winners of a competition between individuals. Of course, when, as happened with Lu Jianjua, a non-Westerner wins a competition dominated by Westerners, there is double reason for rejoicing.[24] Even there, however, note well that we published papers explicitly to represent the younger generation of sociologists. There were older people who did not make the age limit of under 35 and were correspondingly excluded, who otherwise would have appeared in print. No apologies!

I won't carry this abstract argument further into ever-deeper territory in this short memoir. Suffice it to say that it can be pursued up to and including ultimate assumptions about how knowledge is gained, what it is for and, indeed, what it is. And the course of that argument would take us into and beyond ideological issues about competition and collective wisdom. For these reasons, debates about editorial decisions on the content of a journal are never purely 'academic'.

Elsewhere, commenting on the editorial policy of *International Sociology*, I expressed this view provocatively and concretely: 'There is, therefore, something which the young female Indian sociologist working in her own city can give to sociology which is beyond the capacity of the senior male American sociologist working in the same place.'[25]

And further, for an illustration of the consequences of that policy for Chinese sociology, we can refer to the statistics of papers received and accepted by the journal in its first four years, as reported in volume 39 of *Current Sociology*.[26] From the United States, 55 papers were received and 18 accepted, from the USSR six and one respectively, and from China, six received, six accepted.

Enough said. I want rather to dwell on the relatively limited topic (though still enormous in its own right) of the contribution that the Chinese collaboration made to the globalization of sociology at that time and how we can construe it now. It was only then that the discipline was beginning to reflect on the conse-

---

[24] Lu 1991.
[25] Albrow 1991, 'Internationalism as a Publication Project', p. 111.
[26] Ibid. pp. 116–118.

quences of globalization for itself. The term 'globalization' was already being domesticated in the language of sociology in papers from 1985 onwards by Roland Robertson.[27] He was emphasizing consciousness of the globe as an element in the creation of global society, a product of his own dual interest in the sociology of religion and in international relations.

In the pages of *International Sociology* Piotr Sztompka was another pointing to the globalization of society as involving the internationalization of sociology and a revision of older ideas of comparative method.[28] Zsuzsa Hegedus pointed to the new planetary orientation of 1980s movements, 'conflictualizing' global issues and effectively 'globalizing' individuals, something she referred to as empowerment and globalization.[29]

It was papers such as these that prompted me to recommend to the ISA that the volume to be presented to the delegates at the Madrid World Congress should be drawn from papers published in the journal and bear the title *Globalization, Knowledge and Society.30* I believe this was the first time that 'globalization' figured in an English book title. The volume could not have been compiled without the work of Elizabeth King, who had given editorial support from the early planning of the journal and continued through to her tragically early death.[31] In a way, her own biography, spanning Germany, Switzerland, the UK and Greece, epitomized the way I conceptualized the globalization of sociology in the Introduction to the volume: 'It results from the freedom individual sociologists have to work with other individuals anywhere on the globe and to appreciate the worldwide processes within which and on which they work.'[32]

That rather general-sounding formulation actually was intended to represent a concrete stage beyond two others in the development of sociology, which, in succession, were the 'internationalism' and 'indigenization' of the discipline. The former was a post-Second World War I phenomenon associated with modernization in both American and socialist thought, and the latter primarily an assertion of autonomy and the values of traditional culture in Third World societies. The volume reflected both of those orientations but pointed also to an emergent one of a globalized sociology, where there is a diversity of sociological dialects and special visions within a worldwide shared discourse.

While not explicit at that point, my reflections drew on understandings that fitted with and were enhanced by what I was learning about Chinese sociology. Li Lulu emphasized that the combination of a huge population, an ancient culture and socialism meant China was bound to develop a distinctive kind of modernization,

---

[27] Robertson 1992, *Globalization: Social Theory and Global Culture*.
[28] Sztompka 1988, 'Conceptual Frameworks in Comparative Inquiry: Divergent or Convergent'.
[29] Hegedus 1989, 'Social Movements and Social Change in Self-Creative Society'.
[30] Albrow and King 1990.
[31] Albrow 1998. Obituary.
[32] Albrow and King 1990, op. cit. p.7.

but he and colleagues in a later paper argued that the old hierarchical culture still inhibited the creativity required for a successful non-Western modernization.[33] In Pan Jianxiong's account of the dual structure of ancient Chinese culture, its combination of autocracy and a secular humanism meant that a conformity in ethics and mutual goodwill provided stability but also a barrier to Western modernization.[34] These accounts captured cultural specifics but did not yet address the way they could frame the development of sociology.

A later round-table discussion led by Dai directly addressed the conceptual problems of a Chinese sociology under globalized conditions.[35] Dai wrote of a 'bumper harvest' for sociology in the previous decade, recording 15 universities where there was a department of sociology and 31 specialized research institutes. That compares with the Nankai report of 1987, which detailed only five university departments and three research institutes. She reported on the third meeting of the Board of Directors of the Chinese Sociological Association in August 1990, which emphasized the need to integrate theory and practice with the goal of creating a Chinese sociology, and where Fei stressed an overwhelming need for further development.

In the other papers of that symposium we find a discussion of the sinification and globalization of sociology that could almost be taken as a textbook case of the issues involved in indigenization. Bettina Gransow surveyed the different tendencies in intensive debates among Chinese sociologists in Taiwan, Hong Kong, the United States and the People's Republic. She concluded that 'the endeavour towards the sinicization of sociology led to a learning process about sociology's cultural and civilizational ties, a learning process which sharpened the senses for the relative limits set within the context of cultural semantic patterns, even if a universal approach was taken'.[36]

For Chan Hoiman,[37] commenting on Gransow, this debate about globalization and sinification reflected a wider anxiety about the universalistic credentials of sociology, ones which we saw that Archer was concerned to reassert, and which for Chan would be advanced through a reflexive sociology, one that continually reflected on its foundations under the pressure of indigenizing and globalizing forces. Such a sociology, as advocated by Alvin Gouldner and Pierre Bourdieu, would be one of perpetual self-rejuvenation.

And that is an appropriate point to end this short account of an episode in the globalization of sociology, because the reflexivity of a discipline is fundamental to the advance of knowledge and it continues apace. But the case of this particular

---

[33] Li 1989; Li, Yang and Wang 1991.
[34] Pan 1990.
[35] Dai 1993a, 'The Vicissitudes of Sociology in China'.
[36] Gransow 1993, 'Chinese Sociology: Globalization and Sinicization' p. 110.
[37] Chan 1993, 'Some Metasociological Notes on the Sinicization of Sociology'.

encounter between China and a globalizing sociology reveals something about both sociology and reflexivity.

There is a big difference between the reflexivity that arises out of self-examination and the reflectiveness induced through partnership in conversation where each party reflects and reflects on the other. What I think we managed by introducing Chinese sociology into *International Sociology* was to bring the in-culture self-examination into an arena of multiple exchanges. It highlights cultural differences while simultaneously enhancing mutual understanding.

What does this say about universality, the quality regarded as fundamental to true knowledge? Within sociology we may employ mathematical and statistical methods that are acknowledged to have universal validity, but we fail to find the invariant relations that characterize the natural sciences. A goal of shared understandings between all human beings is not achieved by means of a science akin to that of the natural world but only through multiple encounters that are bound always to cross cultural and linguistic barriers.

The shared understandings we arrive at often arise from the recognition of a particular patterning of underlying elements that one culture selects out as strategic, the separate components of which, however, can be identified in any culture. When we recognize such a pattern in another culture, because those individual components are familiar to us in our own, we also see its potential for us in our own culture and often seek to replicate it. We discover possibilities for ourselves through understanding others. The history of East–West relations is therefore one of experimenting with one another's ways of life.

It is in this light that I see in sociology the distinction in early German theory between *Gemeinschaft* and *Gesellschaft* which has generated a wealth of finer distinctions in English. While the original opposition remains embedded in German thought and experience and has no exact equivalent in English, which is why we retain the German terms in English-language publications, it represents a configuration of thought and feeling that may be identifiable in English-speaking cultures but never precisely replicable, and for those who speak both languages it is obvious there can be no exact equivalent.

We can expect many more such examples the more the discipline recognizes indigenous roots to social thought. Recently, Xiangqun Chang's account of the prevalence and durability of *Li shang wanglai* in a Chinese village has provided a fine example of identifying the irreducible distinctiveness of culturally transmitted patterns of social relations.[38] And yet we can still see that this is one possible pattern of social relations, culturally defined in China, but not without approximations elsewhere.

The understanding we achieve of *Li shang wanglai* and its place in Chinese society through Chang's work illuminates cognate patterns, resemblances and dif-

---

[38] Chang 2010, *Guanxi or Li shang wanglai?*

ferences in other cultures. This is what is conveyed through her development of it as an analytical concept in conjunction with ideas of reciprocity and networks. In comparative work it therefore operates for us in Weberian terms as an ideal type. Underlying this intelligibility are generic ideas of individual people, acting in social relations with one another. These are translatable into any language, belonging to a universal sociological thesaurus that conveys an unconfined diversity in the concrete manifestations of those relations in social life.

The most elementary features of the human condition are recognizable across cultures, are pre-linguistic and are shared with other species – birth, bonding, nurture, reproduction, health, death among others – and these enable us to cross cultures in our understanding. We replicate the universal features of our species as much, or even more, as we meet foreigners than we do in engaging with our own countrymen, when we are confined by the oddities of our own culture. Chinese and Westerners are of one humankind and we can rejoice in finding difference and similarity in one another.

But there is another moment in the globalization of sociology, and indeed of globalization in general, namely that, whatever differences there are between our cultures, there are supervening issues that affect the human future on this earth. Both climate change and nuclear security are challenges that require cooperation across all boundaries.

Whatever the unity sociology has found *in and through* diversity, it now has to find unity *beyond* diversity in facing the global challenges. This is what animated my concern 'to respect all peoples as potential sources of wisdom for our own time. Already the Global Age is the first period in human history when both sexes and all peoples have gone a considerable way towards asserting their equal right to make their contribution to the common stock of human knowledge.'[39]

In the 1980s the problem of how we understand one another was uppermost in our drive to globalize sociology. Since then, the need to cooperate to solve global challenges has become a more urgent priority. We cannot dwell forever on the problems of understanding one another before we work together in a common cause. In that sense, achieving an understanding adequate for the challenges facing humankind collectively is a proper ambition for sociology in our times. That has to be the main thrust of a globalized sociology today, and I am as confident of Chinese sociologists as of any national body of sociologists that they will be major contributors to that joint endeavour.

---

[39] Albrow 1996, p. 6.

DOI https://doi.org/10.24103/GCSS.en.2018.22

References

Adair-Toteff, Christopher. 2013. `Sinn der Welt: Max Weber and the Problem of Theodicy'. *Max Weber Studies* 13.1: 87-107.

Albrow, Martin.

    1975. 'Legal Positivism and Bourgeois Materialism: Max Weber's View of the Sociology of Law'. *British Journal of Law and Society* 2.1: 14-31.

    1987a. 'The Application of the Weberian Concept of Rationalization to Contemporary Conditions'. In Sam Whimster and Scott Lash eds. *Max Weber, Rationality and Modernity*, pp. 164-182.

    1987b. 'Sociology for One World'. *International Sociology* 2: 1–12.

    1990. *Max Weber's Construction of Social Theory.* London: Macmillan.

    1991. 'Internationalism as a Publication Project: Experience in Editing an International Sociological Journal'. *Current Sociology* 39: 101–118.

    1996. *The Global Age: State and Society beyond Modernity.* Cambridge: Polity.

    1998. Obituary: 'Elizabeth King, 1949–1998'. *International Sociology* 13: 517–518.

    1999a. *Sociology: The Basics.* London: Routledge.

    1999b. 'The Position of the Moderns in Conditions of Globality'. In Gert Schmidt and Rainer Trinczek eds. *Globalisierung*, pp. 551-564.

    2004. *The Global Age: State and Society beyond Modernity,* Chinese edition.

    2007. 'Unfinished work: The Career of a European Sociologist'. In Mathieu Deflem ed. *Sociologists in a Global Age: Biographical Perspectives.* Aldershot: Ashgate pp.15–28 (also in Chinese).

    2014a. *Global Age Essays on Social and Cultural Change.* Klostermann: Frankfurt-am-Main.

    2014b. 'Globalization or Americanization: The Fate of European Culture'. In *Global Age Essays on Social and Cultural Change,* pp.177-188.

    2015. Speech 'The Architectonic of Ideas - *Xi Jinping: The Governance of China'*, 15 April Global China Press, http://ccpn-global.com/cms.php?articl=1071.

    2016. (in Chinese) 'Bridging the Divides – China's Role in a Fragmenting world', 《弥合分岐——中国在分化世界中的角色》 *Global Communication.*

Albrow, Martin and King, Elizabeth eds. 1990. *Globalization, Knowledge and Society.* London: Sage.

Albrow, Martin and Zhang Xiaoying. 2014. 'Weber and the Concept of Adaptation: the Case of Confucian Ethics'. *Max Weber Studies* 14.2: 199-226.

Anderson, Benedict. 1983. *Imagined Communities: Reflections on the Origins and Spread of Nationalism.*

Andreski, Stanislav. 1984. *Max Weber's Insights and Errors.* London: Routledge.

Archer, Margaret. 1988. *Culture and Agency. The Place of Culture in Social Theory.* Cambridge: Cambridge University Press.

Archer, Margaret. 1991. Presidential Address: 'Sociology for One World: Unity and Diversity.' *International Sociology* 6: 131–147

Arnold, Mattthew. 1869. *Culture and Anarchy.* London: Smith, Elder & Co.

Barbalet, Jack. 2008. *Weber, Passion and Profits: The Protestant Ethic and the Spirit of Capitalism in Context.* Cambridge: Cambridge University Press.

Barbalet, Jack. 2014 forthcoming. 'The Religion of China and the Prospects of Chinese Capitalism' in *The Anthem Companion to Max Weber*, ed. Alan Sica. 28pp. London: Anthem Press.

Barr, Michael. 2011. *Who's Afraid of China? The Challenge of China's Soft Power.* London and New York: Zed Books.

Baumgarten, Eduard. 1964. *Max Weber: Werk und Person.* Tübingen: Mohr.

BBC This World: After Brexit – the Battle for Europe. BBC2 TV broadcast, 9 February17.

Beck, Ulrich. 1992 [1986]. *Risk Society: Towards a New Modernity.* London: Sage.

Beck, Ulrich. 2000. *What is Globalization?* Cambridge: Polity.

Beetham, David. 1974. *Max Weber and the Theory of Modern Politics.* London: Allen and Unwin.

Bell, Daniel. 1973. *The Coming of Post-Industrial Society.* New York: Basic Books,

Bendix, Reinhard. 1960. *Max Weber: An Intellectual Portrait.* London: Heinemann.

Bertaux, Daniel. 1990. 'Designing the Worldwide Competition'. *International Sociology* 5: 373–378.

Boese, Franz. 1939. Geschichte des Vereins für Sozialpolitik. Munich: Duncker and Humblot.

Cardoso, Fernando. 1986. 'Foreword'. *International Sociology* 1: 1–2.

Caruana, Louis. 2008. 'The Jesuits and the Quiet Side of the Scientific Revolution'. In

Castells, Manuel. 1996. *The Rise of the Network Society.* Oxford: Blackwell.

Chan Hoiman. 1993. 'Some Metasociological Notes on the Sinicization of Sociology'. *International Sociology* 8: 113–119.

Channing, William E. 1870. *Complete Works.* London: George Routledge.

The Cambridge Companion to the Jesuits, ed. Thomas Worcester, 243-62.

Chang, Xiangqun. 2010. *Guanxi or Li shang wanglai? Reciprocity, Social Support Networks, & Social Creativity in a Chinese Village.* Taipei: Airiti Press.

Chen, Liangjin. 1990. 'Social Developmental Mechanisms and Social Security Functions'. *International Sociology* 5: 89–100. (First published in *Shehuixue Yanjiu (Sociological Studies)* 1987, Vol. 2, No 1: 85–91.)

China, Government of. 1987. Leaflet 'Family Planning Program in China 1987'. Beijing: State Family Planning Commission.

Clinton, President Bill. 2000. Speech at the University of Nebraska, 8 December.

Collins, Randall. 1986. *Weberian Sociological Theory.* Cambridge: Cambridge Uuniversity Press

Commager, Henry S. 1950. *The American Mind.* New Haven and London: Yale University Press.

Confucius. 2007. *The Analects of Confucius.* Annotated by Cheng Changming. Huhhot: Yuanfang Press, pp. 107, 202.

Corry, Olaf. 2013. *Constructing the Global Polity: Theory, Discourse and Governance.* London: Palgrave Macmillan.

Dai, Kejing. 1991. 'The Life Experience and Status of Chinese Rural Women from Observation of Three Age Groups'. *International Sociology* 6: 5–24.

Dai, Kejing. 1993a. 'The Vicissitudes of Sociology in China'. *International Sociology* 8: 92–100.

Dai, Kejing. 1993b. Portrait: 'Fei Xiaotong 1910–'. *International Sociology* 8: 239–246.

Darmon, Isobel. 2011. 'No "new spirit"? Max Weber's account of the dynamic of contemporary capitalism through "pure adaptation" and the shaping of adequate subjects'. *Max Weber Studies.* 11.2: 193-216.

Darwin, Charles. 1859 [1928]. *The Origin of Species.* London: Dent

Davis, Aeron. 2013. 'Applying a Weberian Perspective to the Analysis of UK Journalism: Hacking and Leveson as Products of Organizational Rationalization'. *Max Weber Studies* 13.2: 176-196.

Dewey, John, 1929. *Characters and Events.* New York: Henry Holt.

Dilthey, Wilhelm. 1958. *Gesammelte Schriften Vol. VII, Der Aufbau der Geschichtlichen Welt in den Geisteswissenschaten.* Stuttgart: Teubner and Göttingen: Vandenhoenck & Ruprecht.

Eisenstadt,Schmuel. 1983. 'Innerweltlich Transzendenz und die Stukturierung der Welt. Max Webers Studie über China und die Gestalt der Chinesischen Zivilization.' In Wolfgang Schluchter ed. *Max Webers Studie über Konfuzianismus und Taoismus,* pp. 363-411.

Eisenstadt, Schmuel. 1984. 'Die Paradoxie von Zivilizationen mit außerweltlichen Orientierungen: Überlegungen zu Max Webers Studie über Hinduismus und Buddhismus.' In Wolfgang Schluchter ed. *Max Webers Studie über Hinduismus und Buddhismus,* pp 333-352.

Engisch, Karl Bernhard Pfister and Johannes Wickelmann, eds. 1996. *Max Weber: Gedächtnisschrift der Ludwig-Maximilians-Universität München zur Wiederkehr seines Geburtstages 1964.* Berlin: Duncker & Humblot.

Etzioni, Amitai. 2004. *From Empire to Community*. New York: Palgrave Macmillan.

Feng Youlan. 2006. *The History of Chinese Philosophy*. Beijing: Commercial Press.

Fischer, H. Karl. 1907. 'Kritische Beiträge zu Professor Max Webers Abhandlung "Die Protestantische Ethik und der Geist des Kapitalismus,,'. *Archiv für Sozialwissenschaft und Sozialpolitik* 25.1: 232-42. In 1972 *Die Protestantische Ethik. II Kritiken und Antikritiken*, ed. Johannes Winckelmann, 11-26.

Fischer, H. Karl. 1908. 'Protestantische Ethik und "Geist des Kapitalismus,,. Replik auf Herrn Professor Max Webers Gegenkritik'. *Archiv für Sozialwissenschaft und Sozialpolitik* 26.1: 270-74. In 1972 *Die Protestantische Ethik. II Kritiken und Antikritiken*, ed. Johannes Winckelmann, pp. 38-43.

Fortescue, Chief Justice Sir John. 1885. Edited by Charles Plummer. *The Governance of England, otherwise called The Difference between and Absolute and a Limited Monarchy*. Oxford. Clarendon Press.

Francke, Herbert. 1996. 'Max Weber's Soziologie der ostasiatischen Religionen'. In Karl Engisch et al. *Max Weber: Gedächtnisschrift*. Pp. 115-130.

Franke, Herbert. 1966. 'Max Webers Soziologie der ostasiastischen Religionen'. In *Max Weber. Gedächtnisschrift der Ludwig Maximilians Universität München*, eds. Karl Engisch, Bernhard Pfister and Johannes Winckelmann, pp.115-130.

Friedman. Thomas L. 1999. *The Lexus and the Olive Tree*. New York: Farrar, Strauss and Giroux.

Fu Peirong. 2010. Expounding on the Concept of Tian in Confucianism and Taoism. Beijing: Beijing Book Press.

Fukuyama, Francis. 1992. *The End of History and the Last Man*. New York: The Free Press.

Gabriel, Markus. 2013. *Warum es die Welt nicht Gibt*. Berlin: Ullstein.

Giddens, Anthony. 1998. *The Third Way*. Cambridge: Polity.

Giddens, Anthony. 1999. *Runaway World*. Cambridge: Polity.

Goethe, Johann Wolfgang. 1949. *Gedenkausgabe der Werke, Briefe und Gespräche*. Ed. Ernst Beutler. Zürich: Artemis.

Goldman, Harvey. 1988. *Max Weber and Thomas Mann*. Berkeley: University of California Press.

Gonzales Garcia, José M. 2011. 'Max Weber, Goethe and Rilke: The Magic of Language and Music in a Disenchanted World'. *Max Weber Studies* 11.2: 267-88.

Gransow, Bettina. 1993. 'Chinese Sociology: Sinicization and Globalization'. *International Sociology* 8: 101–112.

Groot, J. J. M. de. 1918. *Universismus: Die Grundlage der Religion und Ethik, des Staatswesens und der Wissenschaften Chinas*. Berlin: Georg Reimer.

Groot. J.J.M. de. 1910. *The Religion of the Chinese*. New York: Macmillan.

Habermas, Jürgen, 1986/87. *The Theory of Communicative Action*. 2 vols. Cambridge: Polity.

Han, Qi. 1998. Bai Jin De Yi Jing Yan Jiu He Kang Xi Shi Dai De "Xi Xue Zhong Yuan" Shuo (Joachim Bouvet's Study on Yi Jing and the Theory of Western Culture Being of Chinese Origin in Kangxi Period), *Han Xue Yan Jiu* (*The Study of Sinology*), No. 1.

Hawthorne, Nathaniel. [1850] 2000. *The Scarlet Letter*. New York: Modern Library.

He, Fangchuan, ed. 2008, *Zhong Wai Wen Hua Jiao Liu Shi* (*A History of Cultural Exchange between China and Foreign Countries*), Book I--II, Beijing: China International Culture Press Limited.

Hegedus, Zsusza. 1989. 'Social Movements and Social Change in Self-Creative Society: New Civil Initiatives in the International Arena'. *International Sociology* 4: 19–36.

Heidegger, Martin. 1976 [1927]. Sein und Zeit. Frankfurt: Klostermann.

Hodges, H.A. 1944. *Wilhelm Dilthey: An Introduction*, London: Kegan Paul.

Honigsheim, Paul. 1963. `Erinnerungen an Max Weber'. In René König and Johannes Winckelmann eds. *Max Weber zum Gedächtnis*, pp. 161-271. Köln and Opladen: Westdeutscher Verlag.

Hsia, Adrian. 2000. `Das Chinesien bei Leibniz und Max Weber', in Li Wenchao and Hans Poser eds. Das Neueste über China: G.W. Leibnizens Novissima Sinica von 1697, pp. 345-358.

Hu Zhihong and Ding Sixin. 2006. On China and the West -- Interview with Professor Roger T. Ames. *The History of Chinese Philosophy*. No. 4, pp112-119.

Huntington, Samuel. 1996. *Clash of Civilizations and the Remaking of World Order.* New York: Simon and Schuster

Huntington, Samuel. 2004. *Who Are We? America's Great Debate.* New York: Simon & Schuster.

Jacques, Martin. 1993. 'Politicians Stand Still While the World Moves On'. *The Times,* 4 October.

Jacques, Martin. 2012. *When China Rules the World.* London: Penguin.

Jaspers, Karl. 1932. *Philosophische Weltorientierung,* Berlin: Springer.

Jaspers, Karl. 1953. *Einführung in die Philosophie.* Munich: Piper.

Kalberg, Stephen. 1994. *Max Weber's Comparative-Historical Sociology.* Cambridge: Polity.

Kalberg, Stephen. 2012. *Max Weber's Comparative-Historical Sociology Today*. Farnham and Burlington: Ashgate.

Kant, Immanuel 1983. Ed. Ted Humphrey. *Perpetual Peace and Other Essays.* Indianapolis: Hackett.

Lao Tzu. 2013. *The Book of Tao and Teh.* Translated and Annotated by Gu Zhengkun. Beijing: China Translation and Publishing Corporation, p. 121.

Lévi-Strauss, Claude. 1966. *The Savage Mind.* London: Weidenfeld and Nicolson.

Levitt, Theodore. 1983. 'The Globalization of Markets'. *Harvard Business Review*, May-June, 92-102.

Lewin, Kurt. 1951. *Field Theory in Social Science: Selected Theoretical Papers.* New York: Harper Row.

Li Lulu. 1989. 'Theoretical Theses on "Social Modernization"'. *International Sociology* 4: 365–377. (First published in *Shehuixue Yanjiu* (Sociological Studies) 1987, 2, 3: 105–112.)

Li Lulu, Yang Xiao and Wang Fengyu. 1991. 'The Structure of Social Stratification and the Modernization Process in Contemporary China'. *International Sociology* 6: 25–36.

Li Wenchao and Hans Poser eds. 2000. *Das Neueste über China: G.W. Leibnizens Novissima Sinica von 1697.* Stuttgart: Franz Steiner.

Li Tusheng. 2009. *Tusheng Shuo Zi (Tusheng's Study on Chinese Characters).* Beijing: Central Documentary Press.

Lin Yutang. 2009. *The Wisdom of Confucius.* Beijing: Foreign Language and Teaching Press.

Lippmann, Walter. 1955. *The Public Philosophy.* London: Hamish Hamilton.

Löwith, Karl. 1982. *Max Weber and Karl Marx.* London: Allen & Unwin.

Lu Jianhua. 1991. 'Chinese Workers' High Expectations of Enterprise Managers'. *International Sociology* 5: 37–49.

Luhmann, Niklas. 1998. *Die Gesellschaft der Gesellschaft. 2 vols.* Frankfurt am Main: Suhrkamp.

MacIntyre, Alasdair. 1967. *A Short History of Ethics.* London: Routledge & Kegan Paul.

Metzger, Thomas. 1983. 'Max Webers Analyse der Konfuzianische Tradition: Eine Kritik'. In Wolfgang Schluchter ed. *Max Webers Studie* über Konfuzianismus und Taoismus, pp. 229-270.

Modelski, George. 1972. *The Principles of World Politics.* New York: The Free Press.

Molloy, Stephen. 1980. 'Max Weber and the Religions of China: Any Way out of the Maze?', *British Journal of Sociology* 31.3: 377-400.

Mommsen, Wolfgang J. 1984. *Max Weber and German Politics 1890-1920.* Chicago: Chicago University Press.

Mommsen, Wolfgang J. and Jürgen Osterhammel eds. 1987. *Max Weber and his Contemporaries.* London: German Historical Institute and Allen & Unwin.

Mungello, D.E. 1989. *Curious Land: Jesuits' Accommodation and the Origin of Sinology.* Honolulu: University of Hawaii Press.

Münsterberg, Hugo. 1900. *Grundzüge der Psychologie I.* Leipzig: Barth.

Münsterberg, Hugo. 1904. *The Americans.* New York: McClure, Phillips.

Münsterberg, Hugo. 1909. *The Eternal Values.* Boston and New York: Houghton Mifflin.

Nankai University, Investigation Group of. 1989. 'Report on Nationwide Demand for Sociology Graduates during the Period of the Seventh Five-Year Plan'. *International Sociology* 4: 393–418. (First published in *Shehuixue Yanjiu* (Sociological Studies) 1987, 2,4: 21–35.)

Ning, Fang, 2014. *China's Democracy Path.* Beijing: China Social Sciences Press.

Nye, Joseph. 2005. *Soft Power: The Means to Success in World Politics,*

OECD (Organization for Economic Cooperation and Development). 1993. *STI Review, Special Issue on Globalization).*

Ohmae, Kenichi. 1994. *The End of the Nation-State.* New York: The Free Press.

Ortiz, Fernando.1951. *Los Bailes y el Teatro de los Negros en el Folklore de Cuba.* Havana: Cardenas y Cia.

Pan Jianxiong. 1990. 'The Dual Structure of Chinese Culture and its Influence on Modern Chinese Society.' *International Sociology* 5: 75–88. (First published in *Shehuixue Yanjiu* (Sociological Studies) 1987, 3,1: 88–96.

Parsons, Talcott. 1937. *The Structure of Social Action.* New York: McGraw Hill.

Parsons. Talcott. 1951. *The Social System.* London: Routledge.

Parsons, Talcott. 1960. *Structure and Process in Modern Societies,* Glencoe, Ill: The Free Press. Parsons. Talcott. 1951. *The Social System.* London: Routledge.

Parsons, Talcott. 1965. 'Introduction' in Max Weber, *The Sociology of Religion.* London: Methuen xix-lxvii.

Peel, J.D.Y. 1971. *Herbert Spencer: The Evolution of a Sociologist.* London: Heinemann.

Pfister, Bernhard. 1966. '*Max Weber: Persönlichkeit und Werk*'. In Karl Engisch et al. *Max Weber: Gedächtnisschrift*, pp. 5-26.

Pleyers, Geoffrey. 2010. *Alter-Globalization: Becoming Actors in the Global Age.* Cambridge: Polity.

Qi, Xiaoying. 2014. *Globalized Knowledge Flows and Chinese Social Theory.* New York and Abingdon: Routledge.

Qiao Gensuo, Wei Dong and Xu Dongming. 2012. *The Study of the Philosophical Thinking of Tibetan and Han Buddhism.Shanghai*: Ancient Books Press, p. 56.

Radin, Paul. 1957 [1927]. *Primitive Man as Philosopher.* New York: Dover.

Radkau, Joachim. 2009. *Max Weber: A Biography.* Cambridge: Polity.

Ritzer, George. 1993. *The McDonaldization of Society.* Newbury Park, CA: Pine Forge Press.

Ritzer, George. 2007. 'A New "Global Age", but Are There New Perspectives on it'? In Ino Rossi, ed., *Frontiers of Globalization Research: Theoretical and Methodological Approaches.* New York: Springer, pp. 361-369.

Robertson, Roland. 1992, *Globalization: Social Theory and Global Culture.* London: Sage.

Roth, Guenther and Wolfgang Schluchter. 1979. *Max Weber's Vision of History: Ethics and Methods.* Berkeley: University of California.

Roth, Günther. 1999. 'Max Weber und der globale Kapitalismus damals und heute'. In Gert Schmidt and Rainer Trinczek eds. *Globalisierung*, pp. 29-40.

Runciman, W.G. 2001. 'Was Weber a Selectionist in Spite of Himself?' *Journal of Classical Sociology.* 1,1: 13-32.

Russell, Bertrand. 1938. *Power: A New Social Analysis,* 1938

Russell, Bertrand. 1945. *A History of Western Philosophy.* New York: Simon and Schuster.

Scaff, Lawrence A. 1989. *Fleeing the Iron Cage: Culture and Modernity in the Thought of Max Weber.* Berkeley: University of California.

Schluchter, Wolfgang, ed. 1983. *Max Webers Studie über Konfuzianismus und Taoismus.* Frankfurt am Main: Suhrkamp.

Schluchter, Wolfgang, ed. 1984. *Max Webers Studie über Hinduismus und Buddhismus.* Frankfurt am Main: Suhrkamp.

Schluchter, Wolfgang. 1983. 'Einleitung Max Webers Konfuzianismusstudie – Versuch eine Einordnung'. In Wolfgang Schluchter ed. *Max Webers Studie über Konfuzianismus und Taoismus*, Frankfurt am Main: Suhrkamp, pp. 11-54.

Schluchter, Wolfgang. 1984. 'Max Webers Religionssoziologie. Eine werkgeschichtliche Rekonstruktion'. *Kölner Zeitschrift für Soziologie und Sozialpsychologie* 36: 342 .

Schluchter, Wolfgang. 1985. *The Rise of Western Rationalism: Max Weber's Developmental History.* Berkeley: University of California.

Schluchter, Wolfgang. 2014. '"How Ideas become Effective in History": Max Weber on Confucianism and Beyond'. *Max Weber Studies* 14.1: 9-29.

Schmidt-Glintzer, Helwig and Petra Kolonko. 1989. 'Editorisches Bericht'. In Max Weber, *Die Wirtschaftsethik der Weltreligionen, Konfuzianismus und Taoismus: Schriften 1915-20*, 31-73.

Schmidt, Gert and Rainer Trinczek eds. 1999. *Globalisierung, Soziale Welt Sonderband* 13, Baden-Baden: Nomos.

Schroeder, Ralph. 1992. *Max Weber and the Sociology of Culture*. London: Sage.

Schütz, Alfred. 1932, *Der Sinnhafte Aufbau der Sozialen Welt*, Vienna: Springer.

Smith, Adam. 1790[1979]. *The Theory of Moral Sentiments*. Indianapolis: Liberty Fund.

Smith, Adam. 1868 [1776]. *The Wealth of Nations*, London: Nelson.

Smith, Arthur H. 1894. *Chinese Characteristics*. New York: Fleming H. Revell.

Sombart, Werner. 1976 [1906]. *Why Is There no Socialism in the United States?* White Plains, NY: International Arts and Sciences Press.

Sprenkel, Sybille van der. 1956. 'A Sociological Analysis of Chinese Legal Institutions with Special Reference to the Ch'ing Period, 1644-1911'. Unpublished M.Sc. (Econ) thesis, University of London.

Standaert, Nicolas. 2008. 'Jesuits in China'. In Thomas Worcester ed. *The Cambridge Companion to the Jesuits*, pp. 169-85.

Sumner, W.G. 1906. *Folkways*. New York: Ginn.

Sztompka, Piotr. 1988. 'Conceptual Frameworks in Comparative Inquiry: Divergent or Convergent?' *International Sociology* 3: 207–218.

Tenbruck, Friedrich H. 1980. 'The Problem of Thematic Unity in the Works of Max Weber'. *British Journal of Sociology* 31.3: 316-351.

Toynbee, Arnold. 1935. *A Study of History, Vol. 1*. London: Oxford University Press.

Toynbee, Arnold. 1966. *Change and Habit: The Challenge of our Time*. New York: Oxford University Press.

Tu, Weiming. 1983. 'Die Neo-Konfuzianische Ontologie'. In Wolfgang Schluchter ed. *Max Webers Studie über Konfuzianismus und Taoismus*, pp. 271-297.

Turner, Bryan. S. 2007. 'The Enclave Society: Towards a Sociology of Immobility', *European Journal of Social Theory* 10.2: 287-303.

Voltaire, François-Marie Arouet. 2005 [1759].*Candide, or Optimism*. Translated and edited by Theo Cuffe. London: Penguin.

Wang, Yiwei. 2016. *The Belt and Road Initiative. What Will China Offer the World in its Rise?* Beijing: New World Press.

Weber, Marianne. 1926. *Max Weber: Ein Lebensbild*. Tübingen: Mohr (Siebeck).

Weber, Marianne. 1975. *Max Weber: a Biography*. New York: Wiley.

Weber, Max.

1895. 'Der Nationalstaat und die Volkswirtschaftspolitik'. In 1958. *Gesammelte Politische Schriften*. 1-25. In Whimster Collected Methodological Writings, translated and edited by H.H. Bruun and S. Whimster [referred to as 'Freiburg Inaugural'].

1904/5. 'Die protestantische Ethik und der Geist des Kapitalismus', *Archiv für Sozialwissenschaft und Sozialpolitik* [ASwSp] 20.1: 1-54; 21.1:1-110 [referred to as 'early PE'].

1907/8a. 'Kritische Bemerkungen zu den vorstehenden Kritischen Beiträgen', *Archiv für Sozialwissenschaft und Sozialpolitik* 25.1: 243-49. In 1972 *Die Protestantische Ethik. II Kritiken und Antikritiken*, ed. Johannes Winckelmann, 27-37.

b. 'Bemerkungen zu den vorstehenden "Replik"', *Archiv für Sozialwissenschaft und Sozialpolitik* 26.1: 275-283. In 1972 *Die Protestantische Ethik. II Kritiken und Antikritiken*, ed. Johannes Winckelmann, 44-56 [referred to as 'Fischer debate'].

1908/9a. 'Methodologische Erhebungen über Auslese und Anpassung (Berufswahl und Berufsschicksal) der Arbeiterschaft der geschlossenen Großindustrie' (Printed manuscript), In 1924, *Gesammelte Aufsätze zur Soziologie und Sozialpolitik*, 1-60.

b. 'Zur Psychophysik der industriellen Arbeit', *Archiv für Sozialwissenschaft und Sozialpolitik* 27.3: 730-70; 28.1: 219-77, 3:719-61; 29.2 513-42. In 1924, *Gesammelte Aufsätze zur Sociologie und Sozialpolitik,* 109-255 [referred to as 'Workforce studies'].

1913a. 'Ueber einige Kategorien der verstehenden Soziologie', *Logos* 4.3: 253-94. In 1968 *Gesammelte Aufsätze zur Wissenschaftslehre.* Tübingen: J. C. B. Mohr. 427-74. Translated in 2012 *Collected Methodological Writings,* ed. H.H. Bruun and Sam Whimster, 273-301 [referred to as Sociological Categories].

1913b. Manuscript of 'Äußerungen zur Werturteilsdiskussion im Ausschuß des Vereins für Sozialpolitik'. In Eduard Baumgarten. 1964. *Max Weber: Werk und Person,* 102-39 [referred to as Value Judgment Paper]. (Expanded in 1917).

1916 'Die Wirtschaftsethik der Weltreligionen. Religionssoziologische Skizzen' (The Economic Ethics of World Religions. Sociology of Religion Sketches) in *Archiv für Sozialwissenschaft und Sozialpolitik* 41, 1916 [referred to as WeWr1].

(a) 'Einleitung'. *Archiv für Sozialwissenschaft und Sozialpolitik* 41.1: 1-29. As amended in 1920 GARS1 and translated in 1948 *From Max Weber* as 'The Social Psychology of World Religions', pp. 367-301. [Referred to as Introduction (1915a)]

(b) 'Die soziologischen Grundlagen'. *Archiv für Sozialwissenschaft und Sozialpolitik* 41.1: 30-67. As amended in 1920 GARS1 and translated in 1951 *The Religion of China* [Referred to here as early Confucianism Studies (1915b)].

(c) 'Der "Geist" der konfuzianischen Bildung und die Wirtschaft', *Archiv für Sozialwissenschaft und Sozialpolitik* 41.1: 68- 87. Amended in 1920 GARS1 and translated in 1951 *The Religion of China* [Referred to here as early Confucianism Studies (1915c)].

(d) 'Orthodoxie und Heterodoxie in ihren sozialethischen Wirkungen', *Archiv für Sozialwissenschaft und Sozialpolitik* 41.2: 335-371. Amended in 1920 GARS1 and translated in 1951 *The Religion of China* [Referred to here as early Confucianism Studies (1915d)].

(e) 'Zusammenfassung. Konfuzianismus und Puritanismus', *Archiv für Sozialwissenschaft und Sozialpolitik* 41.2: 372-386. Amended in 1920 GARS1 and translated in 1951 *The Religion of China* [Referred to here as Conclusion of early Confucianism Studies (1915e)].

(f) 'Zwischenbetrachtung: Stufen und Richtungen der religiöser Weltablehnung'. *Archiv für Sozialwissenschaft und Sozialpolitik* 41.2: 387-421. Amended in 1920 GARS1 and translated in 1948. *From Max Weber,* ed H.H. Gerth and C. Wright Mills as 'Religious Rejections of the World and Their Directions' 323-362 [Referred to as Intermediate Reflections (1915f)].

1917. 'Der Sinn der "Wertfreiheitt,, der soziologischen und ökonomischen Wissenschaften'. *Logos: Internationale Zeitschrift für Philosophie der Kultur* 7.1: 40-88. In 1968 *Gesammelte Aufsätze zur Wissenschaftslehre* pp. 489-539. Translated in 2012 H. H. Bruun and Sam Whimster eds. *Collected Methodological Writings,* pp. 304-334 [Referred to as Value Freedom article].

1920. *Gesammelte Aufsätze zur Religionssoziologie.* Vol. 1. Tübingen: J. C. B. Mohr. Vol. 1. [Referred to as GARS1].

1921. *Gesammelte Aufsätze zur Religionssoziologie.* Vol. 2. *Hinduismus und Buddhismus.* Tübingen: J. C. B. Mohr. [Referred to as GARS2].

1923. *Wirtschaftsgeschichte.* S. Hellman and M. Palyi eds. Munich and Leipzig: Duncker & Humblot.

1924. *Gesammelte Aufsätze zur Soziologie und Sozialpolitik.* Tübingen: J. C. B. Mohr.

1948. *From Max Weber.* Eds. H. H. Gerth and C. Wright Mills. London: Routledge.

1951. *The Religion of China: Confucianism and Taoism.* Translated and edited by Hans H. Gerth. Glencoe, Ill: Free Press.

1956a. *Wirtschaft und Gesellschaft* 4th ed. 2 Vols Tübingen: J. C. B. Mohr. Translated G. Roth and C. Wittich 1978, *Economy and Society.*

1956b. *Wirtschaft und Gesellschaft* 4th ed. Tübingen: J. C. B. Mohr. Ch 5 'Typen religiöser Vergemeinschaftung (Religionssoziologie)'. Pp 245-381 [referred to as Sociology of Religion].

1958a. *Gesammelte Politische Schriften.* Tübingen: J. C. B. Mohr.

1958b. *The Religion of India: The Sociology of Hinduism and Buddhism.* Translated and edited by Hans H. Gerth and Don Martindale. New York: The Free Press

1961. *General Economic History.* Translated by Frank H. Knight. New York: Collier Books.

1968. *Gesammelte Aufsätze zur Wissenschaftslehre.* Tübingen: J. C. B. Mohr.

1972 *Die Protestantische Ethik. II Kritiken und Antikritiken.* Ed. Johannes Winckelmann. Hamburg: Siebenstern.

1976. *The Protestant Ethic and the Spirit of Capitalism.* London: Allen & Unwin.

1978. *Economy and Society.* Edited and translated by G. Roth and C. Wittich. Berkeley: University of California.

1989. *Die Wirtschaftsethik der Weltreligionen Konfuzianismus und Taoismus: Schriften 1915-20.* Edited with an introduction by Helwig Schmidt-Glintzer and Petra Kolonko. *Max Weber Gesamtausgabe* 19/1.Tübingen: J. C. B. Mohr.

2003. *Ru Jiao Yu Dao Jiao (Confucianism and Daoism).* Translated by Wang Rongfen. The Commercial Press.

2009. *The Protestant Ethic and the Spirit of Capitalism with Other Writings on the Rise of the West.* Translated and introduced by Stephen Kalberg. New York: Oxford University Press.

2012a. *Collected Methodological Writings.* Edited by Hans Henrik Bruun and Sam Whimster. London: Routledge.

2012b. *Confucianism and Taoism.* Translated by Wang Rongfen. Beijing: Central Translation Press.

Whimster, Sam and Scott Lash, eds. 1987. *Max Weber, Rationality and Modernity.* London: Allen & Unwin.

White House Press Office, 2017. 'Remarks by President Trump to the People of Poland', 6 July.

Winckelmann, Johannes, ed. 1972. *Die Protestantische Ethik. II Kritiken und Antikritiken.* Hamburg: Siebenstern.

Worcester, Thomas ed. 2008. *The Cambridge Companion to the Jesuits.* Cambridge: Cambridge University Press.

Xi Jinping. 2014. *Xi Jinping: The Governance of China.* Beijing: Foreign Languages Press.

Xi Jinping. 2016. 'Speech at the Symposium of Social Sciences', Xinhua, http://news.xinhuanet.com/politics/2016-05/18/c/_1118891128.htm.

Xi Jinping, 2017. Speech: 'Jointly Shoulder Responsibility of Our Times, Promote Global Growth', Davos, 17 January.

Xi Jinping. 2017. Speech 'Work Together to Build a Community of Shared Future for Mankind', Geneva, 18 January.

Ye Kelin, Zou Nongjian and Ye Nanke. 1989. 'The Establishment of Market Town Sociology with Chinese Characteristics.' *International Sociology* 4: 379–392. (First published in *Shehuixue Yanjiu (Sociological Studies)* 1987, 2, 2: 36–43.)

Ye Ren Chang. 2003. 'Dong Ya Jing Ji Lun Li De Cheng Qing Yu Bian Si: Weber, Ru Jia Yu Ji Du Xin Jiao' ('Clarification and Thoughts on East Asia's Economic Ethics: Weber, Confucianism and Protestantism'). *Solitudo,* 3. Taipei.

Yu, Shou, 2015. 'Universal Dream, National Dreams and Symbiotic Dream: Reflections on Transcultural Generativity in China-Europe Encounters'. *Journal of China in Comparative Perspective* 1, 1: 44-81, 201-227.

Yu Yingshi 1987. *Zhong Guo Jin Shi Zong Jiao Lun Li Yu Shang Re Jing Shen (Religious Ethics and Entrepreneurial Spirit in China's Modern Times).* Taipei: Taiwai Lian Jing Press.

Zhang Xiaoying and Martin Albrow. 2016. 'Max Weber, China and the World: in Search of Trans-cultural Communication'. *Journal of China in Comparative Perspective* 2.1:31-53.

Zhang Xiping. 2009. *Ou Zhou Zao Qi Han Xue Shi* (A History of Early Sinology in Europe), Bei-jing: Publishing House of China.

Zhang, Joy Y. and Michael Barr. 2013. *Green Politics in China.* London: Pluto.

Zhao Qizheng. 2012. *The Wisdom of Public Diplomacy: Cross Border Dialogues,*

Zhao Tingyang. 2011. *The Tianxia System: An Introduction to the Philosophy of World Institution.* The People's University Press. pp. 27-30.

Zhou Shan. 2002. *The Interpretation of the Yi Jing.* Shanghai: Shanghai Bookstore Publishing House, p. 261.

Zhu Xi. 2011. *The Analects of Zhu Zi, Book IV.* Edited by Li Jingde. Beijing: Beijing Book Press.

Zhuang Zi. 2004. Zhuang Zi, annotated by Lei Zhongkang. Huhhot: Yuanfang Press, p. 12.

DOI https://doi.org/10.24103/GCSS.en.2018.23

Publication History with Abstracts

Chapter One
The architectonic of ideas – *Xi Jinping: The Governance of China*

This is the speaking text for the ceremonial book launch of *Xi Jinping: The Governance of China* (Foreign Languages Press, Beijing, 2014) held at the Chinese Embassy, London, on 15 April 2015. It was published in *Transculturality and the New Global Governance*, edited by Xiangqun Chang and Costanza Pernigotti, Global China Press, London, 2016, pp. 149-151.

Three lessons are drawn from Xi's book of speeches: to understand the present we have to embrace the past; he shows how much we should value systematic thought in political leadership; the world can come together in the idea of global governances

Chapter Two
Philosophical social science as a bridge from 'Belt and Road' to global governance

This paper is the full version of a text prepared as the basis for a presentation to the Chinese Academy of Social Science Symposium on China Studies, 23-29 October 2016, Beijing. I am grateful for their generous assistance to the hosts the Academy (CASS) and the Ministry of Culture MOC of the PRC, and to the conference organizers, the Centre of International Cultural Exchange (CICE). The final shorter version that was delivered at the Symposium has appeared in the *Collected Works at the Symposium on China Studies*, 2016, Chinese Academy of Social Sciences, Beijing, 2017, pp. 11-22.

Abstract: 'Belt and Road' is the most ambitious project yet to link the peaceful development of China with the prosperity and well-being of the world as a whole. But it runs the risk of being regarded as the Chinese equivalent to American globalization. Western globalization as discourse combines story, strategy and ideology: The *story*, the advance of civilization; the *strategy*, going global; the *ideology*, liberal democracy.

'Belt and Road' will require the equivalent intellectual creativity to that which built the response to globalization in the West. China's 'Belt and Road' discourse: *story,* 2000 years of cultural encounters; *strategy*, the Chinese dream; *ideology,* socialism with Chinese characteristics. Every country responds from its own culture to the common challenges that mark out the Global Age.

A community of common destiny must become a transcultural concept, belonging to none, shared by all. Philosophical social science and empirical social research must join together in contributing to the pragmatic universalism of the new global governance. In *Xi Jinping: The Governance of China* we find a model of applied theory that can serve as an example of what is needed for an account of global governance.

Keywords: philosophical social science, 'Belt and Road', globalization, discourse, creativity, global governance, Global Age, culture, ideology, liberal democracy, Third Way, the Chinese Dream, socialism with Chinese characteristics, transculturality, community of common destiny, pragmatic universalism, Xi Jinping,

Chapter Three
Harmonizing goals and values: the challenge for Belt and Road

Revised version of the keynote speech at the opening of the 4th Global China Dialogue, "The Belt and Road – Transcultural Cooperation for Shared Goals" at the British Academy in London, 1 December 2017.

Belt and Road is not just a sharing of technologies, but a journey towards greater understanding between cultures. It extends connectivity to encourage local cultures to find affinities with others but we must also be aware of the challenges this brings with it.

Chapter Four
Bridging the divides: China's role in a fragmenting world

Published in Chinese, 《弥合分歧——中国在分化世界中的角色》 in the journal *Global Communication,* 2016.

Abstract: Multiple factors underlie turmoil in world affairs in the Digital Age. The inability of any one power to shape geopolitics in the way the United State did after the Second World War requires a country to assume a new kind of leadership role, dependent on neither military nor soft power, but with the capacity to mobilize other countries to meet global threats. In its domestic achievements in recent years, and building on the heritage of a 5,000-year-old civilization China has demonstrated Eight Global Leadership Qualities: effectiveness, efficiency, legitimacy, respect, reciprocity, reverence, transcendence, inventiveness. The time has come for China to apply these qualities to global issues and assume a global leadership role.

Chapter Five
Leadership for a people's democracy

Text for a speech to be delivered at the launch of *Xi Jinping: The Governance of China*, Volume 2 at on 11 April, 2018.

Following on from the three lessons drawn from the first volume we can find a fourth: China's democracy path is the on-going demonstration of how leadership of the people is achieved through the Communist Party. It is underpinned by consultative democracy, a genuine alternative to the democratic institutions of the West.

Chapter Six
Chinese social theory in global social science

This appeared as a review article of the book by Xiaoying Qi, *Globalized Knowledge Flows and Chinese Social Theory* (Routledge, Abingdon and New York, 2014) in the *Journal of China in Comparative Perspective,* Volume 1, Issue1, June 2015, pp.146-149.

Qi provides an incisive account of the way classic Chinese concepts such as *lian* and *mianzi* (face), *xin* (heart/mind), *xiangfan xianghe* or *xiangfan yiti* ('paradoxical integration') resonate with cognate ideas in Western thought. She shows how a truly global social science can develop from comparative studies of concept formation.

Chapter Seven
The challenge of transculturality for the USA and China

This is the text of a lecture delivered to the Department of Sociology at Tsinghua University, Beijing on 25 October 2016. My thanks are due to Professor Li Qiang, at that time President of the Chinese Sociological Association, for the invitation to his department and for the richly informative conversations I enjoyed with him then and on several other occasions.

Abstract: The USA and China have world-views that extend far beyond their relations with one another. The USA has often regarded globalization as a simple extension of its own experience. World views in general are ethnocentric. *Tianxia* is also based in Chinese experience, a world of harmony contrasting with American tension between individual and community. Transculturality involves not just exchange between cultures but the creation of new culture beyond them. The world-views of the USA and China were each developed originally in a transcultural experience. When the USA and China reach out to the rest of the world they are creating a new transcultural space where global governance can grow. Americans have a problem with the idea of global governance that depends on equality between nation-states, Chinese have a problem because it lacks a central authority. Projects may serve global governance more effectively than preconceived ideas. A pragmatic universalism may replace the universals of national world views.

Keywords: world-views, *tianxia*, globalization, ethnocentrism, transculturality, global governance, pragmatic universalism

Chapter Eight
Pragmatic universalism and the quest for global governance

Text for presentation at the conference on "Globalization: Social Change and Cultural Construction" held by the School of Philosophy and Sociology at Jilin University in Changchun, China on 12-13 August 2016. I am grateful to the following for making valuable comments on an earlier version of this text: Colin Bradford, Hugh Canham, Graham Leicester, Sam Whimster, Joy Zhang. None of them bears any responsibility for the final version.

The occasion of Britain's vote to leave the European Union and insistence of the EU on the non-negotiable status of four principles prompts a discussion of the place of principle in global governance. In contact between cultures the search for compromise can both illuminate their fluid nature and potential for generating new culture. The Sustainable Development Goals are a prime example of an emergent transculture of the globe.

Chapter Nine
Can there be a public philosophy for global governance?

Speech text for the 2nd Global China Dialogue, held at the British Academy, London, on 23 and 24 November 2015. It was published in *Transculturality and the New Global Governance*, edited by Xiangqun Chang and Costanza Pernigotti, Global China Press, London, 2016, pp. 37-40.

Governance is decentred order. Rules arise out of diversity, and the multiple partners to the global conversation on world social order create a new kind of public philosophy, belonging to no nation or group in particular, and open to all.

Chapter Ten
How do we discover common values?

Speech text for the 'Symposium on China Studies 2017' co-hosted by the Ministry of Culture of the People's Republic of China and the Chinese Academy of Social Sciences with the theme: 'The Belt and Road Initiative from a global perspective', Beijing 24/25 July 2017.

Common values have been a contested sphere in Western culture since the 1960s onwards, their very existence being dispute. We need to understand how values arise and which ones are conducive to social order. Xi's speeches draw effectively on multiple sources for socialist values but Belt and Road offers an indirect way of discovering values positive for peace and well-being via cooperation on tangible goals

Chapter Eleven
The 'community of shared destiny' under conditions of imperfect understanding

Text for Keynote Address to the conference 'Transnationalization and Knowledge': The Ubiquity of Translation and the Crisis it Faces International Conference of the Research Network 'Trans/Wissen' (Trans/Knowledge) at the University of Trier, 12-14 October, 2017. I am grateful to Professor Stefan Köngeter and his colleagues for their cordial invitation.

Xi's *Governance of China* leads us via Marx to global governance. In coming to terms with China's rise the West can draw on aspect of its intellectual heritage that is an alternative German tradition, the theory of values and understanding of the neo-Kantians of Weber's time. Xi's *mingyun gongtongti* has to be translated into the Western experience of community, but as important for mutual understanding for an early theorist, Wilhelm Dilthey were science and the sharing of joint projects.

Chapter Twelve
Max Weber, China and the World: in search of transcultural communication (Co-author Zhang Xiaoying)

This is a much revised version of a paper delivered to the conference 'Max Weber and China: Culture, Law and Capitalism' at the School of Oriental and African Studies, London University, 5-6 September 2014, published in the *Journal of China in Comparative Perspective*, Volume 2, Issue 1, June 2016, pp.32-53. A separate expanded section of that original paper has been published as Albrow and Zhang (2014) and is Chapter 13 below.

Abstract: Weber's research on Confucian economic ethics arose from his hypothesis that Western capitalism owed its unique quality to Puritanism. It led him to search for equivalents in other cultures through the comparative study of world religions. The idea of the world and an ethic that shaped inner-worldly action inspired by hopes of the next world had developed from ancient Western and Christian thought that at one point suggested to Leibniz universal beliefs shared with Chinese classics. That idea was lost with the development of Western rationalism, science and modernity. By Weber's time the idea of the world was conflated with the idea of an objective science of social reality which he projected into his studies of Chinese culture, hence the criticisms of his ethnocentrism. *Tian Xia* and *Shi Jie*, translations of 'world', belong to a distinct world view where the ideal of the consummate person, *Jun Zi*, provides self-transcendence directed towards improving life on this earth rather than life in the next. Weber's receptivity to other cultures changed in accordance with his view that empirical sociology involved understanding the meaning of human action and in studying China to the end of his life he came to recognize that *Ru Jiao* (Confucianism) was more than an adaptation to the everyday world, but an inner-worldly ethic in tension with and shaping the world. He eventually emphasized cultural differences in the definition of ethics and can be seen as a forerunner of phenomenological views of many worlds in which the West and China may find common understandings.

Keywords: Max Weber, Leibniz, *Ru Jiao* (Confucianism), ethics, rationalism, *Tian Xia, Shi Jie*, social reality, *Jun Zi* (consummate person), worldview, ethnocentrism, adaptation, transcendence, universalism, multiculturalism, transcultural communication.

Chapter Thirteen
Weber and the concept of adaptation: the case of Confucian ethics
(Co-author Zhang Xiaoying)

Published as Albrow, Martin and Zhang Xiaoying. 2014. 'Weber and the Concept of Adaptation: the Case of Confucian Ethics'. *Max Weber Studies* 14.2, 199-226. This is a much expanded development of a section of a paper delivered to the conference 'Max Weber and China: Culture, Law and Capitalism' at the School of Oriental and African Studies, 5/6 September 2013. We are grateful for many valuable comments to Jack Barbalet, Hugh Canham, Xiangqun Chang, Anthony Giddens, Stephen Kalberg, Li Xuetao, Sam Whimster, Joy Zhang, none of whom is responsible for mistakes we may have made.

Abstract: Throughout his work Weber made extensive use of a concept of adaptation, usually associated with evolutionism but he was as critical of it as he was of historical materialism and in his concern for identifying the precise importance of ideas in explaining historical developments he rejected both grand narratives. We can detect through examining the sequence of his writing on Chinese ethics how his idea of adaptation to the world evolved over time to the point where he found it of limited use for China but still applicable to the Jesuits, who on their own experience of China were authors of an ethical concept of adaptation that antedated Darwin and coloured Weber's thought. He shifts emphasis from adaptation to tension (*Spannung*) which takes on equivalent importance to autonomy (*Eigengesetzlichkeit*) and rationality in explaining the impact of ethics on economic action.

Keywords: adaptation, autonomy, capitalism, China, Confucianism, ethics, evolutionism, historical materialism, Jesuits, naturalism, rationalization, religion, tension.

Chapter Fourteen
Max Weber, China and the future of global society

This was a keynote address for the Hong Kong Baptist University's Faculty of Social Sciences 8th Global Social Science Conference on Trans-disciplinary Approaches to Global Social Science, 11-12 December 2014. I am grateful to Jack Barbalet for his comments and help before and during this event. I would like to thank Michael Banton, Colin Bradford, Hugh Canham, John Nurser, Geoffrey

Pleyers and Hakan Seckinelgin who commented helpfully on an earlier version of this chapter. An abbreviated version was presented at the 2016 Annual Conference of the British Sociological Association.

Abstract: Although Weber's work was the epitome of the modern Western intellectual outlook a hundred years ago and his account of China has been criticized for its Western ethnocentrism, he developed there what is his true legacy for today, a method of looking at the past to diagnose the future directions contained in the present. He discerned in rationality a force that could drive social transformations and in both individual and collective agents the capacity to take responsibility to shape its direction. He found in the ethics of Confucian rationalism the cultural equivalent to the Protestant rationalism of the West and, even in the acute contrast in their world outlooks, left open the possible future convergence of China and the West in a developing capitalism. A Weberian analysis for the global age highlights rationalization processes, digital communication technology and the multiplicity of agents in the new global governance. The ethical commitments of the agents in this multipolar world are critical for responding to the global challenges of today.

Keywords: agency, bureaucracy, capitalism, charisma, civil society, Confucianism, Digital Age, disenchantment, ethics, geo-politics, global age, global governance, global society, globalization, ideal type, leadership, methodological individualism, modernity, network society, postmodernity, Puritanism, rationality, rationalization, value spheres, world society.

Postscript
A Chinese episode in the globalization of sociology

Published in *Journal of China in Comparative Perspective*, Volume 1, Issue 2, December 2015, pp.79-90. This was written specially for an issue of the journal focusing on the globalization of Chinese social sciences. It describes the author's editorial work in the late 1980s and early 1990s through the journal *International Sociology* to forge links with Chinese scholars.

Abstract: The author's experience in building contacts with social scientists in China in the 1980s assisted in the editorial policy of the new journal of the International Sociological Association, *International Sociology,* establishing collaboration with the new journal *Shehuixue Yanjiu*, both founded in 1986. That policy fed into the theme of the 1990 World Congress in Madrid: 'Sociology for One World: Unity and Diversity'. Chinese papers contributed to a developing debate about the globalization of sociology, its sinification and the universalistic credentials of sociology. This episode illustrates the ongoing reflexivity of sociology when in encounters between cultures it seeks to overcome conceptual differences by attending to common features of the human condition and challenges that confront all humankind.

Keywords: Fei Xiaotong, International Sociological Association, Chinese Sociological Research Association, *International Sociology*, *Shehuixue Yanjiu*, universalism, internationalization, modernization, indigenization, sinification, globalization, reflexivity.

DOI https://doi.org/10.24103/GCSS.en.2018.24

Appendix
The Globalization of Chinese Social Sciences Book Series[1]

Xiangqun Chang

The phrase 'globalization of Chinese social sciences' came out of a discussion with Professor Stephan Feuchtwang at the London School of Economics in 2010 about the title of a book commemorating the 100th anniversary of Professor Fei Xiaotong's birth. The first volume (in both English and Chinese) was published in 2014 by Global China Press alone and in 2015 jointly with New World Press. The dissemination of 'Chinese social sciences' covers a very wide range, in which the promotion of Fei Xiaotong's work is only the first step. We therefore decided to use 'Globalization of Chinese Social Sciences' as the name of a book series in order to promote representative Chinese social scientific works. Here I shall briefly outline the key developments in 'Chinese social sciences' after 1949.[2]

Institutions and resources

In China, the National Philosophy and Social Science Planning Group of the CPC Central Committee is the highest body in the Chinese social sciences. The group operates through the National Planning Office of Philosophy and Social Science. Its National Social Science Foundation is commissioned by the Department of Social Sciences of the Ministry of Education, the Research Bureau of the Chinese Academy of Social Sciences (CASS) and the Research Division of the Central Party School, to be in charge of universities, the institutions of CASS and the central State organs, respectively, with responsibility for the application of research projects, management of funds and evaluation of results. The National Philosophy and Social Science Planning Group also owns the National Social Sciences Database, which was established by CASS and developed by its Library in 2013. It is a national-level, open-information platform for Chinese social sciences. In 2015, the Chinese Social Sciences Year Book series (15 volumes to date) was published, representing the high standard of work in the field. CASS consists of hun-

---

[1] **Editor's note**: This is the General Preface of the Globalization of Chinese Social Sciences Book Series which has been placed at the beginning of each of the previously published volumes. This unusually long piece is to help readers understand the so-called 'Chinese social sciences' and the importance of 'globalization of Chinese social sciences'.

[2] Before 1949 see: *Social Engineering and the Social Sciences in China, 1919-1949*, Yung-chen Chiang, (Cambridge University Press, 2006).

dreds of research institutes, centres and related professional organizations, such as the Social Sciences in China Press (SSCP), Social Sciences Academic Press (SSAP), Chinese Social Sciences Net and its blogs and the journal *Social Sciences in China* and its site and blogs, the English version of which is now published by the Taylor and Francis Group. In 2015, the journal *Social Sciences in China Review* was founded. It aims 'to evaluate Fei Xiaotong Studies based on academic results based on national conditions, introduce a high standard of research results and create a system of academic discourse in contemporary China, comprehensively promoting Chinese philosophical and social scientific work in the world'. In recent years, the CASS Forum has also gained a strong reputation at home and abroad. In addition, there are a huge number of Academies of Social Sciences at province and municipality level.

They also have their own publications on social sciences based on their work at the local level. There are about 2,500 universities of different types in China. Some belong to the Bureau of Higher Education of the Ministry of Education, some to State ministries and commissions and others to provincial and municipal governments; more than a quarter are private universities.[3] In 2001, the Department of Social Sciences, Ministry of Education, built the humanities and social sciences services professional portal, the China Academic Humanities Information Network. It became the centre of information and online publications and for the dissemination, management and public enquiry services for humanities and the social sciences. All the universities have different faculties and departments and research centres for different topics. Almost all have their own publishers, producing academic journals and books. Social scientific work is published in philosophy and social sciences editions. It is worth mentioning a few examples of universities' contributions to providing services or promoting Chinese social sciences at the national level.

In 1998, Nanjing University and the Hong Kong Polytechnic University developed a Chinese Social Sciences Citation Index and the academic series of the Chinese Humanities and Social Sciences Citation index. It led to the foundation of the Chinese Social Science Research Assessment Centre in 2000.

Tsinghua University and Tsinghua Tongfang Holding Group established China's National Knowledge Infrastructure (CNKI) in 1999. It was supported by the Education Ministry, Science and Technology Ministry, Propaganda Ministry and General Administration of Press and Publications, with self-developed cutting-edge Chinese digital library technologies and grid resources as a sharing platform. It built the most comprehensive system of Chinese academic knowledge resources – the China Integrated Knowledge Resources Database – covering journals, dissertations, newspapers, proceedings, yearbooks, reference works, en-

---

[3] See: *2015 National Education Statistics Bulletin* (Ministry of Education of China), 2016-07-06. http://www.moe.gov.cn/srcsite/ A03/s180/moe_633/201607/t20160706_270976.html (见：《2015年全国教育事业发展统计公报》，中国教育部)

cyclopaedias, patents, standards, science and technology achievements and laws and regulations and some well-known foreign-language resources from Springer, Taylor & Francis and Wiley, forming a complete knowledge service network. The system is the core of the China knowledge resource base, totalling 101.9 million articles encompassing a large amount of social scientific work, some of which has been translated into English.

Fudan University is a top locus for the internationalization of Chinese social sciences. It founded China's first national institute for advanced studies of the social sciences (Fudan-IAS for Social Sciences). The founding Dean, Professor Deng Zhenglai, also founded the *Chinese Social Science Quarterly* in Hong Kong as early as 1992, which was re-established in 2008. In the same year, he founded China's first English-language journal on social sciences, the *Fudan Journal of the Humanities and Social Sciences* (FJHSS). Unfortunately, Deng passed away in 2013. His successor in Fudan-IAS, Sujian Guo, Professor of the Department of Political Science at San Francisco State University, USA, also became Editor of the FJHSS, which is now published by Springer.

Methodology

Some recent opinions should be mentioned here. In 2011, Professor QIAO Xiao-chun of the Institute of Population Research at Peking University gave a lecture entitled 'Chinese social science: how far away from science?' at a number of universities, including his own and Shanghai University of International Studies, China Youth University for Political Science, Huazhong University of Science and Technology and Zhongnan University of Economics and Law. He believed that Chinese social science occupies no position or status in world academia, and therefore enjoys no right of discourse. This is because methodologically Chinese social sciences have a strong speculative character, in contrast to the empirical studies on which general social sciences are based. However, in his 'Understanding the future' lecture in 2016, Professor Yu Xie of Princeton University and Peking University issued some more nuanced statements. Scientific studies, he observed, have three characteristics, namely objectivity, experience and repeatability. He also put forward three principles, variability, social grouping and social context, which provide a methodological basis for social scientific research. Xie suggested that in today's China it is more important than ever to carry out social scientific research on China, since Chinese society has undergone comprehensive change and is still rapidly changing.[4]

In 2014, XIONG Yihan, Associate Professor at Fudan University School of International Relations and Public Affairs, published an article entitled 'The inter-

---

[4] Yu XIE, 'Today it is so important and so opportune to be conducting social scientific research in China' (a speech at the Future Forum, Beijing), *Scientific American*, 2016-07-26, http://oicwx.com/ detail/1102356(谢宇: 今天在中国做社会科学太重要了，也太幸运了，环球科学("未来科学"论坛演讲)

nationalization of social science and native language scholarly writing in China'.[5] He criticized the phenomenon of 'academic nationalism' that seeks to boycott internationalization, but also took issue with the 'colonial academic' who lacks local consciousness. He thought it very important that 'Chinese scholars should apply scientific research methods, actively participate in international academic dialogue and competition, invent dominant theoretical paradigms and set up research agendas with international colleagues. Even first-class Chinese writing with a global perspective is an integral part of the internationalization of social science in China.'

In 2015, Biao Xiang, Professor of Social Anthropology at Oxford University, who graduated from the Department of Sociology, Peking University, in the mid-1990s, published an article on 'The ending of the "intellectual youth" era of Chinese social sciences'.[6] Scholars born before the 1960s, who received an incomplete education but had experience in rural China, have nearly all left their leadership or teaching posts. In contrast, post-1970s scholars, who received continuous formal education but had little experience outside educational institutions, became the mainstream of academia. Xiang believes that the evolution of modern Chinese social science resembles the changes that have taken place between different generations of academic practice, knowledge acquisition and accumulation. Nevertheless, as Yefu Zheng, Emeritus Professor of Sociology at Peking University, pointed out, professors in the Department of Sociology at Peking University who were born before 1960 had still not retired; scholars' influence does not depend on their posts. Professor TIAN Song of Beijing Normal University also questioned whether the 'intellectual youth' era had ended. He maintained that the phenomenon of the post-1970s becoming mainstream is more of an academic management change.[7]

The methodological character of Chinese social sciences is a large topic. Recently, a problem arose with translating the phrase '哲学社会科学' into English, which occurred in a speech at the Symposium of Philosophical Social Sciences by Xi Jinping, President of China, on 17 May 2016.[8] Xi obtained a PhD from the Department of Sociology, School of Humanities and Social Science at Tsinghua University, in 2002. Our professional translator translated 哲学社会科学 into English

---

[5] XIONG Yihan. 'The Internationalization of Social Science and Native Language Scholarly Writing in China'. *Fudan Journal (Social Sciences)* 4, 2014. [熊易寒, 中国社会科学的国际化与母语写作,《复旦学报(社会科学版)》, 2014年第4期。]

[6] Biao Xiang. 'The Ending of the "Intellectual Youth" Era of Chinese Social Sciences, *Beijing Cultural Review*, 12, 2015 [项飙, 中国社会科学"知青时代"的终结,《文化纵横》, 2015年第12期。]

[7] Tian Song. 'Are We Experiencing Generational Change or Institutional Change? *Social Science Weekly*, Shanghai Academy of Social Sciences, 10 March 2016: 10.

[8] 习近平,《在哲学社会科学工作座谈会上的讲话》, 2016年5月18日, 新华网 [Xi Jinping, Speech at the Symposium of Philosophical Social Sciences, 18 May 2016. Xinhua Net. http://news.xinhuanet.com/politics/2016-05/18/c_1118891128.htm]

as 'philosophical social sciences', based on the context of the speech. Our editor accepted it, as did our academic adviser, Professor Martin Albrow, a founding editor of *International Sociology* and former President of the British Sociological Association. Moreover, inspired by it, when writing speech notes in preparation for attending a high-end international conference on China studies in October, 2016, he titled his speech 'Philosophical social science as a bridge from "Belt and Road" to global governance'. However, as the editor of this book series, I decided to change 'philosophical social sciences' to 'philosophy and social sciences' in the final English version of Xi's speech. This seemed to coincide with the letter of Xi's speech, although, from the methodological point of view, some important characteristics of Chinese social sciences were lost.

Globalization of Chinese social sciences

The 'globalization of Chinese social sciences' is a live issue. The direction and outcomes of globalization of Chinese social scientific studies are neither Western nor Chinese, but add concepts, theories and methods derived from studying countries like China, which have a long history, huge population and complicated society, to the sum of human knowledge. This idea first appeared in 'A Chinese phase in social anthropology'[9], the Malinowski Memorial Lecture by Maurice Freedman given at the London School of Economics and Political Science in 1962. Two years later, Freedman made another speech on an occasion when area studies were being discussed, with the title 'What social science can do for Chinese studies[10], in which he distinguished sinology from Chinese studies and emphasized the need to study China social-scientifically. Both Martin Albrow and Stephan Feuchtwang were research students in, respectively, the Departments of Sociology and Anthropology at LSE, under the supervision of Maurice Freedman, and this influenced their academic careers throughout their lives. Martin Albrow helped many Chinese scholars to publish their articles in *International Sociology* in the 1980s when he was editor of the journal.[11] After 1990, he devoted himself to promoting the idea of globalization and became one of its international representatives. Nowadays, he helps promote Chinese social scientific work as part of the globalization of Chinese social sciences; at the same time, he attempts to insert the concept of transculturality into mainstream academia, as well as exploring the contributions of Chinese social sciences in the process of transculturalization. Details of this can be seen in my introductory paper launching the *Journal of China*

---

[9] Maurice Freedman, 'A Chinese Phase in Social Anthropology', *British Journal of Sociology*, 14(1), 1963.

[10] Maurice Freedman. 'What Social Science Can Do for Chinese Studies', *Journal of Asian Studies*, 23(4), 1964.

[11] Martin Albrow. 'A Chinese Episode in the Globalization of Sociology', *Journal of China in Comparative Perspective*, 1(2), 2015. Chinese version: 马丁·阿尔布劳, 社会学全球化过程中的中国片段,《中国比较研究》, 2015年第1卷第2期。

in Comparative Perspective, entitled 'Transculturality and the globalization of Chinese social sciences: vocabulary, invention and exploration'.[12]

Stephan Feuchtwang founded the China Research Unit at City University in 1973 when he worked there. It was the first organization dedicated to social scientific studies on China in the UK. Since 1998, when Feuchtwang was at the London School of Economics, he devoted himself to the creation of comparative studies of China. He appreciated Fei Xiaotong's comparative perspectives and theoretical conceptualization of the differential mode of association and the organizational mode of association (Gary G. Hamilton's translation of 差序格局 and 团体格局[13]) and elaborated them with his own translation.[14] In 2013, after the gestation, birth and early years of growth of the China in Comparative Perspective Network (CCPN) at LSE, he supported changing its name from CCPN to CCPN Global, as CCPN completed the process of becoming independent from the LSE.

In the USA also, some scholars are dedicated to Chinese social sciences. For example, Professor Daniel Little, Chancellor at the University of Michigan-Dearborn, presented a paper 'New developments in the Chinese social sciences' at a conference Mapping Difference: Structures and Categories of Knowledge Production, 19–20 May 2006, at Duke University. As early as 1989, he published *Understanding Peasant China: Case Studies in the Philosophy of Social Science*, which was translated into Chinese and published in 2009.[15] In 2010, Gary Hamilton, Professor of Sociology and International Studies at the University of Washington, presented a paper entitled 'What Western social scientists can learn from the writings of Fei Xiaotong'[16] at the international conference at LSE, Commemorating the 100th Anniversary of Professor Fei Xiaotong's Birth. Hamilton speaks highly of Chinese social sciences' methodological contribution to general social science methodology. A recent example was seen at the Young Scholars conference, Social Sciences and China Studies, 20–21 May 2016, organized by the

[12] Xiangqun Chang. 'Transculturality and the Globalization of Chinese Social Sciences: Vocabulary, Invention and Exploration', *Journal of China in Comparative Perspective*, 1(1), 2015. [常向群, 文化与中国社会全球化: 词汇的发明与发掘《中超文化国比较研究》, 2015年第 1卷第2 期]。

[13] Fei Xiaotong. *From the Soil: The Foundations of Chinese Society*, A translation of Fei Xiaotong's *Xiangtu Zhongguo*, by Gary Hamilton and WANG Zheng. University of California Press, 1992.

[14] Stephan Feuchtwang. 'Social Egoism and Individualism: surprises and questions from a Western anthropologist of China – Reading Fei Xiaotong's contrast between China and the West', *Journal of China in Comparative Perspective*, 1(1), 2015. Chinese version: 王斯福, 社会自我主义与个体主义——一位西方的汉学人类学家阅读费孝通"中西对比"观念的惊讶与问题, 《中国比较研究》, 2015年第1卷第1期。

[15] Daniel Little. *Understanding Peasant China: Case Studies in the Philosophy of Social Science*. (Yale University Press, 1989). Chinese version: 李丹《理解农民中国——社会科学哲学的案例研究》, 江苏人民出版社2009年.

[16] Gary Hamilton. 'What Western Social Scientists Can Learn from the Writings of Fei Xiaotong', *Journal of China in Comparative Perspective*, 1(1), 2015. Chinese version: 韩格理 (Gary G. Hamilton), 费孝通著作对西方社会科学家的启示, 《中国比较研究》, 2015年第1卷第1期。

Fudan-UC Centre on Contemporary China at the University of California, San Diego. These are joint efforts to promote Chinese social sciences from both Chinese and American scholars. All in all, a huge amount of work is being done all over the world in different disciplines studying China social-scientifically – too much to be mentioned here.

In the Preface to this book, Feuchtwang states that Fei Xiaotong is probably the highest-ranking policy-influencing anthropologist of all time, who profoundly influenced social policies in China's development.[17] It is no accident that Xi Jinping mentioned in his 2016 speech LSE graduate Fei Xiaotong's name. In his Preface to *Peasant Life in China*, Malinowski noted that Dr Fei promised that, after he returned to China, he would work with Chinese colleagues to undertake a comprehensive reform of China's economic, social, cultural, political and belief systems.[18] Now Dr Xi Jinping, the highest-ranking policy-maker, in his speech on Chinese philosophy and social sciences, has promoted the comprehensive development of Chinese social sciences. We believe that this may not only affect the process of globalization of Chinese social science but could also have far-reaching historic impact on China's participation in global governance and society building and the sustainable development of a global society.

---

[17] Stephan Feuchtwang. Preface, *Journal of China in Comparative Perspective*, 1(1), 2015

[18] Bronislaw Malinowski. Preface, in *Hsiao-Tung Fei [Fei Xiaotong], Peasant Life in China*, London: Routledge, 1939.

DOI https://doi.org/10.24103/GCSS.en.2018.25

Index

DOI https://doi.org/10.24103/GCSS.en.2018.26

About the Author

In a career in sociology spanning over 50 years Martin Albrow, PhD (University of Cambridge), held the Chair in Sociological Theory in the University of Wales in Cardiff before becoming Professor Emeritus in 1989. Since then, he has held visiting positions in numerous institutions, including the Eric Voegelin chair in Munich, and chairs in the London School of Economics, State University of New York, Stonybrook, and the Beijing Foreign Studies University. He has been Fellow at the Woodrow Wilson International Center for Scholars, Washington DC, and the Käte Hamburger Center for Advanced Studies "Law as Culture", Bonn University. He is now based in London.

Currently a Fellow of the Academy of Social Sciences in the UK, in the past he has been President of the British Sociological Association, Editor of the journal *Sociology* and founding editor of *International Sociology*, the journal of the International Sociological Association.

His first visit to China was in 1987 on an observational tour with the State Family Planning Commission and in recent years he has contributed to the annual Symposium on China Studies with the Academy of Social Sciences and the Ministry of Culture of the PRC.

His specialties include social theory, organization theory and Max Weber's thought, and he is internationally known for his pioneering work on globalization. His *The Global Age: State and Society beyond Modernity* (1996) won the European Amalfi Prize in 1997. Other books include *Bureaucracy* (1970), *Max Weber's Construction of Social Theory* (1990), *Globalization, Knowledge and Society* (1990, ed. with E. King), *Do Organizations Have Feelings?* (1997), *Sociology: The Basics* (1999), *Global Civil Society* (co-editor) in 2006/7, 2007/8 and 2011, and *Global Age Essays on Social and Cultural Change* (2014).

CPSIA information can be obtained
at www.ICGtesting.com
Printed in the USA
LVHW021509030719
623119LV00008B/299/P